Robert Gentleman   Kurt Hornik   Giovanni Parmigiani

For further volumes:
http://www.springer.com/series/6991

Use R!

Yuelin Li • Jonathan Baron

Behavioral Research Data Analysis with R

 Springer

Yuelin Li
Memorial Sloan-Kettering Cancer Center
Department of Psychiatry and Behavioral
Sciences
641 Lexington Ave. 7th Floor
New York, New York 10022-4503
USA
liy12@mskcc.org

Jonathan Baron
Department of Psychology
University of Pennsylvania
3720 Walnut Street
Philadelphia, Pennsylvania 19104-6241
USA
baron@psych.upenn.edu

Series Editors:
Robert Gentleman
Program in Computational Biology
Division of Public Health Sciences
Fred Hutchinson Cancer Research Center
1100 Fairview Ave. N, M2-B876
Seattle, Washington 98109-1024
USA

Kurt Hornik
Department für Statistik und Mathematik
Wirtschaftsuniversität Wien Augasse 2-6
A-1090 Wien
Austria

Giovanni Parmigiani
The Sidney Kimmel Comprehensive Cancer
Center at Johns Hopkins University
550 North Broadway
Baltimore, MD 21205-2011
USA

ISBN 978-1-4614-1237-3   e-ISBN 978-1-4614-1238-0
DOI 10.1007/978-1-4614-1238-0
Springer New York Dordrecht Heidelberg London

Library of Congress Control Number: 2011940221

Printed on acid-free paper

Springer is part of Springer Science+Business Media (www.springer.com)

Preface

This book is written for behavioral scientists who want to consider adding R to their existing set of statistical tools, or want to switch to R as their main computation tool. We aim primarily to help practioners of behavioral research make the transition to R. The focus is to provide practical advice on some of the widely used statistical methods in behavioral research, using a set of notes and annotated examples. We also aim to help beginners learn more about statistics and behavioral research. These are statistical techniques used by psychologists who do research on human subjects, but of course they are also relevant to researchers in others fields that do similar kinds of research.

We assume that the reader has read the relevant parts of R manuals on the CRAN website at `http://www.r-project.org`, such as "An Introduction to R", "R Data Import/Export", and "R Installation and Administration". We assume that the reader has gotten to the point of installing R and trying a couple of examples. We also assume that the reader has relevant experiences in using other statistical packages to carry out data analytic tasks covered in this book. The source code and data for some of the examples in the book can be downloaded from the book's website at: `http://idecide.mskcc.org/yl_home/rbook/`. We do not dwell on the statistical theories unless some details are essential in the appropriate use of the statistical methods. When they are called for, theoretical details are accompanied by visual explanations whenever feasible. Mathematical equations are used throughout the book in the hopes that reader will find them helpful in general, and specifically in reaching beyond the scope of this book. For example, matrix notations are used in the chapters covering linear regression and linear mixed-effects modeling because they are the standard notations found in statistics journals. A basic appreciation of mathematical notations may help the readers implement these new techniques before a packaged solution is available. Nevertheless, the main emphasis of this book is on the practical data analytic skills so that they can be quickly incorporated into the reader's own research.

The statistical techniques in this book represent many of statistical techniques in our own research. The pedagogical plan is to present straightforward solutions and add more sophisticated techniques if they help improve clarity and/or efficiency.

As can be seen in the first example in Chap. 1, the same analysis can be carried out by a straightforward and a more sophisticated method. Chapters 1–4 cover basic topics such as data import/export, statistical methods for comparing means and proportions, and graphics. These topics may be part of an introductory text for students in behavioral sciences. Data analysis can often be adequately addressed with no more than these straightforward methods. Chapter 4 contains plots in published articles in the journal *Judgment and Decision Making* (http://journal.sjdm.org/). Chapters 5–7 cover topics with intermediary difficulty, such as repeated-measures ANOVA, ordinary least square regression, logistic regression, and statistical power and sample size considerations. These topics are typically taught at a more advanced undergraduate level or first year graduate level.

Practitioners of behavioral statistics are often asked to estimate the statistical power of a study design. R provides a set of flexible functions for sample size estimation. More complex study designs may involve estimating statistical power by simulations. We find it easier to do simulations with R than with other statistical packages we know. Examples are provided in Chaps. 7 and 11.

The remainder of this book cover more advanced topics. Chapter 8 covers Item Response Theory (IRT), a statistical method used in the development and validation of psychological and educational assessment tools. We begin Chap. 8 with simple examples and end with sophisticated applications that require a Bayesian approach. Such topics can easily take up a full volume. Only practical analytic tasks are covered so that the reader can quickly adapt our examples for his or her own research. The latent regression Rasch model in Sect. 8.4.2 highlights the power and flexibility of R in working with other statistical languages such as WinBUGS/OpenBUGS. Chapter 9 covers missing data imputation. Chapters 10–11 cover hierarchical linear models applied in repeated-measured data and clustered data. These topics are written for researchers already familiar with the theories. Again, these chapters emphasize the practical data analysis skills and not the theories.

R evolves continuously. New techniques and user-contributed packages are constantly evolving. We strive to provide the latest techniques. However, readers should consult other sources for a fuller understanding of relevant topics. The R journal publishes the latest techniques and new packages. Another good source for new techniques is The Journal of Statistical Software (http://www.jstatsoft.org/). The R-help mailing list is another indispensable resource. User contributions make R a truly collaborative statistical computation framework. Many great texts and tutorials for beginners and intermediate users are already widely available. Beginner-level tutorials and how-to guides can be found online at the CRAN "Contributed Documentation" page.

This book originated from our online tutorial "Notes on the use of R for psychology experiments and questionnaires." Many individuals facilitated the transition. We would like to thank them for making this book possible. John Kimmel, former editor for this book at Springer, first encouraged us to write this book and provided continuous guidance and encouragement. Special thanks go to Kathryn Schell and Marc Strauss and other editorial staff at Springer on the preparation of the book. Several annonymous reviewers provided suggestions on how to improve the book.

We are especially indebted to the individuals who helped supply the data used in the examples, including the authors of the R packages we use, and those who make the raw data freely accessible online.

New York   Yuelin Li
Philadelphia   Jonathan Baron

Contents

Chapter 1
Introduction

1.1 An Example R Session

Here is a simple R session.

```
> help(sleep)
> x1 <- sleep$extra[sleep$group == 1]
> x2 <- sleep$extra[sleep$group == 2]
> t.test(x1, x2)
> sleep[c(1:3, 11:13), ]
> with(sleep, t.test(extra[group == 1],
+       extra[group == 2]))
> q()
```

The help() command prints documentation for the requested topic. The sleep dataset is a built-in dataset in R. It comes from William Sealey Gosset's article under the pseudonym Student (1908). It contains the effects of two drugs, measured as the extra hours of sleep as compared to controls. The vectors x1 and x2 are assigned the values of the extra hours of sleep in drugs 1 and 2, respectively. (a less than sign followed by a minus sign, <-, represents assignment) Two equal signs, ==, represent the logical equal operator. The t.test(x1, x2) carries out an independent sample *t*-test of the sleep time between the two groups. The same analysis can be done using with(sleep, t.test(extra[group == 1], extra[group == 2])). sleep[c(1:3, 11:13),] prints observations 1 through 3 and 11 through 13. To exit the R program, type q(). Typing q without the parentheses prints out the contents of the function to quit R. Most functions are visible to the user in this way. The advantage of using built-in datasets is that they have already been imported. The next example describes how to import data from a text file.

The sleep data can be entered into a text file, the variable names on the first row, and the variables are separated by spaces.

Y. Li and J. Baron, *Behavioral Research Data Analysis with R*, Use R,
DOI 10.1007/978-1-4614-1238-0_1, © Springer Science+Business Media, LLC 2012

```
extra group ID
  0.7      1   1
 -1.6      1   2
 -0.2      1   3
 -1.2      1   4
 -0.1      1   5
  3.4      1   6
  3.7      1   7
  0.8      1   8
  0.0      1   9
  2.0      1  10
  1.9      2   1
  0.8      2   2
  1.1      2   3
  0.1      2   4
 -0.1      2   5
  4.4      2   6
  5.5      2   7
  1.6      2   8
  4.6      2   9
  3.4      2  10
```

Suppose the data entries are saved in a file named t1.dat in the directory C:\\Documents and Settings\\usr1\\My Documents, then this command imports the data and assigns it a name called sleep.df.

```
> sleep.df <- data.frame(read.table(file =
+"C:/Documents and Settings/usr1/My Documents/t1.dat",
+header = TRUE))
```

On a Windows platform, the double back slashes (\\) in a path name can be replaced with one forward slash (/). On Unix/Linux and Mac OS, one forward slash works fine. The read.table() function reads the data in file. It uses the first line of the raw data file (header = TRUE) to assign variable names to the three columns. Blank spaces in the raw data file are ignored. The data.frame() function converts the imported data into a data frame. The sleep.df data is now available for analysis (type objects() to see it). The example above shows some of the unique features of R. Most data analytic tasks in R are done through functions, and functions have parameters such as the options of file and header in the read.table() function. Functions can be nested, the output of one function can be fed directly into another. Some other basic R features are covered in the next section. These features make R flexible but more challenging to learn for beginners.

Some things are more difficult with R especially if you are used to using menus. With R, it helps to have a list of commands in front of you. There are lists in the on-line help and in the index of *An introduction to R* by the R Core Development Team, and in the reference cards listed in http://finzi.psych.upenn.edu/.

Some things turn out to be easier in R. Although there are no menus, the on-line help files are very easy to use, and quite complete. The elegance of the language helps too, particularly those tasks involving the manipulation of data. The purpose of this book is to reduce the difficulty of the things that are more difficult at first. Next we will go over a few basic concepts in R. The remainder of this chapter covers a few examples on how to take advantage of R's strengths.

1.2 A Few Useful Concepts and Commands

1.2.1 Concepts

In R, most commands are functions. The command is written as the name of the function, followed by parentheses, with the arguments (inputs) of the function in parentheses, separated by commas when there is more than one, e.g., `plot(swiss)` to plot a pairwise scatterplot of the `swiss` data. When there is no argument, the parentheses are still needed, e.g., `q()` to exit the program. A function is said to "return" its output when the output is printed or when we can set a variable equal to the output. For example, `sqrt(4)` returns (prints) 2 on the screen; and if we say `v1 <- sqrt(4)`, `v1` is set equal to the output of the function, or 2.

Some basic concepts in R are surprising to beginners. For example, the square of $\sqrt{7}$ is not 7.

```
> 7 == sqrt(7)^2
[1] FALSE
```

That is because floating point arithmetic is not exact.

```
> options(digits = 22)
> sqrt(7)^2
[1] 7.00000000000000888178
```

A solution is to compare `all.equal(sqrt(7)^2, 7)`.

In this book, we generally use names such as `x1` or `file1`, that is, names containing both letters and a digit, to indicate variable names that the user makes up. Really, these can be of any form. We use the number simply to clarify the distinction between a made up name and a key word with a predetermined meaning in R. R is case sensitive; for example, `X` and `x` can stand for different things. We generally use upper-case data objects like `X`, `Y`, and `M` to represent matrices or arrays; and lower-case objects to represent vectors. Although most commands are functions with the arguments in parentheses, some arguments require specification of a key word with an equal sign and a value for that key word, such as `source("myfile1.R", echo = T)`, which means read in `myfile1.R` and echo the commands on the screen. It helps to add spaces between input parameters, so that the extra spaces in `echo = T` make it easier to read than `echo=T`. But that is not necessary.

Key words can be abbreviated (e.g., e = T). In addition to the idea of a function, R has objects and modes. Objects are anything that you can give a name. There are many different classes of objects. The main classes of interest here are *vector*, *matrix*, *factor*, *list*, and *data frame*. The mode of an object tells what kind of things are in it. The main modes of interest here are logical, numeric, and character.

We sometimes indicate the class of object (vector, matrix, factor, etc.) by using v1 for a vector, m1 for a matrix, and so on. Most R functions, however, will either accept more than one type of object or will "coerce" a type into the form that it needs.

The most interesting object is a data frame. It is useful to think about data frames in terms of rows and columns. The rows are subjects or observations. The columns are variables, but a matrix can be a column too. The variables in a data frame can be of different classes.

The behavior of any given function, such as plot(), aov() (analysis of variance), or summary() depends on the object class and mode to which it is applied. A nice thing about R is that you almost do not need to know this, because the default behavior of functions is usually what you want. One way to use R is just to ignore completely the distinction among classes and modes, but *check* every step (by typing the name of the object it creates or modifies). If you proceed this way, you will also get error messages, which you must learn to interpret. Most of the time, again, you can find the problem by looking at the objects involved, one by one, typing the name of each object.

Sometimes, however, you must know the distinctions. For example, a factor is treated differently from an ordinary vector in an analysis of variance or regression. A factor is what is often called a categorical variable. Even if numbers are used to represent categories, they are not treated as ordered. If you use a vector and think you are using a factor, you can be misled.

1.2.2 Commands

As a reminder, here is a list of some of the useful commands that you should be familiar with, and some more advanced ones that are worth knowing about. Some of the more basic commands help you organize your work.

1.2.2.1 Working Directory

It helps to get into the habit of separating R sessions into different working directories specific to different projects or data analytic tasks. Here is why. On Windows, R starts in the user's default HOME directory (e.g., getwd() returns C:/Documents and Settings/usr1/My Documents). On exiting R, the user is prompted to save the current session in a .RData file under that directory by default. Eventually, this .RData file collects too many objects to be managed efficiently. You may organize R sessions into subdirectories, for example, called project1, project2, and project3 under your home directory C:/Documents and Settings/usr1/My Documents/. If you are working on project1, you double click the R icon on your Windows desktop to launch R, then you immediately type setwd("C:/Documents and Settings/usr1/My Documents/project1/") to switch your working directory to project1. Then you can type load(".RData") to retrieve a previously saved session. This is probably the first thing you do each time you run R on Windows. These changes can also be set interactively using the menu. Note that R recognizes the forward slashes in the path name.

The setwd() command is usually not necessary if you are running R from a Unix/Linux command line. Typically, you are already in the working directory before R is called from the command line.

On a computer running the Mac OS, it depends on whether or not your R is a binary version with a graphical user interface or a version compiled from source code. R compiled from source on a Macintosh computer works like a Unix/Linux R from a command line terminal and setwd() is not necessary.

Another advantage of separating R sessions in different working directories is that it allows easier tracking of the command history file. All the commands typed in an R session are saved upon exit in a file called .Rhistory under the working directory. You can use a text editor to edit the .Rhistory file into a command syntax script. Then you can run R in batch mode. For example, suppose the .Rhistory file under project1 contains these lines:

```
> help(sleep)
> x1 <- sleep$extra[sleep$group == 1]
> x2 <- sleep$extra[sleep$group == 2]
> t.test(x1, x2)
> sleep[c(1:3, 11:13), ]
> t.test(extra ~ group, data = sleep)
> with(sleep, t.test(extra[group == 1],
+    extra[group == 2]))
> q()
```

We can take out the first and last lines and save the edited file as sleep.R. Then we can run R in batch mode by calling R CMD BATCH sleep.R. The ouput is saved in sleep.Rout under the project1 directory. The output in sleep.Rout file then can be shared with others.

1.2.2.2 Getting Help

help.start() starts the browser version of the help files. (But you can use help() without it.) With a fast computer and a good browser, it is often simpler to open the html documents in a browser while you work and just use the brower's capabilities. `help(plot)` prints the help available about `plot`, or `help(command1)` to print the help for `command1`. Sometimes you only need the names of the parameters, which can be printed by `args(command1)`.

`help.search("keyword1")` searches keywords for help on this topic. `apropos(topic1)` or `apropos("topic1")` finds commands relevant to `topic1`, whatever it is. `example(command1)` prints an example of the use of the command. This is especially useful for graphics commands. Try, for example, `example(contour)`, `example(dotchart)`, `example(image)`, and `example(persp)`.

1.2.2.3 Installing Packages

The R base system is lean. It contains only the essential components. Additional packages can be installed when needed. For example, `install.packages (c("ltm","psych"))` installs the packages called `ltm` and `psych` from an archive of your choice, if your computer is connected to the internet. You do not need the `c()` if you just want one package. You should, at some point, make sure that you are using the CRAN mirror page that is closest to you. If you live in the U.S., you should have a `.Rprofile` file with `options(CRAN = "http://cran.us.r-project.org")` in it. There are other mirror sites in the U.S. On Windows, you have the option to interactively select a mirror site from a list in a menu if one is not already set. Other useful functions for managing packages include `installed.packages()` to show details of all installed packages and `update.packages()` to update the packages that you have installed to their latest version.

To install packages from the Bioconductor set (tools and resources for computational biology), see the online instructions (http://www.bioconductor.org/install/, last accessed, September, 2011).

When packages are not on CRAN, you can download them and use `R CMD INSTALL package1.tar.gz` from a Unix/Linux command line. On Windows, you would need to open a DOS command prompt, change directory to where `package1.tar.gz` is saved, then type the command `C:\"Program Files"\R\R-2.13.0\bin\R.exe CMD BATCH package1.tar.gz`.

1.2.2.4 Assignment, Logic, and Arithmetic

One of the most frequently typed commands is the assignment command, `<-`. It assigns what is on the right of the arrow to what is on the left. (If you use ESS, the `_` key (underscore) will produce this arrow with spaces, a great convenience.) Typing the name of the object prints the object. For example, if you say:

```
> t1 <- c(1, 2, 3, 4, 5)
> t1
```

you will see 1 2 3 4 5. The object t1 gets a numeric vector of five numbers, put together by the c() function. Beginners sometimes do c <- c(1,2,3). R will let you do it, and will not generate an error if you next do x <- c(4, 5, 6). R knows what to do with x because your local copy of c is a numeric vector and the system copy of c is a function. However, it is better not to assign values to c() or any other system functions to minimize confusions.

Logical objects can be true or false. Some functions and operators return TRUE or FALSE. For example, 1 == 1, is TRUE because 1 does equal 1. Likewise, 1 == 2 is FALSE, and 1 < 2 is TRUE. But beware, sqrt(2)^2 == 2 is FALSE because they have different internal floating-point representations in R. A better test for the equality between two floating-point numbers is provided by the function all.equal(), all.equal(sqrt(2)^2, 2) is TRUE.

Use all(), any(), |, ||, &, and && to combine logical expressions, and use ! to negate them. The difference between the | and the || form is that the shorter form, when applied to vectors, etc., returns a vector, while the longer form stops when the result is determined and returns a single TRUE or FALSE. Set functions operate on the elements of vectors: union(v1,v2), intersect(v1,v2), setdiff(v1,v2), setequal(v1,v2), is.element(element1,v1) (or, element1 %in% v1). Arithmetic works. For example, -t1 yields -1 -2 -3 -4 -5. It works on matrices and data frames too. For example, suppose m1 gets the matrix m1 <- matrix(c(1,2,3,4,5,6), nrow=2, byrow=T).

```
1 2 3
4 5 6
```

Then m1 * 2 is

```
2  4  6
8 10 12
```

Matrix multiplication works too. Suppose m2 is the matrix
m2 <- matrix(c(1,1,1,2,2,2), ncol=2)

```
1 2
1 2
1 2
```

then m1 %*% m2 is

```
 6 12
15 30
```

and m2 %*% m1 is

```
9        12        15
9        12        15
9        12        15
```

You can also multiply a matrix by a vector using matrix multiplication, vectors are aligned vertically when they come after the %*% sign and horizontally when they come before it. This is a good way to find weighted sums, as we shall explain.

For ordinary multiplication of a matrix times a vector, the vector is vertical and is repeated as many times as needed. For example m2 * 1:2 yields

```
1 4
2 2
1 4
```

Ordinarily, you would multiply a matrix by a vector when the length of the vector is equal to the number of rows in the matrix.

1.2.2.5 Loading and Saving

Additional functions not activated at startup have to be loaded by library(pkg) or require(pkg), where pkg is the unquoted name of the package. A list of packages can be found online at cran.r-project.org. A useful library for psychology is mva (multivariate analysis). To find the contents of a library such as mva before you load it, say library(help = mva). The ctest library is already loaded when you start R. Other useful functions include:

- source("file1") runs the commands in file1.
- sink("file1") diverts output to file1 until you say sink().
- save(x1,file="file1") saves object x1 to file file1.
- To read in the file, use load("file1").
- q() quits the program. q("yes") saves everything.
- write(object, "file1") writes a matrix or some other object to file1.
- write.table(object1, "file1") writes a table and has an option to make it comma delimited, so that a spreadsheet program can read it. See the help file, but to make it comma delimited, say write.table(object1, "file1", sep=",") or simply write.csv(object1, "file1")
- round() produces output rounded off, which is useful when you are cutting and pasting R output into a manuscript (e.g., round(t.test(v1)$statistic, 2) rounds off the value of t to two places). Other useful functions are format and formatC. For example, if we assign t1 <- t.test(v1) then the following command prints out a nicely formatted result, suitable for dumping into a paper:

```
> x1 <- sleep$extra[sleep$group == 1]
> x2 <- sleep$extra[sleep$group == 2]
> t1 <- t.test(x1, x2)
> print(paste("(t_{",t1[[2]],"}=",
+    formatC(t1[[1]],format="f",digits=2),", p=",
+    formatC(t1[[3]],format="f"),")",sep=""),
+    quote=FALSE)
```

This works because the output of the `t.test()` assigned to `t1` is actually a list, and the numbers in the double brackets refer to the elements of the list.

* `read.table("file1")` reads in data from a file. The first line of the file can (but need not) contain the names of the variables in each column.

1.2.2.6   Dealing with Objects

All objects created by the user are stored in an R environment called `.GlobalEnv` (can also be accessed by `globalenv()`. The `ls()` and `objects()` functions lists all the active objects in `.GlobalEnv`. Other system files, such as the built-in datasets and statistical functions, are stored in various packages. A list of the loaded packages can be found by `search()`. Note that `search()` numbers the packages.

```
> search()
 [1]  ".GlobalEnv"
 [2]  "package:stats"
 [3]  "package:graphics"
 [4]  "package:grDevices"
 [5]  "package:utils"
 [6]  "package:datasets"
 [7]  "package:methods"
 [8]  "Autoloads"
 [9]  "package:base"
```

Thus, `ls(pos = 2)` or simply `ls(2)` shows all objects in the `package:stats` (or by `objects(2)`). To remove one or more data objects, do `rm(object1)` to remove only `object1` or `rm(x1, x2, v1, v2, object2, object3)` to remove multiple objects. Type `rm(list=ls())` to remove all objects in the current environment. Be careful with this because the `rm()` function assumes you know what you are doing so it does not prompt you for a confirmation. `attach(df1)` makes the variables in the data frame `df1` active and available generally. Sometimes you are working in one directory but you need to access data saved in another directory, type `attach("/another/directory/.RData")` to gain access to data objects saved in that directory. `names(obj1)` prints the names, e.g., of a matrix or data frame. `typeof()`, `mode()`, and `class()` tell you about the properties of an object.

1.3   Data Objects and Data Types

One of the most basic data objects in R is a vector. A vector can be put together by the function `c()`. We can calculate its `length`, `mean`, and other properties.

```
> x <- c(1, 2, 3, 4, 5, 6, 7)
> length(x)
[1] 7
> mean(x)
[1] 4
```

We can refer to the elements of a vector in various ways.

```
> x[6]
[1] 6
> x[-6]              # all elements except the 6th
[1] 1 2 3 4 5 7
> x[2:4]             # : represents a sequence
[1] 2 3 4
> x[c(1, 4, 7)]
[1] 1 4 7
```

A colon, :, is a way to abbreviate a sequence of numbers, e.g., 1:5 is equivalent to 1,2,3,4,5. A sequence of evenly spaced numbers can be generated by seq(from = 1, to = 6, length = 20) (20 evenly spaced numbers from 1 to 6) or seq(from = -3, to = 3, by = 0.05) (from −3 to +3 in increment of 0.05). c(number.list1) makes the list of numbers (separated by commas) into a vector object. For example, c(1,2,3,4,5) (but 1:5 is already a vector, so you do not need to say c(1:5)). rep(v1,n1) repeats the vector v1 n1 times. For example, rep(c(1:5),2) is 1,2,3,4,5,1,2,3,4,5. rep(v1,v2) repeats each element of the vector v1 a number of times indicated by the corresponding element of the vector v2. The vectors v1 and v2 must have the same length. For example, rep(c(1,2,3),c(2,2,2)) is 1,1,2,2,3,3. Notice that this can also be written as rep(c(1,2,3),rep(2,3)). (See also the function gl() for generating factors according to a pattern.)

1.3.1 Vectors of Character Strings

R is not intended as a language for manipulating text (unlike Perl, for example), but it is surprisingly powerful. If you know R you might not need to learn Perl. Strings are character variables that consist of letters, numbers, and symbols. A c("one", "two", "3") is a vector of character strings. You can use

```
> paste("one", "two", "3", sep = ":")
[1] "one:two:3"
```

to paste three character strings together into one long character string. Or to unpaste them by

```
> strsplit(paste("one", "two", "3", sep = ":"), ":")
[[1]]
[1] "one" "two" "3"
```

grep(), sub(), gsub(), and regexpr() allow you to search for, and replace, parts of strings.

The set functions such as union(), intersect(), setdiff(), and %in% are also useful for dealing with databases that consist of strings such as names and email addresses.

Calculating date and time differences needs special care because of leap years and other complications. Raw data in character strings of date and time should be converted into the POSIX date time classes using the strptime() function. Suppose, we have the birth dates of two children and today's date.

```
> bdate <- strptime(c("2/28/2002", "3/05/2006"),
+ format = "%m/%d/%Y")
> today <- strptime(c("2/28/2008"),
+ format = "%m/%d/%Y")
```

The option format="%m/%d/%Y" specifies how the date character string is formatted, by month, day, and the four-digit year (separated by forward slashes). The first child was born on 2/28/2002, precisely six years old on 2/28/2008. The second child's age in years is 1 because the child has not yet reached 2 years of age. You might be tempted to calculate age by:

```
> difftime(today, bdate, units="days")/365.25
```

But you get 5.999 and 1.985, which cannot be easily fixed by rounding. As of R-2.13.1, difftime() does not yet offer a "years" unit. Decimal age values of 5.999 and 1.985 may be acceptable for practical purposes, for example, in describing the average age of research study participants. However, they do not match the way we typically treat age as an non-negative integer.

A solution uses the components of a POSIX date.[1]

```
> age <- today$year - bdate$year
> age
[1] 6 2
> t1 <- bdate$mon + bdate$mday/31; t1
[1] 1.56 2.10
> t2 <- today$mon + today$mday/31; t2
[1] 1.56
> ti <- t2 < t1
> age[ti] <- age[ti] - 1
> age
[1] 6 1
```

The $mon component of a date variable takes on numeric values of 0, 1, 2, ..., 11 for January, February, March, and December, respectively. The $mday component

---

represents the day of the month. So the children are 1.56 and 2.10 months from January 1, 2006; and `today` is 1.56 months from January 1, 2008. The division by 31 yields an approximated fraction of a month. So that the first child is 6 years of age and the second child is 1 year of age. The `difftime()` function provides time units in seconds, minutes, hours, days, and weeks. The resolution of weeks is usually enough for a time to event analysis. However, we are not limited by the restrictions of existing functions when we take advantage of the POSIX date components. The `strptime()` function is especially useful when date variables are entered into a spreadsheet program as character strings.

There are many other powerful features of R's character strings. You can even use these functions to write new R commands as strings, so that R can program itself. Just to see an example of how this works, try `eval(parse(text = "t.test(1:5)"))`. The `parse()` function turns the text into an R expression, and `eval()` evaluates and runs the expression. So this is equivalent to typing `t.test(1:5)` directly. But you could replace `t.test(1:5)` with any string constructed by R itself.

1.3.2   Matrices, Lists, and Data Frames

The call to `matrix(v1, nrow = 2, ncol = 3)` makes the vector `v1` into a 2x3 matrix. You do not need to specify both `nrow` and `ncol`. You can also use key words instead of using position to indicate which argument is which, and then you do not need the commas. For example, `matrix(1:10, ncol=5)` represents the matrix

$$\begin{bmatrix} 1 & 3 & 5 & 7 & 9 \\ 2 & 4 & 6 & 8 & 10 \end{bmatrix}.$$

Notice that the matrix is filled column by column. To fill the matrix by rows, do `matrix(1:10, ncol = 5, byrow = TRUE)`.

`cbind(v1,v2,v3)` puts vectors `v1`, `v2`, and `v3` (all of the same length) together as columns of a matrix. You can of course give this a name, such as `mat1 <- cbind(v1,v2,v2)`.

Many R functions require that you collect variables in a `data.frame()` object, for example, `datc <- data.frame(v1, v2, v3)`. Note that `v1`, `v2`, and `v3` must be of the same length. A data frame can include vectors of factors as well as numeric vectors.

```
> ctl <- c(4.17,5.58,5.18,6.11,4.50,4.61,5.17,4.53,
+ 5.33,5.14)
> trt <- c(4.81,4.17,4.41,3.59,5.87,3.83,6.03,4.89,
+ 4.32,4.69)
> group <- gl(2,10,20, labels=c("Ctl","Trt"))
```

```
> datc <- data.frame(weight = c(ctl, trt),
+           group = group)
> datc[1:3, ]
  weight group
1   4.17   Ctl
2   5.58   Ctl
3   5.18   Ctl
```

Inside data.frame(), text strings such as group are automatically converted into a factor() object. So is.factor(datc$group) returns TRUE. We can extract parts of a data frames with matrix operations such that datc[1:3,] extracts the first three rows of data. dim(obj1) prints the dimensions of a matrix, array, or data frame. Alternatively, the data can be entered into a spreadsheet program, saved as a CSV file, and imported into R by:

```
> datc <- data.frame(read.csv(file = "data.csv"))
```

We can refer to variables of a data frame by, for example, datc$weight. We can calculate the average weight across the two groups by:

```
> tapply(datc$weight, datc$group, mean)
Ctl    Trt
5.032 4.661
```

which applies the function mean to datc$weight by the factor datc$group. We can replace mean by sd or length to calculate the standard deviation and the number of observations in the two groups, respectively. Confidence intervals of the group means can also be calculated easily:

```
> tapply(datc$weight, datc$group, function(x) {
+   ans <- t.test(x)$conf.int
+   unlist(ans)    } )
$Ctl
[1] 4.614882 5.449118
attr(,"conf.level")
[1] 0.95

$Trt
[1] 4.093239 5.228761
attr(,"conf.level")
[1] 0.95
```

The function(x) inside tapply() takes x and sends it to t.test() to calculate the 95% confidence intervals of the means by datc$group. Because t.test() returns a list by default, so we unlist() the answer before sending it back. The use of tapply() to calculate confidence intervals is useful in plotting error bars in a graph.

You can refer to parts of objects. m1 [,3] is the third column of matrix m1. m1 [,-3] is all the columns except the third. m1 [m1 [,1]>3,] is all the rows for which the first column is greater than 3. v1 [2] is the second element of vector v1. If df1 is a data frame with columns a, b, and c, you can refer to the third column as df1$c.

Many functions return lists. You can see the elements of a list with unlist (). For example, try unlist (t.test (1:5)) to see what the t.test () function returns. This is also listed in the section of help pages called "Value."

array () seems very complicated at first, but it is extremely useful when you have a three-way classification, e.g., subjects, cases, and questions, with each question asked about each case. We give an example later.

outer (m1, m2, "fun1") applies fun1, a function of two variables, to each combination of m1 and m2. The default is to multiply them.

mapply ("fun1", o1, o2), another very powerful function, applies fun1 to the elements of o1 and o2. For example, if these are data frames, and fun1 is "t.test", you will get a list of t tests comparing the first column of o1 with the first column of o2, the second with the second, and so on. This is because the basic elements of a data frame are the columns.

1.3.2.1 Summaries and Calculations by Row, Column, or Group

summary (x1) prints statistics for the variables (columns) in x1, which may be a vector, matrix, or data frame. See also the str () function, which is similar, and aggregate (), which summarizes by groups.

table (x1) prints a table of the number of times each value occurs in x1. table (x1, y1) prints a cross-tabulation of the two variables. The table function can do a lot more. Use prop.table () when you want proportions rather than counts. ave (v1, v2) yields averages of vector v1 grouped by the factor v2. cumsum (v1) is the cumulative sum of vector v1.

You can do calculations on rows or columns of a matrix and get the result as a vector. apply (x, 2, mean) yields just the means of the columns. Similarly, apply (x, 2, sum) calculates the sums of the columns. Shown in the diagram below, apply (x, 2, sum) takes the matrix x_{ij} (the rectangle on top) and applies the sum () function on each column from the top row to the bottom row.

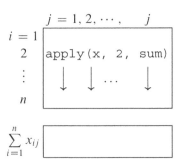

The sums of j columns are reduced into a vector of j numbers (the rectangle at the bottom). Therefore, `apply(x, 2, sum)` is equivalent to the mathematical notation $\sum_{i=1}^{n} x_{ij}$. We get the sum of x_{ij} over index i, keeping j. Abstract mathematical calculations can be visualized as operations performed on data objects. For sums and means, it is easier to use `rowSums()`, `colSums()`, `rowMeans()`, and `colMeans` instead of `apply()`. Next time you have to track many summation symbols, you might consider getting help from `apply()` and others.

You can use other functions aside from `mean`, such as `sd`, `max`, or `min`. To ignore missing data, use `apply(x1, 2, mean, na.rm = T)`, etc. Note that you can use apply with a function, e.g., `apply(x1, 1, function(x) exp(sum(log(x))))` (which is a roundabout way to write `apply(x1,1,prod)`). The same thing can be written in two steps, e.g.:

```
> newprod <- function(x) {exp(sum(log(x)))
> apply(x1, 1, newprod)
```

You can refer to a subset of an object in many ways. One way is to use a square bracket at the end, e.g., `matrix1[,1:5]` refers to columns 1 through 5 of the matrix. A new object like `(matrix1+matrix2)[,1:5]` refers to the first five columns of the sum of the two matrices. Another important method is the use of `by()` or `aggregate()` to compute statistics for subgroups defined by vectors or factors. You can also use `split()` to get a list of subgroups. Finally, many functions allow you to use a `subset` argument.

1.4 Functions and Debugging

Use `function()` to write your own functions. For example, we can define a function to calculate the standard error of a sample mean.

```
se <- function(x, Warn = T)
{
  y <- x[!is.na(x)]
  if(Warn) {
  D <- length(x) - length(y)
  xn <- deparse(substitute(x))
  if(D >= 1)
  warning(paste(D, "missing values omitted in", xn))
  }
  # browser()
  sqrt(var(as.vector(y))/length(y))
}
```

Several functions are useful for debugging your own functions or scripts: `debug()`, `traceback()`, `browser()`, and `recover()`. In the above

example, a `browser()` is commented out. You can use `fix(se)` to edit `se()`
and uncomment that line. Then `se()` will pause when it reaches `browser()` and
prompts `Browse[1]>` for user input. At this point you can test how the rest of the
program works. An upper case Q quits the `browser()` debugger.

```
> se(c(1, 2, 3, 4, 5, 6, NA))
Called from: se(c(1, 2, 3, 4, 5, 6, NA))
Browse[1]> sqrt(var(as.vector(y)))
[1] 1.870829
Warning message:
In se(c(1, 2, 3, 4, 5, 6, NA)) :
  1 missing values omitted in c(1, 2, 3, 4, 5, 6, NA)
Browse[1]> sqrt(var(as.vector(x)))
[1] NA
Browse[1]> Q
```

Exercises

1.1. Indexing vectors
Suppose we have three vectors, `v1`, `v2`, and `v3`.

```
> v1 <- 1:7
> v2 <- 6:12
> v3 <- c("new", "old", "old", "old", "new", "new",
+          "new")
```

(a) Use the `intersect()` function to find the elements of `v1` that have the same
    value as elements of `v2`.
(b) Use the `%in%` operator to find the elements of `v1` that have the same value as
    elements of `v2`.
(c) List all `v3` elements whose `v1` and `v2` values are the same.
(d) List all `v1` elements whose `v3` elements are `"new"`.

1.2. Viewing data
R's default data management method is by command line, not by a spreadsheet-
like user interface. For example, `datc[which(datc$group == "Ctl"),]`
prints all control group observations.

(a) Write the command to view control group subjects whose weight is greater or
    equal to 5.
(b) List all subjects in the `sleep` data frame whose extra sleep time is more than
    1 h.
(c) List all Group 1 subjects in the `sleep` data frame whose extra sleep time is
    reduced by 1 h or more.

1.3. Use `tapply()` to Calculate Descriptive Statistics

Let us revisit the `sleep` data frame to calculate descriptive statistics.

(a) Use the `tapply()` and `mean()` functions to calculate the group means.
(b) Use the `tapply()` and `sd()` functions to calculate the group standard deviations.
(c) Use the `tapply()` and `length()` functions to calculate the number of subjects per group.
(d) Calculate the standard errors of the group means.
(e) Calculate the 95% confidence intervals of the group means using the `t.test()` function within `tapply()`.

1.4. Array Indexing

Suppose we create an array x by `x <- array(c(1:24), c(3, 4, 2))`. So x is a 3×4×2 array with subscripts $i = 1, 2, 3$; $j = 1, 2, 3, 4$; and $k = 1, 2$ representing the three dimensions of x, respectively.

(a) How do you use R to calculate $\sum_{i=1}^{n} x_{ijk}$?
(b) How about summing over two dimensions, such as $\sum_{k}\sum_{i} x_{ijk}$?

1.5. Finding `which` Elements

Suppose x is drawn randomly from a normal distribution, say `x <- rnorm(30)`.

(a) Use the `which()` function to determine which elements of x are negative.
(b) Do the same with the `seq()` function with the `along=x` option.

Suppose x is converted into a matrix by `x <- matrix(x, ncol = 5)`.

(a) Use `which()` with the `arr.ind = TRUE` option to retrieve the row and column indices of elements of x that are negative.

Chapter 2
Reading and Transforming Data Format

2.1 Reading and Transforming Data

2.1.1 Data Layout

R, like Splus and S, represents an entire conceptual system for thinking about data. You may need to learn some new ways of thinking. One way that is new for users of Systat, SAS, and (probably) SPSS concerns two different ways of laying out a data set. In the Systat way, each subject is a row (which may be continued on the next row if too long, but still conceptually a row) and each variable is a column. You can do this in R too, and most of the time it is sufficient.

But some the features of R will not work with this kind of representation, in particular, repeated-measures analysis of variance or hierarchical linear modeling. So you need a second way of representing data, which is that each row represents a single datum, e.g., one subject's answer to one question. The row also contains an identifier for all the relevant classifications, such as the question number, the subscale that the question is part of, and the subject. Thus, "subject" becomes a category with no special status, technically a factor (and remember to make sure it is a factor, lest you find yourself studying the effect of the subject's number).

The former is referred to as the *wide* layout and the latter the *long* layout to be consistent with the terms used by the reshapde() function.

2.1.2 A Simple Questionnaire Example

Let us start with an example of the old-fashioned way. In the file ctest3.data, each subject is a row, and there are 134 columns. The first four are age, sex, student status, and time to complete the study. The rest are the responses to four questions

Y. Li and J. Baron, *Behavioral Research Data Analysis with R*, Use R,
DOI 10.1007/978-1-4614-1238-0_2, © Springer Science+Business Media, LLC 2012

about each of 32 cases. Each group of four is preceded by the trial order, but this is ignored for now.

```
> c0 <- read.table(file = "ctest3.data")
```

The file can be downloaded from the data file has no labels, so we can read it with read.table. You can also try read.csv or read.delim. The file parameter can be ignored. If the data file is found online then the file parameter can be the complete URL address to that file.

```
> age1 <- c0[,1]
> sex1 <- c0[,2]
> student1 <- c0[,3]
> time1 <- c0[,4]
> nsub1 <- nrow(c0)
```

We can refer to elements of c0 by c0[row,column]. For example, c0[1,2] is the sex of the first subject. We can leave one part blank and get all of it, e.g., c0[,2] is a vector (column of numbers) representing the sex of all the subjects. The last line defines nsub1 as the number of subjects.

```
> c1 <- as.matrix(c0[,4+1:128])
```

Now c1 is the main part of the data, the matrix of responses. The expression 1:128 is a vector, which expands to 1 2 3 ... 128. By adding 4, it becomes 5 6 7 ... 132.

2.1.2.1 Extracting Subsets of Data

```
> rsp1 <- c1[,4*c(1:32)-2]
> rsp2 <- c1[,4*c(1:32)-1]
```

The above two lines illustrate the extraction of sub-matrices representing answers to two of the four questions making up each item. The matrix rsp1 has 32 columns, corresponding to columns 2 6 10 ... 126 of the original 128-column matrix c1. The matrix rsp2 corresponds to 3 7 11 ... 127.

Another way to do this is to use an array. We could say a1 <- array(c1, c(ns, 4, 32)). Then a1[,1,] is the equivalent of rsp1, and a1[20,1,] is rsp1 for subject 20. To see how arrays print out, try the following:

```
> m1 <- matrix(1:60,5,)
> a1 <- array(m1,c(5,2,6))
> m1
> a1
```

You will see that the rows of each table are the first index and the columns are the second index. Arrays seem difficult at first, but they are very useful for this sort of analysis.

2.1.2.2 Finding Means (or Other Things) of Sets of Variables

```
> r1mean <- apply(rsp1,1,mean)
> r2mean <- apply(rsp2,1,mean)
```

The above lines illustrate the use of `apply` for getting means of subscales. In particular, `abrmean` is the mean of the subscale consisting of the answers to the second question in each group. The `apply` function works on the data in its first argument, then applies the function in its third argument, which, in this case, is `mean`. (It can be `max` or `min` or any defined function.) The second argument is 1 for rows, 2 for columns (and so on, for arrays). We want the function applied to rows.

```
> r4mean <- apply(c1[,4*c(1:32)], 1, mean)
```

The expression here represents the matrix for the last item in each group of four. The first argument can be any matrix or data frame. (The output for a data frame will be labeled with row or column names.) For example, suppose you have a list of variables such as `q1`, `q2`, `q3`, etc. Each is a vector, whose length is the number of subjects. The average of the first three variables for each subject is `apply(cbind(q1,q2,q3),1,mean)`. (This is the equivalent of the Systat expression `avg(q1, q2, q3)`. A little more verbose, to be sure, but much more flexible.)

You can use apply to tabulate the values of each column of a matrix `m1`: `apply(m1, 2, table)`. Or, to find column means, `apply(m1, 2, mean)`.

There are many other ways to make tables. Some of the relevant functions are `table`, `tapply`, `sapply`, `ave`, and `by`. Here is an illustration of the use of `by`. Suppose you have a matrix `m1` like this:

```
1 2 3 4
4 4 5 5
5 6 4 5
```

The columns represent the combination of two variables, `y1` is 0 0 1 1, for the four columns, respectively, and `y2` is 0 1 0 1. To get the means of the columns for the two values of `y1`, say `by(t(m1), y1, mean)`. You get 3.67 and 4.33 (labeled appropriately by values of `y1`). You need to use `t(m1)` because by works by rows. If you say `by(t(m1), data.frame(y1,y2), mean)`, you get a cross tabulation of the means by both factors. (This is, of course, the means of the four columns of the original matrix.)

Of course, you can also use by to classify rows; in the usual examples, this would be groups of subjects rather than classifications of variables.

2.1.2.3 One Row Per Observation

The next subsection shows how to transform the data from the *wide* layout (one row per subject) to the *long* layout (one row per observation). We will use the matrix rsp1, which has 32 columns and one row per subject. Here are the data from five subjects:

```
1 1 2 2 1 2 3 5 2 3 2 4 2 5 7 7 6 6 7 5 7 8 7 9 8 8 9 9 8 9 9 9
1 2 3 2 1 3 2 3 2 3 2 3 2 3 2 4 1 2 4 5 4 5 5 6 5 6 6 7 6 7 7 8
1 1 2 3 1 2 3 4 2 3 3 4 2 4 3 4 4 4 5 5 5 6 6 7 6 7 7 8 7 7 8 8
1 2 2 2 2 3 3 3 3 4 4 4 4 5 5 5 5 6 6 6 6 7 7 7 7 8 8 8 8 9 9 9
1 1 1 2 2 2 2 3 3 3 3 4 4 4 4 5 5 5 5 6 6 6 6 7 7 7 7 8 8 8 8 9
```

We will create a matrix with one row per observation. The first column will contain the observations, one variable at a time, and the remaining columns will contain numbers representing the subject and the level of the observation on each variable of interest. There are two such variables here, r2 and r1. The variable r2 has four levels, 1 2 3 4, and it cycles through the 32 columns as 1 2 3 4 1 2 3 4 ... The variable r1 has the values (for successive columns) 1 1 1 1 2 2 2 2 3 3 3 3 4 4 4 4 1 1 1 1 2 2 2 2 3 3 3 3 4 4 4 4. These levels are ordered. They are not just arbitrary labels. (For that, we would need the factor function.)

```
> r2 <- rep(1:4,8)
> r1 <- rep(rep(1:4,rep(4,4)),2)
```

The above two lines create vectors representing the levels of each variable for each subject. The rep command for r2 says to repeat the sequence 1 2 3 4, eight times. The rep command for r1 says take the sequence 1 2 3 4, then repeat the first element four times, the second element four times, etc. It does this by using a vector as its second argument. That vector is rep(4,4), which means repeat the number 4, four times. So rep(4,4) is equivalent to c(4 4 4 4). The last argument, 2, in the command for r1 means that the whole sequence is repeated twice. Notice that r1 and r2 are the codes for one row of the matrix rsp1.

```
> nsub1 <- nrow(rsp1)
> subj1 <- as.factor(rep(1:nsub1,32))
```

nsub1 is just the number of subjects (5 in the example), the number of rows in the matrix rsp1. The vector subj1 is what we will need to assign a subject number to each observation. It consists of the sequence 1 2 3 4 5, repeated 32 times. It corresponds to the columns of rsp1.

```
> abr1 <- data.frame(ab1 = as.vector(rsp1),
+ sub1 = subj1, dcost1 = rep(r1,rep(nsub1,32)),
+ abcost1 = rep(r2,rep(nsub1,32)))
```

The data.frame function puts together several vectors into a data frame, which has rows and columns like a matrix.[1] Each vector becomes a column. The as.vector function reads down by columns, that is, the first column, then the

---

[1]The cbind function does the same thing but makes a matrix instead of a data frame.

second, and so on. So ab is now a vector in which the first nsub1 elements are the same as the first column of rsp1, that is, 1 1 1 1 1. The first 15 elements of ab are: 1 1 1 1 1 1 2 1 2 1 2 3 2 2 1. Notice how we can define names within the arguments to the data.frame function. Of course, sub1 now represents the subject number of each observation. The first ten elements of sub1 are 1 2 3 4 5 1 2 3 4 5. The variable abcost1 now refers to the value of r2. Notice that each of the 32 elements of r2 is repeated nsub1 times. Thus, the first 15 values of abcost1 are 1 1 1 1 1 2 2 2 2 2 3 3 3 3 3. Here are the first ten rows of abr1:

```
    ab1 sub1 dcost1 abcost1
1    1    1     1       1
2    1    2     1       1
3    1    3     1       1
4    1    4     1       1
5    1    5     1       1
6    1    1     1       2
7    2    2     1       2
8    1    3     1       2
9    2    4     1       2
10   1    5     1       2
```

The following line makes a table of the means of abr1, according to the values of dcost1 (rows) and abcost1 (columns).

```
> ctab1 <- tapply(abr1[,1],list(abr1[,3],abr1[,4]),
    mean)
```

It uses the function tapply, which is like the apply function except that the output is a table. The first argument is the vector of data to be used. The second argument is a list supplying the classification in the table. This list has two columns corresponding to the columns of abr representing the classification. The third argument is the function to be applied to each grouping, which in this case is the mean. Here is the resulting table:

```
    1   2   3   4
1 2.6 3.0 3.7 3.8
2 3.5 4.4 4.4 5.4
3 4.5 5.2 5.1 5.9
4 5.1 6.1 6.2 6.8
```

The following line provides a plot corresponding to the table.

```
> matplot(ctab1, type = "l")
```

Type l means lines. Each line plots the four points in a column of the table. If you want it to go by rows, use t(ctab1) instead of ctab1. The function t() transposes rows and columns.

Finally, the following line does a regression of the response on the two classifiers, actually an analysis of variance.

```
> summary(aov(ab1 ~ dcost1 + abcost1 +
+        Error(sub1/(dcost1 + abcost1)), data = abr))
```

The function aov, like lm, fits a linear model, because dcost1 and abcost1 are numerical variables, not factors (although sub1 is a factor). The model is defined by its first argument (to the left of the comma), where ~ separates the dependent variable from the predictors. The second element defines the data frame to be used. The summary function prints a summary of the regression. (The lm and aov objects themselves contains other things, such as residuals, many of which are not automatically printed.) We explain the Error term later in Sect. 5.1, but the point of it is to make sure that we test against random variation due to subjects, that is, test "across subjects." Here is some of the output, which shows significant effects of both predictors:

```
Error: sub1
          Df Sum Sq Mean Sq F value Pr(>F)
Residuals  4 52.975  13.244

Error: sub1:dcost1
          Df  Sum Sq Mean Sq F value      Pr(>F)
dcost1     1 164.711 164.711  233.63 0.0001069 ***
Residuals  4   2.820   0.705
---

Error: sub1:abcost1
          Df Sum Sq Mean Sq F value    Pr(>F)
abcost1    1 46.561  46.561    41.9 0.002935 **
Residuals  4  4.445   1.111
---

Error: Within
           Df Sum Sq Mean Sq F value Pr(>F)
Residuals 145 665.93    4.59
```

Note that, in many examples in this section, we used rep() to generate repeated values. We can also use the gl() function for this. For example, instead of subj1 <- as.factor(rep(1:nsub1,32)), we could say subj1 <- gl(nsub1,1,nsub1*32). The first argument specifies the number of levels, which in this case is the number of subjects. The second argument specifies the number of immediate repetitions of each level (within each cycle, when there are cycles – not the total number of repetitions), and the third argument specifies the total length, which is here the number of subjects times the number of items. If we wanted a code for each item, we could say gl(32,nsub1,nsub1*32). But here we do not need the last argument because there is only one cycle. Each item number is immediately repeated nsub1 times. Thus, we could say gl(32,nsub1). The gl() function is useful because it avoids having to say as.factor, which is often forgotten.

2.1.3 Other Ways to Read in Data

First example. Here is another example of creating a matrix with one row per observation.

```
> symp1 <- read.table("symp1.data",header=T)
> sy1 <- as.matrix(symp1[,c(1:17)])
```

The first 17 columns of symp1 are of interest. The file symp1.data contains the names of the variables in its first line. The header=T (an abbreviation for header=TRUE) makes sure that the names are used; otherwise the variables will be names V1, V2, etc.

```
> gr1 <- factor(symp1$group1)
```

The variable group1, which is in the original data, is a factor that is unordered.

The next four lines create the new matrix, defining identifiers for subjects and items in a questionnaire.

```
> syv1 <- as.vector(sy1)
> subj1 <- factor(rep(1:nrow(sy1),ncol(sy1)))
> item <- factor(rep(1:ncol(sy1),rep(nrow(sy1),
+         ncol(sy1))))
> grp <- rep(gr1,ncol(sy1))
> cgrp <- ((grp==2) | (grp==3))+0
```

The variable cgrp is a code for being in grp 2 or 3. The reason for adding 0 is to make the logical vector of T and F into a numeric vector of 1 and 0.

The following three lines create a table from the new matrix, plot the results, and report the results of an analysis of variance.

```
> sytab <- tapply(syv,list(item,grp),mean)
> matplot(sytab,type="l")
> svlm <- aov(syv ~ item + grp + item*grp)
```

Second example. In the next example, the data file has labels. We want to refer to the labels as if they were variables we had defined, so we use the attach function.

```
> t9 <- read.table("tax9.data",header=T)
> attach(t9)
```

Third example. In the next example, the data file has no labels, so we can read it with scan. The scan function just reads in the numbers and makes them into a vector, that is, a single column of numbers.

```
> abh1 <- matrix(scan("abh1.data"),,224,byrow=T))
```

We then apply the matrix command to make it into a matrix. (There are many other ways to do this.) We know that the matrix should have 224 columns, the number of variables, so we should specify the number of columns. If you say help(matrix) you will see that the matrix command requires several arguments, separated by commas. The first is the vector that is to be made into a matrix, which in this case is scan("abh1.data"). We could have given this vector a name, and then used its name, but there is no point. The second and third arguments are the number of rows and the number of columns. We can leave the number of rows blank. (That way, if we add or delete subjects, we do not need to change anything.) The number of columns is 224. By default, the matrix command fills the matrix by columns, so we need to say byrow=TRUE or byrow=T to get it to fill by rows, which is what we want. (Otherwise, we could just leave that field blank.)

We can refer to elements of abh1 by abh1[row,column]. For example, abh1[1,2] is the sex of the first subject. We can leave one part blank and get all of it, e.g., abh1[,2] is a vector (column of numbers) representing the sex of all the subjects.

2.1.4 Other Ways to Transform Variables

2.1.4.1 Contrasts

Suppose you have a matrix t1 with four columns. Each row is a subject. You want to contrast the mean of columns 1 and 3 with the mean of columns 2 and 4. A *t*-test would be fine. (Otherwise, this is the equivalent of the cmatrix command in Systat.) Here are three ways to do it. The first way calculates the mean of the columns 1 and 3 and subtracts the mean of columns 2 and 4. The result is a vector. When we apply t.test() to a vector, it tests whether the mean of the values is different from 0.

```
> t1 <- matrix(rnorm(40), ncol = 4)
> t.test(apply(t1[c(1,3),], 2, mean) -
+ apply(t1[c(2, 4), ], 2, mean))
```

The second way multiplies the matrix by a vector representing the contrast weights, 1, -1, 1, -1. Ordinary multiplication of a matrix by a vector multiplies the rows, but we want the columns, so we must apply t() to transform the matrix, and then transform it back.

```
> t.test(t(t(t1)*c(1,-1,1,-1)))
```

or

```
> contr1 <- c(1,-1,1,-1)
> t.test(t(t(t1)*contr1))
```

The third way is the most elegant. It uses matrix multiplication to accomplish the same thing.

```
> contr1 <- c(1,-1,1,-1)
> t.test(t1 %*% contr1)
```

2.1.4.2   Averaging Items in a Within-Subject Design

Suppose we have a matrix t2, with 32 columns. Each row is a subject. The 32 columns represent a 8x4 design. The first eight columns represent eight different levels of the first variable, at the first level of the second variable. The next eight columns are the second level of the second variable, etc. Suppose we want a matrix in which the columns represent the eight different levels of the first variable, averaged across the second variable.

First method: loop

One way to do it – inelegantly but effectively – is with a loop. First, we set up the resulting matrix. (We cannot put anything in it this way if it doesn't exist yet.)

```
> m2 <- t2[,c(1:8)]*0
```

The idea here is just to make sure that the matrix has the right number of rows, and all 0's. Now here is the loop:

```
> for (i in 1:8) m2[,i] <- apply(t2[,i+c(8*0:3)],1,
    mean)
```

Here, the index i is stepped through the columns of m2, filling each one with the mean of four columns of t2. For example, the first column of m2 is the mean of columns 1, 9, 17, and 25 of t2. This is because the vector c(8*0:3) is 0, 8, 16, 24. The apply function uses 1 as its second argument, which means to apply the function mean across *rows*.

Second method: matrix multiplication

Now here is a more elegant way, but one that requires an auxiliary matrix, which may use memory if that is a problem. This time we want the means according to the second variable, which has four levels, so we want a matrix with four columns. We will multiply the matrix t2 by an auxiliary matrix c0.

The matrix c0 has 32 rows and four columns. The first column is 1,1,1,1,1,1,1,1 followed by 24 0's. This is the result of rep(c(1,0,0,0),rep(8,4)), which repeats each of the elements of 1,0,0,0 eight times (since rep(8,4) means 8,8,8,8). The second column is 8 0's, 8 1's, and 16 0's.

```
> c0 <- cbind(rep(c(1,0,0,0), rep(8,4)), rep(c(0,1,0,0),
+              rep(8,4)), rep(c(0,0,1,0), rep(8,4)),
+              rep(c(0,0,0,1), rep(8,4)))
> c2 <- t2 %*% c0
```

The last line above uses matrix multiplication to create the matrix c2, which has four columns and one row per subject. Note that the order here is important; switching t2 and c0 will not work.

2.1.4.3 Selecting Cases or Variables

There are several other ways for defining new matrices or data frames as subsets of other matrices or data frames.

One very useful function is which(), which yields the indices for which its argument is true. For example, the output of which(3:10 > 4) is the vector 3 4 5 6 7 8, because the vector 3:10 has a length of 8, and the first two places in it do not meet the criterion that their value is greater than 4. With which(), you can use a vector to select rows or columns from a matrix (or data frame). For example, suppose you have nine variables in a matrix m9 and you want to select three submatrices, one consisting of variables 1, 4, 7, another with 2, 5, 8, and another with 3, 6, 9. Define mvec so that it is the vector 1 2 3 1 2 3 1 2 3.

```
> m9 <- matrix(rnorm(90), ncol = 9)
> mvec9 <- rep(1:3,3)
> m9a <- m9[,which(mvec9 == 1)]
> m9b <- m9[,which(mvec9 == 2)]
> m9c <- m9[,which(mvec9 == 3)]
```

You can use the same method to select subjects by any criterion, putting the which() expression before the comma rather than after it, so that it indicates rows.

2.1.4.4 Recoding and Replacing Data

Suppose you have m1 a matrix of data in which 99 represents missing data, and you want to replace each 99 with NA. Simply say m1[m1==99] <- NA. Note that this will work only if m1 is a matrix (or vector), not a data frame (which could result from a read.table() command). You might need to use the as.matrix() function first.

Sometimes you want to recode a variable, e.g., a column in a matrix. If q1[,3] is a 7-point scale and you want to reverse it, you can say

```
> q1[,3] <- 8 - q1[,3]
```

In general, suppose you want to recode the numbers 1,2,3,4,5 so that they come out as 1,5,3,2,4, respectively. You have a matrix m1, containing just the numbers 1 through 5. You can say

```
> c1 <- c(1,5,3,2,4)
> apply(m1,1:2,function(x) c1[x])
```

In this case c1[x] is just the value at the position indicated by x.

Suppose that, instead of 1 through 5, you have A through E, so that you cannot use numerical positions. You want to convert A,B,C,D,E to 1,5,3,2,4, respectively. You can use two vectors:

```
> c1 <- c(1,5,3,2,4)
> n1 <- c("A","B","C","D","E")
> apply(m1,1:2,function(x) c1[which(n1)==x])
```

Or, alternatively, you can give names to c1 instead of using a second vector:

```
> c1 <- c(1,5,3,2,4)
> names(c1) <- c("A","B","C","D","E")
> apply(m1,1:2,function(x) c1[x])
```

The same general idea will work for arrays, vectors, etc., instead of matrices.

Here are some other examples, which may be useful in simple cases, or as illustrations of various tricks.

In this example, q2[,c(2,4)] are two columns that must be recoded by switching 1 and 2 but leaving responses of 3 or more intact. To do this, say

```
> q2[,c(2,4)] <- (q2[,c(2,4)] < 3) * (3 - q2[,c(2,4)]) +
+     (q2[,c(2,4)] >= 3) * q2[,c(2,4)]
```

Here the expression q2[,c(2,4)] < 3 is a two-column matrix full of TRUE and FALSE. By putting it in parentheses, you can multiply it by numbers, and TRUE and FALSE are treated as 1 and 0, respectively. Thus, (q2[,c(2,4)] < 3) * (3 - q2[,c(2,4)]) switches 1 and 2, for all entries less than 3. The expression (q2[,c(2,4)] >= 3) * q2[,c(2,4)] replaces all the other values, those greater than or equal to 3, with themselves.

Here is an example that will switch 1 and 3, 2 and 4, but leave 5 unchanged, for columns 7 and 9

```
> q3[,c(7,9)] <- (q3[,c(7,9)]==1)*3 +
+     (q3[,c(7,9)]==2)*4 + (q3[,c(7,9)]==3)*1 +
+     (q3[,c(7,9)]==4)*2 + (q3[,c(7,9)]==5)*5
```

Notice that this works because everything on the right of <- is computed on the values in q3 before any of these values are replaced.

2.1.4.5   Replacing Characters with Numbers

Sometimes you have questionnaire data in which the responses are represented as
(for example) "y" and "n" (for yes and no). Suppose you want to convert these to
numbers so that you can average them. The following command does this for a
matrix q1, whose entries are y, n, or some other character for "unsure." It converts
y to 1 and n to -1, leaving 0 for the "unsure" category.

```
> q1 <- (q1[,]=="y") - (q1[,]=="n")
```

In essence, this works by creating two new matrices and then subtracting one
from the other, element by element.

A related issue is how to work with date and time variables. A timestamp
value like "2009-02-01 15:22:35" is typically shown as a character string in a
spreadsheet program. Character variables of date and time can be converted into
DateTimeClasses.

```
> x <- c("2008-02-28 15:22:35", "2008-03-01 15:30:35")
> fmt <- "%Y-%m-%d %H:%M:%S"
> y <- strptime(x, format = fmt)
> y[2] - y[1]
Time difference of 2.0056 days
```

Note the time difference of approximately 2 days because there are 29 days
in February 2008. The strptime() function filters the character variable x
by a specific timestamp format. A "mm/dd/yyyy" date would need a format of
"%m/%d/%Y", and a "mm/dd/yy" date would need "%m/%d/%y".

Timestamp variables are often imported from the text output of a spreadsheet
program. Text variables imported through read.csv() and read.table() are
automatically converted into factors when the imported data are turned into a data
frame. strptime() does not accept factors. One workaround is to deactivate the
automatic conversion by setting read.csv(..., as.is = TRUE).

2.1.5   Using R to Compute Course Grades

Here is an example that might be useful and instructive. Suppose you have a set
of grades including a midterm with two parts m1 and m2, a final with two parts,
and two assignments. You told the students that you would standardize the midterm
scores, the final scores, and each of the assignment scores, then compute a weighted
sum to determine the grade. Here, with comments, is an R file that does this. The
critical line is the one that standardizes and computes a weighted sum, all in one
command.

```
> g1 <- read.csv("grades.csv",header=F)
> a1 <- as.vector(g1[,4])
```

```
> m1 <- as.vector(g1[,5])
> m2 <- as.vector(g1[,6])
> a2 <- as.vector(g1[,7])
> f1 <- as.vector(g1[,8])
> f2 <- as.vector(g1[,9])
> a1[a1=="NA"] <- 0 # missing assignment 1 gets a 0
> m <- 2*m1+m2 # compute midterm score from the parts
> f <- f1+f2
> gdf <- data.frame(a1,a2,m,f)
> gr <- apply(t(scale(gdf))*c(.10,.10,.30,.50),2,sum)
 # The last line standardizes the scores and computes
 # their weighted sum.
 # The weights are .10, .10, .30, and .50 for
 # a1, a2, m, and f
> gcut <- c(-2,-1.7,-1.4,-1.1,-.80,-.62,-.35,-.08,.16,
+          .40,.72,1.1,2)
 # The last line defines cutoffs for letter grades.
> glabels <- c("f","d","d+","c-","c","c+","b-","b",
+              "b+","a-","a","a+")
> gletter <- cut(gr,gcut,glabels) # letter grades
> grd <- cbind(g1[,1:2],round(gr,digits=4),gletter)
 # g1[,1:2] are students' names
> grd[order(gr),] # sorts & prints matrix in rank order
> round(table(gletter)/.83,1) # prints, with rounding
 # the .83 is because there are 83 students
> gcum <- as.vector(round(cumsum(table(gletter)/.83),1))
> names(gcum) <- glabels
> gcum # cumulative sum of students w/ different grades
```

2.2   Reshape and Merge Data Frames

The reshape() function reshapes a data frame between the wide and long layouts.

```
> data1 <- c(
+    49,47,46,47,48,47,41,46,43,47,46,45,
+    48,46,47,45,49,44,44,45,42,45,45,40,
+    49,46,47,45,49,45,41,43,44,46,45,40,
+    45,43,44,45,48,46,40,45,40,45,47,40)
> data1 <- data.frame(subj = paste("s", 1:12, sep=""),
+  matrix(data1, ncol = 4))
> names(data1) <- c("subj","sq.red", "circ.red",
+       "sq.blue", "circ.blue")
> data1
```

```
      subj sq.red circ.red sq.blue circ.blue
 1     s1     49       48      49        45
 2     s2     47       46      46        43
 3     s3     46       47      47        44
 4     s4     47       45      45        45
 5     s5     48       49      49        48
 6     s6     47       44      45        46
 7     s7     41       44      41        40
 8     s8     46       45      43        45
 9     s9     43       42      44        40
10    s10     47       45      46        45
11    s11     46       45      45        47
12    s12     45       40      40        40
```

The data come from a hypothetical study of reaction time in working with control panels of different shape (square and circle) and color (red and blue). Each subject works with all all types of controls and the reaction time is collected. Details of this example are described in Sect. 5.1.

You can tell reshape to convert columns 2 through 5 into a single long variable called rt, with 4 records per subj.

```
> data1.long <- reshape(data1, direction = "long",
+   idvar = "subj", varying= 2:5, v.names = "rt")
```

The command takes columns 2 through 5 (varying = 2:5) and collapses them into a single variable called v.names = "rt" in the long format (direction = "long"). The varying option can be variable names, e.g., varying = c("sq.red", "circ.red", "sq.blue", "circ.blue"). The subj ids are repeated in the long format. A new variable (named time by default) is created to index the collapsed columns. The index values of 1, 2, 3, and 4 represent the second (sq.red) through the 5th columns (circ.blue), respectively. The default variable name time can be changed by specifying timevar = "groups" if you want the new variable be named as groups. To convert data1.long back into the wide format, type reshape(data1.long, direction = "wide", ids = "subj"). We will see this data frame again in Sect. 5.1 when we deal with repeated-measures ANOVA.

Another useful function is merge(), which joins data frames. Suppose you have in a separate data frame the gender information of subjects 1 through 9. By default the two data frames are matched by common variable(s), in this case one single variable subj.

```
subj.char <- data.frame(subj = paste("s", 1:9,
    sep = ""), sex = c("F","F","M","F","F","F","M",
    "M","M"))
merge(x = data1.long, y = subj.char, all = TRUE)
```

```
     subj time rt   sex
1     s1    1 49      F
2     s1    2 48      F
3     s1    3 49      F
4     s1    4 45      F
5    s10    2 45   <NA>
6    s10    1 47   <NA>
7    s10    4 45   <NA>
8    s10    3 46   <NA>
...
15   s12    4 40   <NA>
16   s12    3 40   <NA>
...
47    s9    2 42      M
48    s9    1 43      M
```

Note that all = TRUE retains all subject ids from both data frames. The default is all = FALSE, which would drop subjects 10 through 12. Set only all.x = TRUE if you want to keep all subjects in data1.long but you are fine with subjects in subj.char being dropped. The all.y option works the opposite way. Note also that R sorts character strings by one character at a time, so that subject id "s10" comes after id "s1." We can force the subject ids to contain one "s" and two digits by paste("s", sprintf("%02d", 1:12), sep = "") when data1 and subj.char are created. (although subj.char only contains subjects 1 through 9) You get "s01," "s02," ..., "s10," and so on.

2.3 Data Management with a SQL Database

The last sections of this chapter deals with data management with a SQL database. These advanced data management topics can be skipped without loss of continuity or context.

Researchers working with Ecological Momentary Assessment (EMA) data (Shiffman et al. 2008) may find this section especially useful. In this section we cover how to work with PostgreSQL, an open-source database program that can be freely downloaded and installed on computers running Unix/Linux, Mac OS, and Windows. To fully appreciate how this works, you need to install a PostgreSQL server program on your computer, run the SQL commands in Appendix A to build a database, and run the R query commands below to retrieve data from the PostgreSQL database program. It is a different method of data management. You have the option to retrieve only a handful of variables you need to run an analysis. You no longer need to use R to manage many variables in one large data frame, most of which are anyways not needed in a specific analysis.

Subjchar

id	sex	edu	race
s001	F	3	W
s002	F	2	A
s003	M	1	W
s004	M	4	B
s005	F	2	B

EMA

id	tstamp	smoke
s001	2009–06–29 09:20:25	1
s001	2009–06–29 09:35:35	1
...		
s001	2009–06–29 10:35:55	1
s002	2009–06–19 07:35:35	1
s002	2009–06–19 08:05:15	1
...		
s002	2009–06–19 09:42:32	0
...		
s005	2009–07–14 11:07:03	1
s005	2009–07–14 11:32:23	1
...		
s005	2009–07–14 12:42:19	0
s005	2009–07–14 13:29:07	1

Baseassess

id	bsi	bdi	basedate
s001	10	13	2009–06–28
s002	12	15	2009–06–17
s003	12	10	2009–07–09
s004	14	16	2009–07–12
s005	11	10	2009–07–12

Fig. 2.1 An example SQL database with three data tables

Figure 2.1 shows the design of a hypothetical database with three data tables. Each table can be thought of as a spreadsheet. The subchar table contains information on subject characteristics. The baseassess table contains baseline assessments. These two tables are simple. The ema table contains repeated measures of intensive EMA data. For example, subject 001 was asked whether or not she was smoking on June 29, 2009 at 9:20 and she responded "yes" (coded 1). Another entry is timestamped at 9:35, and another at 10:35. EMA is typically collected through an electronic device such as a hand-held computer or a cellular phone to capture behaviors as they happen in real time. An obvious advantage of EMA is that it minimizes recall bias or noncompliance. A data analysis challenge is that the ema table can be very long. Another complication is that different subjects can produce different numbers of assessments. It would not make sense to format the data in a *wide* layout.

Appendix A describes how to create this hypothetical database called test on a PostgreSQL server program. The syntax in Appendix A should also work with other database programs such as MySQL. Once created, the database test can be linked to R by the library(RPostgreSQL) package.

```
> library(RPostgreSQL)
Loading required package: DBI
> conn <- dbConnect(PostgreSQL(), user = "usr1",
        password = "**********", dbname = "test")
```

A connection is first established between R and the PostgreSQL server program. In this example we use a user name and a password to provide data safety protection.

Next, a Standard Query Language (SQL) query is sent to the server through conn to retrieve a result set.

```
> rs <- dbSendQuery(conn, "SELECT subjchar.id, sex,
+ edu, race, bsi, bdi, bdate, tstamp, smoke
+ FROM subjchar, baseassess, ema
+ WHERE subjchar.id = baseassess.id AND
+ subjchar.id = ema.id
+ ORDER BY subjchar.id, tstamp;")
> dat <- fetch(rs, n = -1)
> dbDisconnect(conn)
```

A result set `rs` is retrieved and `fetch()` actually gets all data in the result set into `dat`. A great convenience is that any timestamp variable such as `tstamp` in this example is automatically and seamlessly converted by the `RPostgreSQL` package into `DateTimeClasses` in R. There is no need to do the often tedious manual conversion. The `tapply()` command shows that the five consecutive assessments for subject 001 are separated by approximately 15–25 minutes apart.

```
> tapply(dat.del$tstamp, list(dat.del$id),
+     function(x) {
+     x[2:length(x)] - x[1:(length(x)-1)] } )
$s001
Time differences in mins
[1] 15.167 15.000 24.500 20.833
attr(,"tzone")
[1] ""
....
$s005
Time differences in mins
[1] 25.333 30.167 39.767 46.800 34.783
attr(,"tzone")
[1] ""
```

R can also work with an ACCESS database or any other ODBC-compliant database programs. An example on how to set up and ODBC connection on a standalone PC running Windows XP is provided in Appendix A.3.

2.4 SQL Database Considerations

Data management by a SQL-based database requires some preparations and basic knowledge of SQL. Would it not be much easier just to save the data in spreadsheet files, export each file into a comma-separated file (CSV) and use `read.csv()` and `merge()` to combine them?

The answer to this question depends on a few things. A database management system has several advantages over a spreadsheet program. A database management system also deals with different variable types more efficiently, especially variables marked by timestamps. There is limited gain in efficiency if you only have a small dataset in a fixed format, with mostly numeric, binary, and categorical variables. Managing complex data with spreadsheet programs can be frustrating. For example, reading character string variables into R and converting them into `DateTimeClass` format is tedious and error prone. Timestamps variables have to be converted one by one from text strings by `strptime()`. Sometimes the user of a spreadsheet program inadvertently changes the format of a date variable so that some entries are entered as "mm/dd/yyyy" and others as "mm/dd/yy". A "%d/%m/%Y" string in `strptime()` requires a "mm/dd/yyyy" format so that it fails with entries in "mm/dd/yy". Furthermore, sometimes the person who enters the data accidentally type a space in one of the cells in a blank column. The resulting CSV file may contain many blank variables. It certainly takes time to set up a SQL-based database, but the prevention of common problems in managing data with a spreadsheet program may more than compensate for the upfront cost in setting up a SQL-based database.

Exercises

2.1. Importing data from a website
In the first exercise of this chapter, we will try importing data directly from a website. Online data repositories make it easy to share de-identified data. The `read.table()` and `read.csv()` functions in R can directly import data from a file on the internet. For example, the `ctest3.data` file in this chapter can be directly accessed from http://idecide.mskcc.org/yl_home/.

(a) Try the command below to read the `ctest3.data` file.

```
c0 <- read.table("http://idecide.mskcc.org/yl_home/
                    rbook/ctest3.data")
```

2.2. Importing data from an online data repository
Online data repository is common. Many authors now make their data available online. One example is the online data repository for the book by Fitzmaurice et al. (2004a). Its URL is http://www.biostat.harvard.edu/~fitzmaur/ala/ (last accessed April 20, 2011).

(a) Click on the "Datasets" icon, and you will find a link called "Television School and Family Smoking Prevention and Cessation Project." That link points to a raw data file called `tvsfp.txt`.
(b) Click on the link to the TVSFP dataset to view its contents.
(c) What is the complete URL that goes into the `file` option in your `read.csv()` function?

(d) The first 44 lines of text in that file are the authors' notes. They will have to be skipped by the `skip` option. How can this be done?

(e) Write the complete `read.csv()` command with the `skip` option set.

(f) Would you set the `header` option to TRUE or FALSE?

(g) Convert the retrieved data into a `data.frame` in R.

(h) Add variable names to the final data frame if necessary.

2.3. Read and merge two data files

Read two data files from http://idecide.mskcc.org/yl_home/rbook/. The first is `subjchar.dat`, the second is `ema.dat`. The first row of each file contains the variable names.

(a) The `ema.dat` file should be imported with an `as.is=T` to keep the timestamp variable as a character string.

(b) Try the commands below.

```
url <- paste("http://idecide.mskcc.org/yl_home/",
       "rbook/ema.dat", sep="")
ema <- read.table(url, as.is=T, sep="\t",
       header=TRUE)
t1 <- strptime(ema$tstamp,
       format="%Y-%m-%d %H:%M:%S")
ema <- data.frame(id=ema$id, tstamp=t1,
       smoke=ema$smoke)
```

(c) Explain why we need the `strptime()` function for ema$tstamp?

(d) Use `merge()` to combine the two data frames into one.

2.4. Change data layout through `reshape()`

In this exercise we practice how to use `reshape()` to convert the ema data in the previous problem into a *wide* format.

(a) First, create a new variable called `time` that contains the chronological order of each subject's `tstamp` variable. Try the command below and explain what it does.

```
ema$time <- unlist(tapply(ema$tstamp, list(ema$id),
       function(x) { order(x) })).
```

(b) Next, build the `reshape()` command that converts ema into the wide format. (hint: You will need `timevar="time"`, `idvar="id"`, `v.names="smoke"`, and an optional `drop="tstamp"`).

(c) Note that the reshaped wide layout contains additional variable(s), particularly the one associated with the reshaped `smoke` variable. Explain why extra variable(s) were created automatically as part of `reshape()`?

(d) Explain what the `drop="tstamp"` option does?

(e) Explain why you do not need to set the `varying` option?

Chapter 3
Statistics for Comparing Means and Proportions

3.1 Comparing Means of Continuous Variables

In Chap. 1, we apply `t.test()` to the `sleep` dataset to compare the effects of two drugs on sleep time. We revisit it and give it a more detailed analysis. The first steps in comparing the means of two continuous variables often involve plotting the data to check their distributional properties. Histograms stacked one on top of the other is a good way to visually compare two distributions.

```
> par(mfcol = c(2, 1))
> brk <- seq(-2, 6.0, by = 0.5)
> hist(x1, br = brk, ylim = c(0, 0.6), prob=T)
> lines(density(x1), lwd = 2)
> hist(x2, br = brk, ylim = c(0, 0.6), prob=T)
> lines(density(x2), lwd = 2)
```

The `par(mfcol = c(2, 1))` command partitions the main plotting area into two sub-plots; `mfcol = c(2, 1)` represents the partitioning into two rows and one column. The `brk` sets up the x-axis for the histogram from -2 to 6 in increment of 0.5. Coupled with `ylim = c(0, 0.6)`, the two options ensure that the histograms are mapped onto the same x and y axes so that they are comparable. There appears to be a sizeable overlap between the two somewhat skewed distributions. The `lines(density(x1))` command adds a smoothed density curve.

The two smoothed distributions in Fig. 3.1 are not unimodal. A nonparametric method such as the Wilcoxon rank sum test using `wilcox.test()` may also be used.

```
> wilcox.test(x1, x2)

Wilcoxon rank sum test with continuity
correction
```

Y. Li and J. Baron, *Behavioral Research Data Analysis with R*, Use R,
DOI 10.1007/978-1-4614-1238-0_3, © Springer Science+Business Media, LLC 2012

Fig. 3.1 Histograms and
superposed density estimates
showing a sizeable overlap
between the distributions of
the two samples

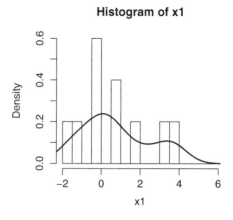

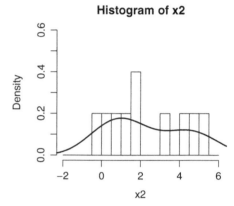

```
data:   x1 and x2
W = 25.5, $p$-value = 0.06933
alternative hypothesis: true location shift
is not equal to 0

Warning message:
In wilcox.test.default(x1, x2)  : cannot
compute exact $p$-value with ties
```

The warning message states that an exact *p*-value cannot be calculated
because of ties in x1 and x2. Normal approximation is used instead (see
help(wilcox.test)). The null hypothesis of zero location shift difference
is not rejected at the 0.05 level.

This finding is consistent with the parametric, Welch's *t*-test using t.test(x1,
x2). Another form of the same *t*-test can be done using a formula to compare the
extra sleep time by group:

```
> t.test(extra ~ group, data = sleep)

Welch Two Sample $t$-test

data:  extra by group
t = -1.8608, df = 17.776, $p$-value = 0.0794
alternative hypothesis: true difference in means is
not equal to 0
95 percent confidence interval:
 -3.3654832  0.2054832
sample estimates:
mean in Group 1 mean in Group 2
          0.75            2.33
```

Group 2 has an average of 2.33 extra hours of sleep whereas Group 1 has an average of 0.75 extra hours. However, the 95% confidence interval of the difference does not exclude 0.00. The null hypothesis that the true difference in means is equal to zero is not rejected. The t.test() results can be checked manually by the following formula:

$$t = \frac{\bar{x}_1 - \bar{x}_2}{\sqrt{\frac{s_1^2}{n_1} + \frac{s_2^2}{n_2}}}.$$

```
> x1 <- sleep$extra[sleep$group %in% "1"]
> x2 <- sleep$extra[sleep$group %in% "2"]
> m1 <- mean(x1)
> m2 <- mean(x2)
> n1 <- length(x1)
> n2 <- length(x2)
> S  <- sqrt(sd(x1)^2/n1 + sd(x2)^2/n2)
> (m1 - m2) / S
[1] -1.8608
```

Note the resemblance between the mathematical formulae and the R commands. The $\bar{x}_1$ is represented by mean(x1), $\bar{x}_2$ by mean(x2), and so on. The match between mathematical notations and R syntax is useful in teaching. Beginners are often intimidated by mathematical symbols. R helps to convert symbols into data objects that are more tangible and easier to work with than the abstract mathematical symbols. This manual verification also makes clear that Welch's t-test does not assume a common standard deviation between the two samples.

3.2   More on Manual Checking of Data

Some things are easy to do in R. For example, you can quickly check the accuracy of some results in a manuscript you are reviewing. A simple example shows how to do it. Dutton and Aron (1974) tested the Schachter-Singer theory of emotion in a now classic social psychology experiment. A crude description of the theory is that a person's physical arousal is labeled a specific emotion depending on the situation. Part of the experiment involved interviews between male subjects and an attractive female confederate working with the psychologists. The interviews occurred either on a fear-arousing suspension bridge or a nonfear-arousing bridge. At the end of the interview, the interviewer gave the subject her phone number in case he wanted to discuss the interview further. Dutton and Aaron found that, in the experimental group, 9 out of 18 (50%) called whereas in the control group only 2 out of 16 (12%) called. They reported a χ^2 statistic of 5.7, $p < 0.02$. The experimenters took the observed behavior and other results as evidence in support of their hypothesis that male subjects interpreted fear arousal on the suspension bridge as attraction to the interviewer. The χ^2 result reported in the published paper can be verified easily by:

```
> mcnemar.test(M[, 1], M[, 2], correct = FALSE)

        McNemar's Chi-squared test

data:  M[, 1] and M[, 2]
McNemar's chi-squared = 0.0625, df = 1, p-value = 0.8026
```

Note that M contains the number of callers and noncallers across the two groups. By default the chisq.test() carries out a continuity correction. But in this incidence it is deliberately deactivated in order to match the χ^2 statistic reported by Dutton and Aaron. If you were reviewing their paper, the lack of the continuity correction might be a reason for you to ask for further clarifications and offer the fisher.test() as a more appropriate alternative due to the small sample size.

```
> fisher.test(M)

Fisher's Exact Test for Count Data

data:  M
$p$-value = 0.02959
alternative hypothesis: true odds ratio is not equal
  to 1
95 percent confidence interval:
  1.0265 76.4815
sample estimates:
odds ratio
    6.5954
```

3.3 Comparing Sample Proportions

Another way to compare sample proportions is by prop.test(). The χ^2 reported by Dutton and Aaron can also be calculated as follows:

```
> prop.test(x = c(9, 2), n = c(18, 16), correct = FALSE)

2-sample test for equality of proportions
without continuity correction

data:  c(9, 2) out of c(18, 16)
X-squared = 5.4427, df = 1, $p$-value = 0.01965
alternative hypothesis: two.sided
95 percent confidence interval:
 0.092841 0.657159
sample estimates:
prop 1 prop 2
 0.500  0.125
```

The number of successes (number of subjects who called) is entered as x and the total number of subjects is entered as n. The x and n parameters can contain more than two proportions. When they do, prop.test() carries out a comparison of proportions from several independent samples. The null hypothesis being tested is that all proportions are equal.

Another useful function is binom.test() for the calculation of an exact binomial test of a proportion. Suppose we roll a dice 100 times and the number 6 comes up 20 times (the expected is 16.67 times). Is there a reason to suspect that the dice is loaded? One method to test it is binom.test(x = c(20, 80), p = 1/6) to test the 20/80 split against the expected one sixth proportion. The p-value is 0.35, which is against the suspicion.

The binom.test() function can also perform the *sign test* for two related proportions, for example, in Moore and McCabe (1993, Example 7.3). A sample of 20 high school French language teachers participated in a 4-week French training program. After the training, 17 teachers showed a change in a spoken French comprehension test (16 improved and 1 declined). The two-sided exact binomial probability of 16 teachers who improved out of 17 teachers is 0.00027.

```
> binom.test(16, 17, p = 0.5, alt = "two.sided")

        Exact binomial test

data:  16 and 17
number of successes = 16, number of trials = 17,
$p$-value = 0.0002747
alternative hypothesis: true probability of success
    is not equal to 0.5
```

```
95 percent confidence interval:
 0.71311 0.99851
sample estimates:
probability of success
                 0.94118
```

The sign test can also be applied to matched pairs (e.g., husband and wife pairs in decision-making) or to comparisons made by the same individuals over two consumer products (e.g., each subject evaluates and indicates his/her preference in products A and B).

The exact binomial test is particularly useful in calculating the 95% confidence intervals of proportions for graphing. For example, Meltzer et al. (2008) asked 68 pediatric physicians and 85 pediatric nurses on how they would address patient/family's psychosocial concerns in hypothetical vignettes of complex medical problems. Respondents were asked whether or not they would do the following:

(a) Use conversation to ease the patient's and/or family's intense emotions and pain?
(b) Call a family meeting to review/address medical care and/or psychosocial issues?
(c) Talk with a colleague about how to work with the patient/family's emotional response?
(d) Make a referral to a professional who is specially trained to manage the psychosocial aspects of pediatric specialty care?

Each response was dichotomized into either "likely" or "unlikely." Percentages of "likely" responses and their exact binomial 95% confidence intervals can be plotted (see Fig. 3.2) using these commands:

```
> rn <- c(68, 69, 72, 66)
> md <- c(50, 53, 49, 65)
> rn.ci <- matrix(NA, nrow = 4, ncol = 2)
> md.ci <- matrix(NA, nrow = 4, ncol = 2)
> for (i in 1:length(rn))
+    rn.ci[i, ] <- binom.test(x=rn[i], n=85)$conf.int
> for (i in 1:length(md))
+    md.ci[i, ] <- binom.test(x=md[i], n=68)$conf.int
> prp <- rbind(rn/85, md/68)
> bx <- barplot(prp, beside = T, ylim=c(0, 1), axes=F)
> segments(bx[1,], rn.ci[,1], bx[1,], rn.ci[,2])
> segments(bx[2,], md.ci[,1], bx[2,], md.ci[,2])
> axis(1, at = c(2, 5, 8, 11), label = rep("",4))
> mtext(c("Ease\nEmotion", "Family\nMeeting",
+        "Consult\nColleague", "Psych\nReferral"),
+    side = 1, at = c(2, 5, 8, 11), line = 2, cex=1.2)
> axis(2, at = seq(0, 1, by=.2), las = 1)
```

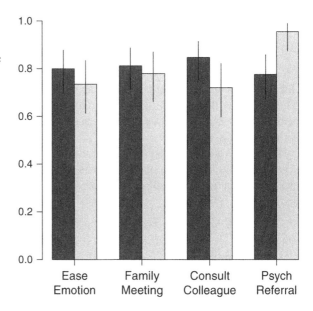

Fig. 3.2 Barplot of the percentages of physicians (*light bars*) and nurses (*dark bars*) who would take specific actions to provide psychosocial support in pediatric complex care. The error bars represent exact binomial 95% confidence intervals. Physicians and nurses differ on how likely they may refer a patient/family to a professional who is specially trained to manage the psychosocial aspects of pediatric specialty care

Physicians represented by light grey bars and nurses (dark grey) agree on the first two actions. They differ slightly on consulting a colleague about the patient/family's emotional response. But the overlapping confidence intervals suggest no discernible difference. Physicians are more likely than nurses to refer the patient/family to psychological consultation. The nonoverlapping confidence intervals indicate a statistically reliable difference between the two proportions.

3.4   Moderating Effect in `loglin()`

R can help simplify complex data analysis tasks. The elegance of the language helps, particularly those tasks involving the manipulation of data. Below is an example in contingency table analysis from Wickens (1989, p.78, Table 3.2).

	Department 1		Department 2	
	Accept	Reject	Accept	Reject
Male	23	16	3	25
Female	7	4	7	47

This 2 by 2 by 2 contingency table summarizes the number of female and male applicants who are accepted or rejected by two hypothetical academic departments in their graduate programs. The data can be pooled across the two departments.

	Accept	Reject
Male	26	41
Female	14	51

This 2×2 table suggests that female applicants are more likely to get rejected ($51/65 = 78\%$) than males ($41/67 = 61\%$). With the data collapsed over departments, a Chi-square test raises the concern of sex discrimination in graduate school admission ($\chi^2_{\mathrm{df}=1} = 3.88$, $p = 0.049$).

However, Wickens (1989) shows that this association is illusory. The difference of gender and graduate school admission is *moderated* by the academic department under consideration.[1] We will go over how to test this effect using R. First, we enter the raw data.

```
> tab3.2 <- array(c(23, 7, 16, 4, 3, 7, 25, 47),
+                 dim = c(2, 2, 2))
> dimnames(tab3.2) <- list( c("Male", "Female"),
+     c("Accept", "Reject"), c("Dept1", "Dept2") )
```

Type tab3.2 to print the contents of the data array.

```
, , Dept1

        Accept Reject
Male        23     16
Female       7      4


, , Dept2

        Accept Reject
Male         3     25
Female       7     47
```

The array() function takes Wickens' $2 \times 2 \times 2$ table and converts it into an array of the same shape (dim = c(2, 2, 2)). The dimnames() function assigns names to the array's three dimensions, also called margins. The three margins represent gender, acceptance, and academic department, respectively. We can collapse the data over the two departments.

```
> apply(tab3.2, MARGIN = c(1, 2), FUN = sum)
        Accept Reject
Male        26     41
Female      14     51
```

---

[1] Wickens used the term '*mediated*' but we believe "*moderated*" is a better fit because mediation relationships typically imply temporal causation which is not available in this example. Either way, it is really about the *conditional independence* hypothesis in a 3-way contingency table.

The apply() function keeps margins 1 and 2 of tab3.2 and add data over the 3rd margin by the function sum(). A Chi-square test of the pooled data raises the concern of sex discrimination.

```
> chisq.test(apply(tab3.2, MARGIN = c(1, 2), FUN = sum))

Pearson's Chi-squared test with Yates'
continuity correction

data:  apply(tab3.2, MARGIN = c(1, 2), FUN = sum)
X-squared = 3.876, df = 1, $p$-value = 0.04898
```

However, this apparent gender difference goes away if you look at the data within academic departments. In department one, female and male applicants are rejected at about the same rate ($4/11 = 36\%$ vs. $16/39 = 41\%$). A similar pattern is seen in department two ($47/54 = 87\%$ vs. $25/28 = 89\%$).

Looking at tab3.2 again shows that department one is popular among male applicants while department two is popular among females. The overall gender difference is in part because department two only accepts 12% of its applicants, while department one accepts 60% of its applicants. Overall, females get rejected more often than males because department two is harder to get into. Looking at only data from department one, a Fisher's exact test[2] indicates no gender difference.

```
> fisher.test(tab3.2[, , "Dept1"])

Fisher's Exact Test for Count Data

data:  tab3.2[, , "Dept1"]
$p$-value = 1
alternative hypothesis: true odds ratio is not equal
  to 1
95 percent confidence interval:
 0.1508734 3.9163416
sample estimates:
odds ratio
  0.824631
```

In this example, we say that the gender difference in graduate school admission is *moderated* by the acceptance rates across academic departments (see Wickens (1989, p.61)). A more formal test of the moderation effect can be carried out with the following loglinear model.

```
> loglin(tab3.2, margin = list(c(2,3), c(1,3)))
2 iterations: deviation 0
$lrt
[1] 0.1670179
```

---

[2]Fisher's test is versatile; fisher.test() is not limited to 2×2 tables, it can handle tables more complex than a 2×2 table.

```
$pearson
[1] 0.1647739

$df
[1] 2

$margin
$margin[[1]]
[1] 2 3

$margin[[2]]
[1] 1 3
```

The Pearson $X^2_{(df=2)}$ is 0.16 with a p-value of 0.92.

```
> 1 - pchisq(0.16477, df = 2)
[1] 0.9209173
```

The margin = list(c(2, 3), c(1, 3)) parameter specifies the null hypothesis, which states that gender and graduate school acceptance are *unrelated* at every department. To set this up in loglin(), we specify that graduate school acceptance and department are related (c(2, 3)) and that gender and department are related (c(1, 3)); but gender and acceptance are *not* related given the departments. Note that there is no c(1, 2) in the margins. The nonsignificant Pearson X^2 shows that the null hypothesis cannot be rejected. Therefore, graduate school acceptance and applicants' gender are unrelated at every department. There is no sufficient statistical evidence to suggest sex discrimination in graduate school admission.

Paradoxical findings such as the example above are common. Mittal (1991) describes the general cases in which paradoxes arise when data are pooled over multiple tables. This may be a concern in exploratory studies using Chi-squares to look for potential associations between pairs of variables. It may be worth the effort to explore further to minimize the false discovery of associations between two factors (e.g., outcome and treatment) that is unrelated to a third factor (e.g., self-efficacy), using a test of *conditional independence*.

This example shows several features of R. R only prints the most essential output. The input data format often matches how the statistical problem is posed. In this case the loglin() function analyzes contingency table data in an array. This can be useful if you want to check the calculations of published articles (or the article you are reviewing for a journal). You can plug in the published numbers and verify the accuracy of the statistics.

This example examines only a very small part of loglinear models and methods to test moderation effects. Extensions to the basic loglinear modeling routines are also not covered. For example, the loglm() function in package MASS extends loglin(). If you have the raw data then you can run something like loglm(count ~ sex+accept+dept+sex:dept+sex:accept) to test the same hypothesis. Additional details on loglinear models can be found elsewhere (Wickens 1989; Agresti 2002). There is a large literature in psychology on how to analyze mediation and moderation effects (Baron and Kenny 1986; MacKinnon et al. 2002).

3.5 Assessing Change of Correlated Proportions

Another frequently used statistic for proportions is the McNemar's test of correlated proportions . Here is an example on students' algebra test performance (Levin and Serlin 2000). Each of the 186 students is given five pairs of items, one item of a pair is presented in a verbal format and the other presented in a symbolic format. The items are randomly arranged in the ten-item test. Separate total scores are calculated for the five verbally and five symbolically presented items. The total scores are dichotomized as "mastery" and "nonmastery." Table 3.1 contains the number of students showing mastery of the algebra test.

Out of the total of 186 students, 74 students master both the verbally presented items and the symbolically presented items, 33 students master the verbally presented items but not the symbolically presented items, and so on. The two bolded numbers, 33 and 31, tell you where the differences are: 33 students master only the verbal items but not the symbolic items and 31 students master only the symbolic items but not the verbal items.

The following R command tests whether or not the probability of passing the algebra test depends on the verbal vs. symbolic format of the items presented.

```
> M <- matrix(c(74, 33, 31, 48), ncol = 2)
> mcnemar.test(M, correct = FALSE)

    McNemar's Chi-squared test

data:  M
McNemar's chi-squared = 0.0625, df = 1,
    $p$-value = 0.8026
```

There is no statistically discernible difference. The McNemar change test is appropriate because the two test formats are matched by the students. The test focuses on the probability of change in mastery of the algebra test when the format

Table 3.1 Number of students who master the two subscales of the ten-item algebra test			Verbal Format	
			Mastery	Nonmastery
Symbolic	Mastery		74	**31**
Format	Nonmastery		**33**	48

Table 3.2 Number of students who master the two subscales, separated by students' recall on the results of prior SAT aptitude assessments

		Higher Verbal Students		Higher Quantitative Students	
		Verbal Format		Verbal Format	
		Mastery	Nonmastery	Mastery	Nonmastery
Symbolic	Mastery	34	**13**	38	**17**
Format	Nonmastery	**21**	37	**5**	3

of the items changes. The `help(mcnemar.test)` page shows that R can work with either a contingency table or raw data:

```
> M <- matrix(c(rep(c(1,1), 74), rep(c(1,0), 33),
+ rep(c(0,1), 31), rep(c(0,0), 48)), ncol=2, byrow=T)
> mcnemar.test(M[, 1], M[, 2], correct = FALSE)

        McNemar's Chi-squared test

data:  M[, 1] and M[, 2]
McNemar's chi-squared = 0.0625, df = 1,
p-value = 0.8026
```

By default, the continuity correction option is set to `correct = TRUE`. It is disabled here (by setting `correct = FALSE`) to show that the output is the same as in Levin and Serlin (2000).

3.5.1 McNemar Test Across Two Samples

Levin and Serlin (2000) show how the McNemar test in Table 3.1 can be calculated across two samples. Here is the example in their Sect. 3.1. They asked students taking the algebra test to recall which of their SAT subtest score was higher. Then they stratified the students into two samples, the "higher verbal students" and the "higher quantitative students" based on their recall of the SAT aptitude assessments. The stratified algebra test results are presented in Table 3.2.

Among the 105 "higher verbal students," 21 mastered the verbal format but not the quantitative format whereas 13 mastered the symbolic format but not the verbal format. The reverse pattern was found in the "higher quantitative students." The overall pattern in Table 3.2 suggests that students' differences in mastery of verbal vs. symbolic algebra problem formats is related to students' baseline verbal vs. quantitative skills. Levin and Serlin (2000) show that this hypothesis can be tested by a χ^2 test on the differences.

```
> chisq.test(matrix(c(13, 21, 17, 5), ncol = 2),
+          correct = FALSE)

        Pearson's Chi-squared test

data:   matrix(c(13, 21, 17, 5), ncol = 2)
X-squared = 8.1838, df = 1, $p$-value = 0.004227
```

Exercises

3.1. Comparing two percentages

Hardin et al. (2008) describe a smoking cessation trial for Medicaid-eligible pregnant women who smoke. A sample of 1,017 pregnant women were recruited from 9 Medicaid maternity care sites, randomized to receive either standard public health care pamphlets (C group) or enhanced patient education materials (E group). The primary outcome was smoking abstinence at 60-day follow-up, biochemical verified by saliva cotinine. Abstinence rates were 9% (44/493) in the E group and 8% (43/524) in the C group.

(a) Compare the abstinence rates across the two groups, assuming independence among women recruited from the same site.
(b) Is there evidence that enhanced patient education materials work better than the standard public health pamphlets in helping pregnant women quit smoking?
(c) What is the 95% confidence interval for the difference in the two abstinence rates?

3.2. Husband and wife decision-making

Suppose a researcher asks 20 husband and wife pairs about the decisions they make, such as the decision about family vacations. The data are as follows, where a 1 represents the response that the wife usually makes the decision and a 0 represents that the husband usually makes the decision. A variable called sign is created to represent the agreement (coded 1) and disagreement (coded 0) between the husband–wife pairs. The first data entry for pair p01 shows that the husband reports that usually the wife makes the decision, which agrees with the wife's report and thus gets a sign of 1.

pair	husband	wife	sign
p01	1	1	1
p02	1	1	1
p03	1	1	1
p04	0	0	1
p05	0	0	1
p06	0	0	1
p07	0	1	0

p08	1	1	1
p09	1	1	1
p10	1	0	0
p11	0	0	1
p12	0	1	0
p13	1	0	0
p14	1	0	0
p15	1	1	1
p16	1	1	1
p17	0	0	1
p18	0	0	1
p19	0	1	0
p20	1	1	1

(a) What is the percentage of agreement in the 20 husband–wife pairs?
(b) Is the percentage of agreement significantly greater than 50%?
(c) What is the 95% confidence interval of the percentage of agreement?

3.3. Changes in asthma trigger prevention in children

Suppose a pediatrician wants to minimize common asthma triggers in the homes of children with asthma. She enrolls 50 children with moderate to severe asthma and provides them with pillow and mattress covers. A nurse makes home visits to observe whether or not the pillow and mattress covers are used in the child's bed. The nurse observes that, 7 (14%) of children use pillow covers in the first home visit. In the second home visit, the frequency of pillow cover use increases to 19 (38%). The frequencies and percentages for mattress cover use are lower than those for pillow cover use, at 6 (12%) and 9 (18%) for the first and second home visits, respectively.

(a) Based on the frequencies and percentages above, and suppose that seven children use pillow covers at both the first and the second home visits, construct a table similar to Table 3.1.
(b) How many children do not use the pillow cover at the first home visit but do use the pillow cover at the second home visit?
(c) How many children do use the pillow cover at the first home visit but do not use it at the second home visit?
(d) Enter the table of pillow cover use into a matrix for analysis.
(e) Is there a significant change in the use of pillow covers?
(f) Suppose that five children use mattress covers at both the first and the second home visits, construct a table similar to Table 3.1.
(g) Enter the table of mattress cover use into a matrix for analysis.
(h) Is there a significant change in the use of mattress covers?

3.4. Changes in asthma trigger prevention across two groups of children

Suppose that the asthma trigger prevention data above are part of a randomized controlled trial. The study team is particularly interested in the difference in the changes in asthma trigger prevention between the intervention and the control conditions. Suppose, the frequencies of changes in pillow cover use are as follows. The `freq` variable represents the number of children in a specific change pattern of pillow cover use between the `first` and the `second` home visits.

```
Intervention                    Control
first second freq               first second freq
"use" "use"    7                "use" "use"    8
"use" "no"     0                "use" "no"     1
"no"  "use"   12                "no"  "use"    4
"no"  "no"    31                "no"  "no"     37
```

The raw data above can be summarized in a tabular format:

		Intervention		Control	
		first visit		first visit	
		Use	No use	Use	No use
second	Use	7	12	8	4
visit	No use	0	31	1	37

(a) Based on the information above, fill in the blanks in the following summary of the results.

"The percentage of pillow cover use changes from _____ % at the first home visit to _____ % at the second home visit for children randomized to the intervention condition; whereas pillow cover use changes from _____ % to _____ % for children randomized to the control condition."

Is there a greater change in pillow cover use among children in the intervention condition than children in the control condition?

(b) Is there a greater change in pillow cover use among children in the intervention condition than children in the control condition?

3.5. Weight changes

In a hypothetical diet and weight loss study, 60 participants are randomized into either the special diet intervention condition or the no special diet control condition. Columns 1 and 2 are the baseline and postintervention, respectively, weight in kilograms for the control group. Columns 3 and 4 are the baseline and postintervention weight in kilograms for the intervention group.

```
61   78   50   15
66   34   75   38
32   69   67   53
61   80   86   30
31   73   69   45
65   56   54   67
53   54   44   48
86   32   42   49
59   55   70   47
70   75   40   60
```

74	65	52	42
81	56	61	53
50	88	54	52
43	78	32	49
46	60	32	64
59	70	58	47
49	65	22	56
67	53	61	22
50	73	61	42
54	2	70	22
77	64	65	51
57	57	40	66
69	48	62	53
60	37	47	62
46	24	62	51
101	49	46	39
59	59	55	40
57	55	51	56
55	62	65	46
71	72	76	52

(a) Use `apply()` to calculate the means and standard deviations of the four columns.
(b) What is the mean weight change for the control group?
(c) What is the mean weight change for the intervention group?
(d) Is there evidence in support of greater weight reduction in participants randomized to the intervention condition than the control condition?

Chapter 4
R Graphics and Trellis Plots

4.1 Default Behavior of Basic Commands

One trick with graphics is to know how each of the various graphics commands responds (or fails to respond) to each kind of data object: `data.frame`, `matrix`, and `vector`. Often, you can be surprised. Here is the default behavior for each object for each of some of the plotting commands, e.g., `plot(x1)` where `x1` is a vector, matrix, or data frame.

	vector	matrix	data.frame
`plot`	values as function of position	2nd column as function of 1st	plots of each column as function of others
`boxplot`	one box for whole vector	one box for all values in matrix	one box for each column (variable)
`barplot`	one bar for each position, height is value	one bar for each column, summing successive values in colors	error
`matplot`	one labeled point for each position, height is value	X axis is row, Y is value, label is column	X axis is row, Y is value, label is column

The `barplot()` of a matrix is an interesting display worth studying. Each bar is a stack of smaller bars in different colors. Each smaller bar is a single entry in the matrix. The colors represent the row. Adjacent negative and positive values are combined. (It is easier to understand this plot if all values have the same sign.)

Another common use of a `barplot` is in displaying group averages. Error bars can be added to the barplot by the `plotCI()` function in `library(gplots)`. Sometimes we may need an elaborate design to highlight special features, or to have better control over the exact appearance of a graph. This, typically, requires a few lines of code. An example is in Fig. 5.1 on page 94. It is better to cover the details when we describe how to carry out ANOVA in Chap. 5.

Y. Li and J. Baron, *Behavioral Research Data Analysis with R*, Use R,
DOI 10.1007/978-1-4614-1238-0_4, © Springer Science+Business Media, LLC 2012

4.2 Other Graphics

To get a bar plot of the column means in a data frame `df1`, you need to say `barplot(height=apply(df1),2,mean)`. To get a nice parallel coordinate display like that in Systat, use `matplot` but transform the matrix and use lines instead of points, that is: `matplot(t(mat1), type = "l")`. You can abbreviate `type` with `t`. The `matplot(v1, m1, type="l")` function also plots the columns of the matrix `m1` on one graph, with `v1` as the horizontal axis. This is a good way to get plots of two functions on one graph.

To get scatterplots of the columns of a matrix against each other, use `pairs(x1)`, where `x1` is a matrix or data frame. (This is like "splom" in Systat, which is the default graph for correlation matrices.)

Suppose you have a measure `y1` that takes several different values, and you want to plot histograms of `y1` for different values of `x1`, next to each other for easy comparison. The variable `x1` has only two or three values. A good plot is `stripchart(y1 ~ x1, method='stack')`. When `y1` is more continuous, try `stripchart(y1 ~ x1, method='jitter')`.

Here are some other commands in their basic form. There are several others, and each of these has several variants. You need to consult the help pages for details.

`plot(v1,v2)` makes a scatterplot of `v2` as a function of `v1`. If `v1` and `v2` take only a small number of values, so that the plot has many points plotted on top of each other, try `plot(jitter(v1),jitter(v2))`.

`hist(x1)` gives a histogram of vector `x1`.

`coplot(y1 ~ x1 | z1)` makes several plots of `y1` as a function of `x1`, each for a different range of values of `z1`.

`interaction.plot(factor1,factor2,v1)` shows how `v1` depends on the interaction of the two factors.

Many wonderful graphics functions are available in the Grid and Lattice packages. Many of these are illustrated and explained in Venables and Ripley (2002).

4.3 Saving Graphics

To save a graph as a `png` file, say `png("file1.png")`. Then run the command to draw the graph, such as `plot(x1,y1)`. Then say `dev.off()`. You can change the width and height with arguments to the function. There are many other formats aside from png, such as pdf, and postscript. See `help(Devices)`.

There are also some functions for saving graphics already made, which you can use after the graphic is plotted: `dev.copy2eps("file1.eps")` and `dev2bitmap()`.

4.4 Multiple Figures on One Screen

The par() function sets graphics parameters. One type of parameter specifies the number and layout of multiple figures on a page or screen. This has two versions, mfrow and mfcol. The command par(mfrow=c(3,2)), sets the display for three rows and two columns, filled one row at a time. The command par(mfcol=c(3,2)) also specifies three rows and two columns, but they are filled one column at a time as figures are plotted by other commands.

Here is an example in which three histograms are printed one above the other, with the same horizontal and vertical axes and the same bar widths. The breaks are every 10 units. The freq=FALSE command means that densities are specified rather than frequencies. The ylim commands set the range of the vertical axis. The dev.print line prints the result to a file. The next three lines print out the histogram as numbers rather than a plot; this is accomplished with print=FALSE. These are then saved to hfile1.

```
> par(mfrow=c(3,1))
> brk <- 10*1:10
> hist(vector1,breaks=brk,freq=FALSE,ylim=c(0,.1))
> hist(vector2,breaks=brk,freq=FALSE,ylim=c(0,.1))
> hist(vector3,breaks=brk,freq=FALSE,ylim=c(0,.1))
> dev.print(png,file="file1.png",width=480,height=640)
> h1 <- hist(vector1,breaks=brk,freq=FALSE,
+           ylim=c(0,.1),plot=FALSE)
> h2 <- hist(vector2,breaks=brk,freq=FALSE,
+           ylim=c(0,.1),plot=FALSE)
> h3 <- hist(vector3,breaks=brk,freq=FALSE,
+           ylim=c(0,.1),plot=FALSE)
> sink("hfile1")
> h1
> h2
> h3
> sink()
```

For simple over-plotting, use par(new=T). Of course, this will also plot axis labels, etc. To avoid that, you might say par(new=T,ann=F). (Apparent undocumented feature: this setting conveniently disappears after it is used once.) To plot several graphs of the same type, you can also use points(), lines(), or matplot().

4.5 Other Graphics Tricks

When you use plot() with course data (e.g., integers), it often happens that points fall on top of each other. There are at least three ways to deal with this. One is to use stripchart() (see above). Another is to apply jitter() to one or both of

the vectors plotted against each other, e.g., plot(jitter(v1),v2). A third is
to use sunflowerplot(v1,v2), which uses symbols that indicated how many
points fall in the same location.

Use identify() to find the location and index of a point in a scatterplot made
with plot(). Indicate the point you want by clicking the mouse on it. The function
locator() just gives the coordinates of the point. This is useful for figuring out
where you want to add things to a plot, such as a legend.

text() uses a vector of strings instead of points in a plot. If you want a
scatterplot with just these name, first make an empty plot (with type="n") to
get the size of the plot correct and then use the text command, e.g.:

```
> x <- 1:5
> plot(x,x^2,type="n")
> text(x,x^2, col = x,
+     labels=c("one","two","three","four","five"))
```

In this case, the col=x argument plots each word in a different color.

To put a legend on a plot, you can use the legend= argument of the
plotting function, or the legend() function, e.g., legend(3, 4, legend =
c("Self", "Trust"), fill = c("gray25", "gray75")). This ex-
ample illustrates the use of gray colors indicated by number, which is convenient for
making graphics for publication. (For presentation or data exploration, the default
colors are usually excellent.) See help(grey) on how to create greyscales. Several functions draw various things on graphs. segments() draws line segments.
polygon() draws polygons, 2-dimensional shapes made up of line segments
connected end to end. The two functions differ in the kind of input they want, and
the first one closes the polygon it draws.

4.6   Examples of Simple Graphs in Publications

This section illustrates some practical techniques for making publication-quality
graphs with very basic graphics commands.

The second author, as the editor of the open-access journal *Judgment and
Decision Making* (http://journal.sjdm.org), has found it necessary to
redraw some graphs. Usually the originals were made with expensive proprietary
software, most of which is designed for printing on paper but sometimes is difficult
to use for publication graphics, which usually must be re-sized to fit the journal's
format. For this purpose, the best format is encapsulated PostScript (eps).

However, the eps format itself is not enough because of the two types of graphics
formats. *Vector* graphics describe images in terms of commands, of the form "draw
a black line from point x1,y1 to point x2,y2." Of course, these commands are
abbreviated in different ways for different formats. The details of which points
should be black are left to other software (or to a printer), which is usually designed
to do the best possible job of displaying the element in question. On the other hand

raster (or "bitmap") images specify all the points. This works fine if the result is printed on paper or if the computer software plots the image point by point on the user's display. If the image must be re-sized, however, the display program cannot fully recover the original information, and plots are usually somewhat messy. Common raster formats are tiff, png, gif, and bmp. Common vector formats are eps, svg (scalable vector graphics), wmf (Windows meta-file), and emf (extended wmf). But *all* of these "vector formats" can include raster images within them. Unfortunately, software that claims to produce eps often does it simply by making a raster image and including it in an eps file. R is one of the few that makes true vector images correctly. (Others are Stata and SigmaPlot.)[1]

To produce good eps with R, we generally use the following format:

```
> postscript(file="fig1.eps", width=8, height=8,
+   horiz=F, onefile=F, pointsize=16, paper="special")

[plotting commands here]

> dev.off()
> system("bbox fig1.eps")
```

All of these options are described in the help file for `postscript()` (in the graphics package), but some comments are needed. First, `pointsize` controls the size of the font. A setting of 14 or 16 is good for a large figure that covers the width of a page, but usually 18 or 20 is better for a figure that will go in a single column of a two-column text. Note that the advantage of eps is that you can resize it, without loss, to fit wherever it goes.[2] The `dev.off()` command is necessary to save the result to disk.

For all the niceties of R, there is one thing it does not do, which is to make a "tight bounding box" around a plot. The difference between eps and ordinary Postscript is the specification of a bounding box, which is a description of the box containing the plot. You can see these commands by looking at the top of almost any eps file, which is just text. The problem is that R's default bounding box includes a blank margin, which you usually do not want. To remove the margin, we use the following script

---

[1]Note that the jpeg (or jpg) format, commonly used for photographs, is a third category. It is closer to a raster image and is definitely not vector format. But it re-codes the images into a more compact format by using interesting mathematical transformations (involving singular value decomposition), which preserve the useful information found in most photographs. It is called a "lossy" format because it loses some information. It should not be used for "line art," that is, graphs, but it is practically necessary for photos. Although most digital cameras now have a tiff (raster) option, it is rarely used because it requires much more storage space than jpeg.

[2]In LATEX, the usual way to do that is with the `\includegraphcis[width=\textwidth]{fig1.eps}` command to scale the width of the graph by the width of the text or the `\includegraphcis[width= \columnwidth]{fig1.eps}`. The latter is for inclusion in a single column of a two-column text.

(which requires Ghostscript and uses Linux shell commands, which can probably
be translated for other operating systems):

```
#!/bin/bash
cat $1 | sed -r -e
"s/BoundingBox:[\ ]+[0-9]+[\ ]+[0-9]
+[\ ]+[0-9]+ [\ ]+\[0-9]+/'gs -sDEVICE=bbox -dBATCH
-dNOPAUSE -q'/" > temp.eps

gs -sDEVICE=bbox -sNOPAUSE -q $1 $showpage -c quit 2>
bb.out

sed -e"1 r bb.out" temp.eps > $1

/bin/rm bb.out
/bin/rm temp.eps
```

Note that the first line of this script is folded to make it easier to read here. It should
be unfolded. This script removes the original bounding box and replaces it with the
smallest possible box. The `system()` command above simply calls the script.

Each of the following examples is listed according to the URL of the paper in
which it appears. The complete R scripts for these and other figures are linked from
`http://journal.sjdm.org/RX.html`

4.6.1 `http://journal.sjdm.org/8827/jdm8827.pdf`

```
> postscript(file="fig1.eps",width=8,height=8,
> horiz=F,onefile=F,pointsize=16,paper="special")
> c1 <- c(683,605)
> c2 <- c(648,594)
> c3 <- c(619,577)
> c4 <- c(520,489)
> c5 <- c(525,507)
> plot(c1,xlab=expression(bold("Distance from target")),
+     ylab=expression(bold("Mean RT (milliseconds)")),
+     ylim=c(475,700),xlim=c(.8,2.2),type="b",xaxt="n")
> axis(1,at=c(1,2),labels=c("Near","Far"))
> lines(c2,type="b")
> lines(c3,type="b")
> lines(c4,type="b")
> lines(c5,type="b")
> text(c(.92,2.08),c1,labels=c1)
> text(c(.92,2.08),c2,labels=c2)
> text(c(.92,2.08),c3,labels=c3)
> text(c(.92,2.08),c4,labels=c4)
```

```
> text(c(.92,2.08),c5,labels=c5)
> text(1.5,mean(c1)+8.6,srt=-23,
> labels="First quintile: Largest distance-effect
  slope")
> text(1.5,mean(c2)+7,srt=-16,labels="Second
  quintile")
> text(1.5,mean(c3)+7,srt=-12,labels="Third quintile")
> text(1.5,mean(c4)-7.4,srt=-9.2,labels="Fourth
  quintile")
> text(1.5,mean(c5)+8.8,srt=-5.4,
> labels="Fifth quintile: Smallest distance-effect
  slope")
> dev.off()
> system("bbox fig1.eps")
```

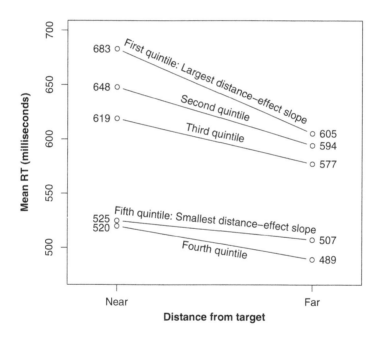

This figure illustrates the use of the text() function. Here we adjusted the slope with srt by trial and error, although the initial errors got smaller after the first one.

```
> postscript(file="fig2.eps",width=8,height=8,
+ horiz=F,onefile=F,pointsize=16,paper="special")
> c1 <- c(0.9,2.0,2.6,3.3,4.0)
> c2 <- c(-1.6,-1.3,-1.1,-1.0,-0.8)
> c1t <- c("0.9","2.0","2.6","3.3","4.0")
> c2t <- c("-1.6","-1.3","-1.1","-1.0","-0.8")
> par(oma=c(3,0,0,0))
```

```
> plot(c1,ylab=expression(bold("Predicted
  preference")),
+    xlab="", ylim=c(-2,4),xlim=c(.8,5.2),
+    type="b",xaxt="n")
> axis(1,at=c(1:5),padj=1, labels=
+  c("1st quintile\nLargest\ndistance-\neffect
  \nslope",
+  "2nd quintile","3rd quintile","4th quintile",
+  "5th quintile\nSmallest\ndistance-\neffect
  \nslope"))
> mtext(side=1,line=5, text=
+ expression(bold("Distance-effect slope quintile
  split")))
> lines(c2,type="b")
> text(1:5,c1-.25,labels=c1t)
> text(1:5,c2+.25,labels=c2t)
> abline(h=0,lty=2)
> text(3,mean(c1)+.65,labels="$10/$15 choice")
> text(3,mean(c2)-.5,labels="$100/$110 choice")
> dev.off()
> system("bbox fig2.eps")
```

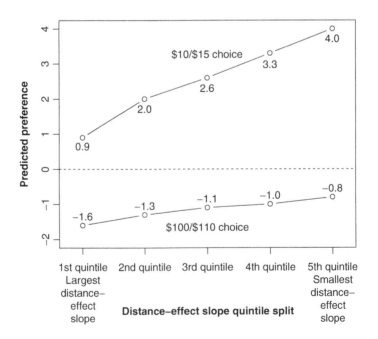

This figure illustrates the use of padj and multiline labels.

4.6.2 `http://journal.sjdm.org/8814/jdm8814.pdf`

```
> Intent <- array(c(7.32,7.60,7.80,5.28,7.44,8.24,7.96,
+ 7.40,8.08, 7.50,6.76,7.48,7.52,7.28,6.48,6.80,7.72,
+ 7.48),c(3,3,2))
> dimnames(Intent) <- list(Arguments=c(2,4,6),
+  Background=c("Positive","Negative","None"),
+  Frame=c("Positive","Negative"))
> Intention <- c(Intent)
> Arguments <- rep(c(2,4,6),6)
> Background <- rep(rep(c("Positive","Negative","None"),
+             c(3,3,3)),2)
> Frame <- rep(c("Positive","Negative"),c(9,9))

> postscript(file="fig0.eps",width=8,height=8,
+    horiz=F,onefile=F,pointsize=18,paper="special")
> plot(c(2,4,6),Intention[1:3],xlim=c(2,18),
+    ylim=c(5,8.5),pch=19,col="maroon",
+    xlab="Number of arguments",
+    ylab="Behavioral intention",xaxt="n")
> y.lm <- fitted(lm(Intention[1:3] ~ c(2,4,6)))
> segments(2, y.lm[1], 6, y.lm[3],col="maroon")
> points(c(8,10,12),Intention[4:6],col="maroon",pch=19)
> y.lm <- fitted(lm(Intention[4:6] ~ c(8,10,12)))
> segments(8, y.lm[1], 12, y.lm[3],col="maroon")
> points(c(14,16,18),Intention[7:9],col="maroon",pch=19)
> y.lm <- fitted(lm(Intention[7:9] ~ c(14,16,18)))
> segments(14, y.lm[1], 18, y.lm[3],col="maroon")

> points(c(2,4,6),Intention[10:12],col="blue")
> y.lm <- fitted(lm(Intention[10:12] ~ c(2,4,6)))
> segments(2, y.lm[1], 6, y.lm[3],col="blue",lty=2)
> points(c(8,10,12),Intention[13:15],col="blue")
> y.lm <- fitted(lm(Intention[13:15] ~ c(8,10,12)))
> segments(8, y.lm[1], 12, y.lm[3],col="blue",lty=2)
> points(c(14,16,18),Intention[16:18],col="blue")
> y.lm <- fitted(lm(Intention[16:18] ~ c(14,16,18)))
> segments(14, y.lm[1], 18, y.lm[3],col="blue",lty=2)

> mtext(side=1,line=1,at=c(1,2,3,3.5,4,5,6,6.5,7,8,9)*2,
+     text=c(2,4,6,"|",2,4,6,"|",2,4,6))
> abline(v=7)
> abline(v=13)
> text(c(4,10,16),5.15,labels=c("Positive\nbackground",
+     "Negative\nbackground","No\nbackground"))
> legend(14,6.42,legend=c("Gain","Loss"),title="Frame:",
```

```
+          col=c("maroon","blue"),pch=c(19,1))
> dev.off()
> system("bbox fig0.eps")
```

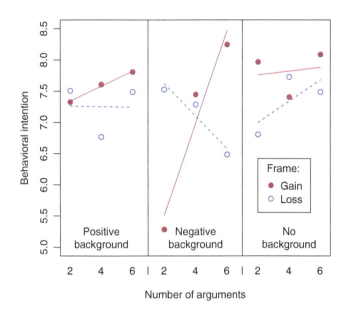

This is a fairly complicated example, which illustrates several things. One is the use of lm() to get properties of best-fitting lines to superimpose on a plot. In simple cases, it is usually sufficient to say something like abline (lm(Y ~ X)). But here the origin is different for each part of the plot, so we use fitted values and segments() instead of abline(). Also shown here is the use of mtext() to add text around the margins of a plot, just as text() adds test internally. Finally, we use legend() to specify more carefully where the legend should go.

4.6.3 http://journal.sjdm.org/8801/jdm8801.pdf

```
> library(gplots)
> c1 <- c(66,69,63,78,40,70,53)
> e1 <- c(3,4,4,4,3,4,8)
> postscript(file="fig4.eps",width=10.8,height=8,
+   horiz=F,onefile=F,pointsize=16,paper="special")
> barplot2(height=c1,plot.ci=T,ci.u=c1+e1,ci.l=c1-e1,
+ xaxt="n",yaxt="n",
+ ylab="Prediction accuracy",ylim=c(0,100),
+ width=c(.5,.5),space=1)
```

```
> axis(1,at=(1:7)-.25,padj=.5,lty=0,
+ labels=c("Total\n","Mouselab\n","Eye\ntracking",
+  "Consistent\ntrials", "Inconsistent\ntrials",
+  "Choice\ntrials","Deferral\ntrials"))
> axis(2, at=c(0,25,50,75,100),
+      labels=c("0%","25%","50%","75%","100%"))
> text((1:7)-.25,10,labels=paste(c1,"%",sep=""))
> text(3.15,72,labels="n.s.")
> text(3.15,65.6,labels="}",cex=1.75,lwd=.1)
> dev.off()
> system("bbox fig4.eps")
```

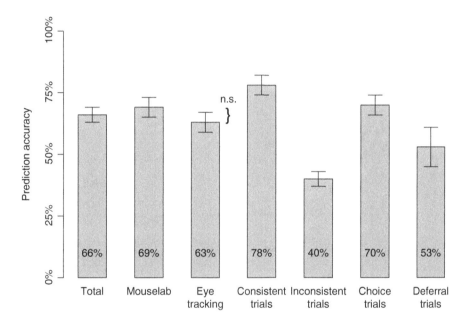

For adding confidence intervals, the easiest way is to use the gplots package, as illustrated here. This plot also illustrates the use of axis(), and the use of cex to make a large character, in this case a bracket. The lwd option is necessary to keep the bracket from being too thick. Trial and error are needed.

4.6.4 http://journal.sjdm.org/8319/jdm8319.pdf

```
> postscript(file="fig1.eps",family="NimbusSan",
+    width=8,height=8, horiz=F,onefile=F,
+    pointsize=16,paper="special")
> plot(0:100,0:100,type="n",axes=F,,xlab="",ylab="")
```

```
> rect(0,30,20,70,col="#EEEEFF",border=NA)
> rect(20,30,45,70,col="#FFFFDD",border=NA)
> rect(45,30,95,70,col="#EEEEFF",border=NA)
> lines(c(0,0),c(25,75))
> lines(c(0,100),c(30,30),col="red",lty=2)
> lines(c(0,100),c(70,70),col="red",lty=2)
> lines(c(0,100),c(50,50))
> segments(x0=c(0,20,45),y0=c(50,60,45),x1=c(20,45,95),
+          y1=c(60,45,70),lwd=2)
> points(95,70,cex=4)
> mtext("r(t) = value(Left - Right)",side=2)
> text(4,65, pos=4, expression(
+ r(t) == r(t-1) + f(v[target],v[non-target]) + u[t]))
> text(10,25,"barrier right",pos=4,col="red")
> text(10,75,"barrier left",pos=4,col="red")
> text(95,77,"choose left")
> text(c(0,20,45,85),c(33,33,33,47),
+     labels=c("left","right","left","time"),pos=4)
> lines(c(20,20),c(30,70),lty=3)
> lines(c(45,45),c(30,70),lty=3)
> dev.off()
> system("bbox fig1.eps")
```

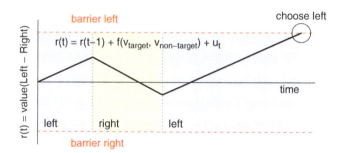

This plot illustrates the inclusion of a mathematical expression as text, as well as the use of rect to make shaded rectangles.

4.6.5 `http://journal.sjdm.org/8221/jdm8221.pdf`

```
> Ch=14
> postscript(file="fig1.eps",family="NimbusSan",
+  width=8, height=8, horiz=F,onefile=F,pointsize=16,
+  paper="special")
```

```
> plot(c(0,110),c(0,100),type="n",axes=F,xlab="",
  ylab="")
> rect(0,80,20,100,col="gray80")
> rect(0+Ch,80-Ch,20+Ch,100-Ch,col="gray80")
> rect(0+2*Ch,80-2*Ch,20+2*Ch,100-2*Ch,col="gray80")
> rect(0+3*Ch,80-3*Ch,20+3*Ch,100-3*Ch,col="gray80")
> rect(0+4*Ch,80-4*Ch,20+4*Ch,100-4*Ch,col="gray80")
> text(20,98,pos=4,labels="fixation cue appears")
> text(20+Ch,98-Ch,pos=4,labels="saccad targets
  appear")
> text(20+2*Ch,98-2*Ch,pos=4,labels="go cue
  presented")
> text(20+3*Ch,98-3*Ch,pos=4,labels="saccade
  executed")
> text(20+4*Ch,98-4*Ch,pos=4,labels="reward
  delivered")
> points(c(10,  10+Ch,10+Ch-6,10+Ch+6,  10+2*Ch-6,
+        10+2*Ch+6,  10+3*Ch-6),  c(90,  90-Ch,
+        90-Ch-6,90-Ch+6,  90-2*Ch-6,90-2*Ch+6,
+        90-3*Ch-6),  pch=20)
> arrows(0,70,3.5*Ch,70-3.5*Ch,lwd=2)
> text(25,80-3*Ch,labels="time")
> arrows(10+3*Ch,90-3*Ch,10+3*Ch-5,90-3*Ch-5,
  length=0.1)
> par(new=TRUE)
> xspline(87+c(0,2,0,-2),33+c(4,0,-2,0), open=F,
+        shape=c(0,1,1,1))
> dev.off()
> system("bbox fig1.eps")
```

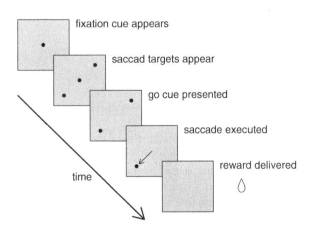

This shows how rectangles can overlap. The droplet of sweetened water in the last rectangle was a bit of a problem because no character seemed to have the shape of a droplet. Thus, we used `xspline()` to draw it piece by piece (with much trial and error). Another feature is the setting of the constant Ch, which helped get the dimensions right.

4.6.6 `http://journal.sjdm.org/8210/jdm8210.pdf`

```
> P <- c(0.0000616649,0.0012931876,0.0014858932,
+        0.0034575074,0.0095432743,0.0112784208,
+        0.0198140078,0.0260565422,0.0378525090,
+        0.0476971273,0.0665802025,0.1160787054,
+        0.1561110462,0.1741858728,0.2592136466,
+        0.3849843314,0.3970805883,0.4387950690,
+        0.5686058809,0.5880746208,0.6367807765,
+        0.7164637107,0.7548314071,0.8594174096,
+        0.8637551603,0.8852179374,0.8854362373,
+        0.8904200780,0.9319782385,0.9411071229,
+        0.9474470330,0.9605232158,0.9621474910,
+        0.9716238220,0.9750371388,0.9800862502,
+        0.9856935080,0.9923052342,0.9993104279,
+        0.9994746329,0.9997647547,0.9999417310,
+        0.9999506389,0.9999650462,0.9999825779,
+        0.9999967088,0.9999994243,0.9999999681)
> ordinate <- sort(P)
> n <- length(ordinate)
> plotpos <- seq(0.5/n, (n - 0.5)/n, by = 1/n)
> postscript(file="fig1.eps",family="NimbusSan",
+ width=8,height=8,horiz=F,onefile=F,
+ pointsize=16,paper="special")
> plot(ordinate, plotpos,
+     xlab="Expected probability",
+     ylab="Observed probability")
> abline(0,1,lty=3)
> grid(); dev.off(); system("bbox fig1.eps")
```

This example is of substantive interest. It shows the p-values for a set of t-tests, one for each subject. The abscissa is the percentile rank of the p-value. If the data were random, the plot would be on the diagonal. The 5th percentile would have $p = 0.05$, because 5% of the p-values would be significant at the 0.05 level. As is apparent, the curve departs from the expectation at both ends, showing that subjects show significant effects in both directions. This example is discussed in Baron (2010).

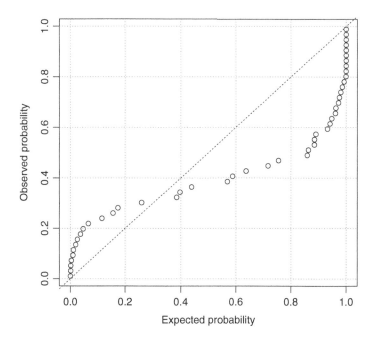

4.7 Shaded Areas Under a Curve

The `polygon()` function is versatile. It can be used to draw highly complex graphs for teaching statistics. Let's begin with a simple example.

```
> plot(c(0, 1), c(0, 2), type = "n")
> polygon(x = c(0, 1, 0), y = c(0, 0, 2), density=-1,
+          border = "blue", col="grey")
```

These commands draw a triangle in blue filled with grey. The three vertices of the triangle are $(x_1, y_1) = (0, 0)$, $(x_2, y_2) = (1, 0)$, and $(x_3, y_3) = (0, 2)$. We use `density = -1` and `border = "blue"` to fill the inside of the blue triangle with `col = "grey"`. Note that the x and y vectors must be of the same length. The length of the x and y vectors determines the number of sides of the polygon.

We can use `polygon()` to plot the shaded areas under probability density functions, like those in Fig. 4.1. An instructor may use a graph like Fig. 4.1 to illustrate the concept of tail probability in a density function. In this example, the density function is a *t*-distribution with 98 degrees of freedom. The `polygon()` function is used to plot histograms to approximate the continuous density functions.

```
> x0 <- seq(-0.52, 3, length=200)
> y0 <- dt(x0, df = 98)
> plot(x0, y0, type = "n", axes=F, xlab="", ylab="")
> lines(x0, y0, lwd = 3)
```

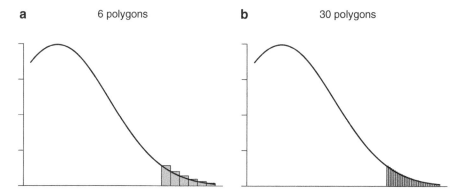

a   6 polygons   **b**   30 polygons

Fig. 4.1 Area under the curve plotted by a series of *rectangles* using polygon(). The two subplots are plotted with 6 and 30 polygons, respectively. The histogram in (**b**) is a closer approximation to the continuous density function than (**a**)

The six grey rectangles in Fig. 4.1a illustrate a crude approximation of the area under the curve from a *t*-statistic of 1.98–3. We set the *x*-coordinates of the rectangles. The vertical heights of the rectangles are calculated from their *t* density.

```
> x <- seq(1.98, 3, length = 7)
> y <- dt(x, df = 98)
```

Next, the rectangles are superimposed one by one on the density curve along the horizontal axis. The vertical heights of the rectangles are calculated from their *t* density. The individual rectangles are added one at a time.

```
> polygon(x=c(x[1],x[1],x[2],x[2]),  y=c(0,y[1],y[1],0),
+      density = -1, col="grey")
> polygon(x[c(2,2,3,3)],  c(0,  y[c(2,2)],  0),
+      density=-1, col="grey")
> polygon(x[c(3,3,4,4)],  c(0,  y[c(3,3)],  0),
+      density=-1, col="grey")
> polygon(x[c(4,4,5,5)],  c(0,  y[c(4,4)],  0),
+      density=-1, col="grey")
> polygon(x[c(5,5,6,6)],  c(0,  y[c(5,5)],  0),
+      density=-1, col="grey")
> polygon(x[c(6,6,7,7)],  c(0,  y[c(6,6)],  0),
+      density=-1, col="grey")
> lines(x0, y0, lwd = 3)
```

The density curve gets painted over by the rectangles. The density curve can be brought back to the foreground by redrawing it with lines(x0, y0, lwd = 3).

There are obvious problems in Fig. 4.1. The shaded area is far from smooth. The total area of the six rectangles, calculated by sum(diff(x) * y[1:6]), is 0.028. This is only a crude approximation of the more precise estimate of the area under the curve by `1 - pt(1.98, df = 98)`, or a one-sided tail probability of 2.5%. A smoother effect can be easily achieved when the length of x and y are increased to something like 100. But it is tedious to run `polygon()` 100 times. A more efficient solution is described next.

4.7.1 Vectors in `polygon()`

The six rectangles in Fig. 4.1a have the following vertices:

Rectangle	x-coordinates				y-coordinates			
1:	x[1],	x[1],	x[2],	x[2]	0,	y[1],	y[1],	0
2:	x[2],	x[2],	x[3],	x[3]	0,	y[2],	y[2],	0
3:	x[3],	x[3],	x[4],	x[4]	0,	y[3],	y[3],	0
⋮	⋮				⋮			
6:	x[6],	x[6],	x[7],	x[7]	0,	y[6],	y[6],	0

Note that the x-positions of the six rectangles follow a highly regular pattern. For the first rectangle, they are `x[1], x[1], x[2], x[2]`. For the second rectangle, they are `x[2], x[2], x[3], x[3]`; for the third, `x[3], x[3], x[4], x[4]`, and so on until rectangle number 6, `x[6], x[6], x[7], x[7]`. Note that `x[1]` is repeated twice in the beginning, then `x[2:6]` is repeated four times each, and `x[7]` is repeated twice at the end. So we can put the x-positions of all rectangles into one long vector `x <- x[c(1,1, rep(2:6, each = 4), 7, 7)]`, or more generally:

```
> x <- c(x[1], x[1], rep(x[2:(length(x)-1)],
+         each=4), x[length(x)], x[length(x)])
```

We also see a regular pattern in y. The first rectangle covers `0, y[1], y[1], 0`. The second rectangle covers `0, y[2], y[2], 0`, the third covers `0, y[3], y[3], 0`, and so on. The last rectangle covers `0, y[6], y[6], 0`. We should repeat each element of y twice and sandwich them with zeros (so that you get something like `(<- 0, y[1], y[1], 0)`. However, there is one extra y at the end that should be taken out. The long vector of y-positions can be put together by:

```
> y <- t(cbind(y[1:(length(y) - 1)], 0))
> y <- c(0, rep(y, each = 2))
> y <- y[-length(y)]
```

All of the rectangles can be plotted at once with only one line of `polygon()`.

```
> polygon(x, y, density=-1, border=T, col="grey")
```

In this way, a histogram with 30 rectangles in Fig. 4.1b is easy to plot. We can easily create 100 or more rectangles to achieve a much smoother effect. A `for()`

loop with 100 `polygon()` commands can certainly plot the same graph, but it gets intolerably slow. Besides, the one-line `polygon()` call is a neat illustration of the power of R.

4.8   Lattice Graphics

The `lattice` package offers several other powerful graphics functions to plot Trellis Graphics (Cleveland 1993). One of the most frequently used functions in the `lattice` package is `xyplot()`. In this section we cover one example on how to use `xyplot()` to visualize clustered multivariate data. Detailed use of lattice graphics are described in the book written by the author of the `lattice` package (Sarkar 2008). Additional resources on R graphics can also be found in the R Graph Gallery at http://addictedtor.free.fr/graphiques/.

4.8.0.1   Mathematics Achievement and Socioeconomic Status

Many behavioral scientists are familiar with the High School & Beyond dataset in Raudenbush and Bryk (2001). High school students' mathematics achievement scores are associated with their socioeconomic status. Students from families with higher SES tend to score higher in mathematics achievement than students from lower SES families. Raudenbush and Bryk (2001) showed that the association is stronger among students attending public schools than among students attending Catholic schools. Figure 4.2 plots data from 20 randomly sampled schools. Each circle represents one student.

This command plots all available schools in the dataset.

```
> xyplot(MathAch ~ SES | School, data=MathAchieve)
```

The High School & Beyond example is available in `library(nlme)`. There are two datasets. The `MathAchSchool` dataset contains variables describing the 160 schools, 90 of which are public schools and the remaining 70 are Catholic schools. The `MathAchieve` dataset contains information on the 7,185 students. Descriptions of the variables can be found by asking for `help(MathAchSchool)`. The students are clustered within schools.

School ids beginning with a "P" and a "C" represent public and Catholic schools, respectively. Public schools are plotted with grey strips. The slope of each regression line represents the strength of association between mathematics achievement and SES in that school. Figure 4.2 suggests that the slopes are steeper in public schools than in catholic schools. Mathematics achievement appears to have a stronger association with SES in public schools than in Catholic schools.

Raudenbush and Bryk use a two-level hierarchical linear model to compare the magnitude of the slopes between public and Catholic schools. Their approach is supported by the visible differences shown in Fig. 4.2. It is often useful to plot pairs

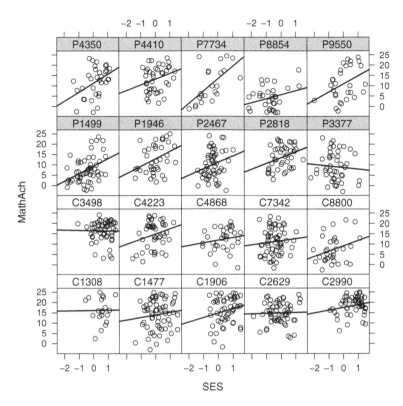

Fig. 4.2 An `xyplot()` of students' mathematics achievement scores against their socioeconomic status. The school identification numbers are plotted in the *strips*. A least-square regression line is fitted to each school

of variables across sample clusters to help guide hypothesis testing. `xyplot()` is well-suited for pairwise plots. Next we describe how to plot Fig. 4.2.

```
> library(nlme)
> set.seed(7)  # reproduce school samples

> dat <-
+ merge(MathAchieve[,c("School","SES","MathAch")],
+     MathAchSchool[, c("School", "Sector")],
+     by = "School")

> p.i <- which(MathAchSchool$Sector == "Public")
> pub.s <- sample(MathAchSchool$School[p.i], size=10)
> pub.s <- as.character(pub.s)
> c.i <- which(MathAchSchool$Sector == "Catholic")
> cath.s <- sample(MathAchSchool$School[c.i], size=10)
> cath.s <- as.character(cath.s)
```

These commands merge school data with student data into a new dataset dat. The variable MathAchSchool$Sector codes the school type, with it we sample ten schools from each sector.

The next few lines add P's or C's to the id numbers of the sampled schools.

```
> sch <- c(pub.s, cath.s)
> dat <- dat[(dat$School %in% sch), ]
> dat$School <- paste(substring(dat$Sector, first = 1,
+              last = 1), dat$School, sep = "")
> dat$School <- factor(dat$School)
```

The lattice package is loaded before we can use xyplot(). We specify in tcol the background shades of grey in the strips and match them to the Catholic schools (grey100, or white) and public schools (grey75, 75% grey) by the first character of their school ids. Note that in bg.col the first ten schools will be plotted with a background of "grey100" and the next ten schools with "grey75."

```
> library(lattice)
> sch.lev <- levels(dat$School)
> tcol <- c("grey100", "grey75")
> bg.col <- tcol[match(substring(sch.lev, 1, 1),
+                c("C", "P"))]
> print(bg.col)  # show each panel's background color
 [1] "grey100" "grey100" "grey100" "grey100" "grey100"
 [6] "grey100" "grey100" "grey100" "grey100" "grey100"
[11] "grey75"  "grey75"  "grey75"  "grey75"  "grey75"
[16] "grey75"  "grey75"  "grey75"  "grey75"  "grey75"
```

We can use panel to control what goes into each subplot. The default is panel = panel.xyplot(), which produces scatterplots only. Other features can be added. For example, with panel.lmline() we can add a least-square regression line for each panel. With panel.xyplot() we add the circles. There are many other panel functions, for example, panel.grid() for adding grid lines and panel.loess() for adding smoothed curves. The panel is a function with two internal parameters x and y, which in our example are assigned the SES and MathAch variables, respectively.

```
> xyplot(MathAch ~ SES | School, data = dat,
+ panel = function(x, y)
+ {
+ panel.lmline(x, y, lwd = 2);
+ panel.xyplot(x, y, col = "black")
+ },
+ strip = function(..., which.panel, bg)
+ {
+ strip.default(..., which.panel = which.panel,
+ bg = bg.col[which.panel])
+ })
```

We can use `strip` to control the appearance of the strips, including the background color of each strip. We need to manipulate the internal variables `which.panel` and `bg`. When `xyplot()` makes the first strip, `which.panel` takes on the value of 1; when `xyplot()` moves on to the next strip, `which.panel` increments by one, and so on. The `bg` parameter specifies the background color of each strip. Thus, `bg.col[which.panel]` assigns `bg.col[1]` (which points to the character string `"grey100"`) to `bg` of the first panel, another `"grey100"` to the second panel, and so on.

If you want to plot two lines per panel, add one more dependent variable before the tilde, like

```
> xyplot(MathAch + I(MathAch+3) ~ SES | School,
+    subset=School %in% c("8367","8854","4458","5762"),
+    data = MathAchieve)
```

The `I(MathAch+3)` creates a new variable which is the original `MathAch` variable plus 3. The `I()` function tells `xyplot()` that the variable within should be treated "as is."

Global settings in `xyplot()` can be changed by `trellis.par.set()`. The settings can be retrieved by `trellis.par.get()`. Customization may not be necessary because the default settings already produce visually appealing graphics. Customization is usually a matter of personal preference. The example above shows how it can be done, and how customizations in `xyplot()` take effect.

Figure 4.2 shows that `xyplot()` is ideally suited for plotting clustered data. An example of using R to visualize clustered data can be found in Atkins (2005), where the author uses `xyplot()` to display couple dyads data over time. Generally, `xyplot()` should be useful in other areas of behavioral research that involves clustered data, including cluster-randomized clinical trials (e.g., Flay et al. 1995), family therapy research (Atkins and Gallop 2007), support group psychotherapy, and Ecological Momentary Assessments (EMA). The `library(nlme)` package and the book by Pinheiro and Bates (2004) contain numerous other examples of using `xyplot()` to help visualize clustered data.

Exercises

4.1. Pairwise scatterplots

Pairwise scatterplots are often useful in exploratory data analysis. They help explain how the variables in a data frame are associated with one another. In this exercise we will try a few basic plots with the `swiss` dataset. `help(swiss)` to learn what

(a) Try `help(swiss)` to learn what the variables represent.
(b) Try `pairs(swiss)` to plot the `swiss` data (or simply `plot(swiss)`). Which variables appear to be positively (or negatively) associated with fertility?

(c) Try `coplot (Fertility~ Education|Agriculture,data=swiss)`
and describe whether or not the association between fertility and education is
independent of the percentage of males whose occupations involve agriculture.

4.2. Association between two variables conditional on the third
The `coplot ()` function (part of the default `package:graphics`) is useful in
visualizing the association between two variables conditional on the values of a third
variable.

(a) Try the following to plot the `Orthodont` data for boys and girls

```
> library(nlme)
>      coplot(distance ~ age | Sex, data = Orthodont,
+             panel = panel.smooth)
```

(b) Does the graph indicate different growth patterns for boys and girls?
(c) Try `xyplot(distance   age | Sex, data = Orthodont`.
(d) Add a `panel` function with `panel.lmline ()` to plot separate regression
lines for boys and girls.
(e) Do boys appear to show a more rapid growth rate than girls?
(f) Try the following plotting command. Do boys appear to show a more rapid
growth rate than girls?

```
> plot(Orthodont, outer = ~ Sex, layout = c(2, 1),
+       aspect = 1, data = Orthodont)
```

(g) In the plot above, does there appear to be a greater variability in the growth
patterns in boys than in girls?

4.3. Change default `strip` color
In plotting the High School & Beyond data in Fig. 4.2 on page 73, we use grey scales
to represent the Catholic and public schools in an `xyplot ()`. Catholic schools are
plotted with `grey100` strips and public schools are plotted with `grey75` strips. In
this exercise we try something different.

(a) Change the `tcol` object so that Catholic schools are plotted with light green
strips (hint: try the HTML color code `#ccffcc`) and public schools are plotted
with salmon pink (`#ffe5cc`).

4.4. Shaded areas under a *t* distribution
Use Fig. 4.1 on page 70 as a guide, plot the area under the curve:

(a) First, plot the area under the curve with 30 polygons, the same as in Fig. 4.1.
(b) Calculate the sum of the areas of the 30 polygons.
(c) Plot the area under the curve with 100 polygons instead of the 30 polygons.
(d) Calculate the sum of the areas of the 100 polygons.

4.5. Plotting mathematics
Mathematical equations and symbols can be plotted easily. The following command
plots $\mu = 0$ $\sigma = 1$ at the bottom of a histogram.

```
hist(rnorm(100), freq = FALSE, main ="",
     xlab= expression(mu == 0 ~~ sigma == 1))
```

Call up help(plotmath) and find answers on how to do the following:

(a) Modify the hist() command above so that it also contains a main title of "Distribution of θ."

(b) Replace the main title with "$N(\mu, \sigma)$" to represent a normal distribution with mean μ and standard deviation σ.

(c) Here is a more challenging exercise that may require some trial-and-error to find a solution. Replace the main title with the equation of the normal distribution:

$$f(x) = \frac{1}{\sqrt{2\pi\sigma^2}}e^{-\frac{(x-\mu)^2}{2\sigma^2}}$$

(d) Add to the histogram a normal density curve with a mean of 0 and a standard deviation of 1.

Chapter 5
Analysis of Variance: Repeated-Measures

5.1 Example 1: Two Within-Subject Factors

The data are presented in Hays (1988, Table 13.21.2, p. 518). The example is simplified as follows. Suppose a psychologist is asked to conduct a study to help in designing the control panel of a machine that delivers medicine by intravenous infusion. The main purpose of the study is to find the best shape and color of the buttons on the control panel to improve efficiency and prevent potential errors. The psychologist wants to know how quickly users (physicians) respond to buttons of different colors and shapes. Suppose that the psychologist hypothesizes that bright colors are easier to see than dark colors so the users respond to them faster. In addition, she thinks that circles are easier to work with than squares. These hypotheses may seem trivial, but they involve the same statistical techniques that can be extended to more complicated experiments.

The psychologists knows that she will not be able to recruit many physicians to run the test apparatus. Thus she wants to collect as many test results as possible from each participating physician. Each participant works with the test apparatus four times, one with round red buttons, once with square red buttons, once with round gray buttons, and once with square gray buttons. Here the users only try each arrangement once, but the psychologist could ask them to repeat the tests several times in random order to get a more stable response time. In that case she would have another effect and she may choose to test (repetition, or the effect of learning).

In psychology, an experimental design like this is often called a "repeated-measures" or "within-subject" design because the measurements are made repeatedly within individual subjects. The variables `shape` and `color` are therefore called within-subject variables. It is possible to do the experiment between subjects. Each data point comes from a different physician. A completely between-subject experiment is also called a randomized design. However, the experimenter would need to recruit four times as many physicians, which is not efficient. This example has two within-subject variables and no between subject variable.

Y. Li and J. Baron, *Behavioral Research Data Analysis with R*, Use R,
DOI 10.1007/978-1-4614-1238-0_5, © Springer Science+Business Media, LLC 2012

We first enter the reaction time data into a vector `data1`. Then we transform `data1` into appropriate format for the repeated analysis of variance using `aov()`.

```
> data1 <- c(
+ 49,47,46,47,48,47,41,46,43,47,46,45,
+ 48,46,47,45,49,44,44,45,42,45,45,40,
+ 49,46,47,45,49,45,41,43,44,46,45,40,
+ 45,43,44,45,48,46,40,45,40,45,47,40)
```

We can take a look at the data in a layout that is easier to read. Each subject takes up a row in the data matrix.

```
> hays.mat <- matrix(data1, ncol = 4)
> dimnames(hays.mat) <-
+    list(paste("subj", 1:12, sep=""),
+       c("S1.C1", "S2.C1", "S1.C2", "S2.C2"))
> hays.mat
          S1.C1 S2.C1 S1.C2 S2.C2
subj1       49    48    49    45
subj2       47    46    46    43
subj3       46    47    47    44
subj4       47    45    45    45
subj5       48    49    49    48
subj6       47    44    45    46
subj7       41    44    41    40
subj8       46    45    43    45
subj9       43    42    44    40
subj10      47    45    46    45
subj11      46    45    45    47
subj12      45    40    40    40
```

Next we use the `data.frame()` function to create a data frame `Hays.df` that is appropriate for the `aov()` function.

```
> Hays.df <- data.frame(rt = data1, subj =
+ factor(rep(paste("subj", 1:12, sep=""), 4)),
+ shape = factor(rep(rep(c("shape1", "shape2"),
+ c(12, 12)), 2)),
+ color = factor(rep(c("color1", "color2"),
+ c(24, 24))))
```

The experimenter is interested in knowing if the shape (`shape`) and the color (`color`) of the buttons affect the reaction time (`rt`). The syntax is:

```
> aov(rt ~ shape*color + Error(subj/(shape * color)),
+      data=Hays.df)
```

The model formula, rt ~ shape * color + Error(subj/(shape * color)), can be divided into two parts. The first part, rt ~ shape * color, states that reaction time is affected by the shapes and colors of the buttons. The asterisk is a shorthand for shape + color + shape:color, representing the shape and color main effects and the shape by color interaction. The second part, Error(subj/(shape * color)), separates residual error into parts for appropriate statistical tests.

The Error(subj/(shape * color)) statement is used to separate the residual sums of squares into several components called error strata. It is equivalent to Error(subj+subj:shape+subj:color+subj:shape:color), meaning that we want to separate the following error terms: one error stratum for subject, another for subject by shape interaction, another for subject by color interaction, and the last one for subject by shape and by color interaction.

This syntax generates the appropriate tests for the within-subject variables shape and color. You get

```
> summary(aov(rt ~ shape*color +
+          Error(subj/(shape * color)), data=Hays.df))

Error: subj
          Df Sum Sq Mean Sq F value Pr(>F)
Residuals 11  226.5    20.6

Error: subj:shape
          Df Sum Sq Mean Sq F value Pr(>F)
shape      1  12.00   12.00    7.54  0.019
Residuals 11  17.50    1.59

Error: subj:color
          Df Sum Sq Mean Sq F value Pr(>F)
color      1  12.00   12.00    13.9 0.0033
Residuals 11   9.50    0.86

Error: subj:shape:color
            Df  Sum Sq  Mean Sq F value Pr(>F)
shape:color  1 1.2e-27 1.2e-27 4.3e-28      1
Residuals   11   30.50    2.77
```

Note that the shape effect is tested against the residuals of the subject by shape interaction, shown in the subj:shape error stratum. Similarly, the color effect is tested against subject by color stratum. The last error stratum offers a test of the shape:color interaction.

In essence, the Error() function matches the individual effects of interest with the appropriate error terms. Hoaglin et al. (1991, Chap. 10) discuss in detail the derivation and appropriate use of denominator error terms.

These denominator error terms is typically discussed in the context of "fixed" and "random" effects. The discussion can be confusing and counterproductive (see Gelman and Hill, 2007, Sect. 11.3). Here we offer a simple and intuitive explanation in the hopes that it will help you understand why `Error()` is needed in repeated-measures ANOVA. More details on the distinction of "fixed" and "random" effects can be found elsewhere (e.g., Searle et al. (1992, Sect. 1.4); Gelman and Hill (2007, Sect. 11.4)). The `shape` effect is treated as a "fixed" effect because the psychologist only wants to compare the reaction time differences between round and square buttons. She is not concerned about the population reaction time distribution for buttons of different shapes. In this case the number of possible shapes is fixed to two – round and square. The reaction time differences between the two conditions do not generalize beyond these two shapes. Similarly, the variable `color` is also considered fixed (again the effect not generalizable to colors other than red and gray).

When `color` and `shape` are both considered fixed, they are tested against the `subj:color` and `subj:shape` mean squares, respectively. The `Error()` function allows you to do these comparisons. In this example the only random effect is the `subj` effect. The 12 subjects reported here belong to a random sample of numerous other potential users of the device. The study would not be very useful without this generalizability because the results of the experiments would only apply to these particular 12 test subjects.

Without the `Error(subj/(shape * color))` formula, you get the wrong statistical tests. Note that both `color` and `shape` are tested against a common entry called "Residuals," which is the sum of all the pieces of residuals in the previous output of `Error(subj/(shape * color))`, with 11 degrees of freedom in each of the four error strata.

```
> summary(aov(rt ~ shape*color, data=Hays.df))
            Df    Sum Sq    Mean Sq    F value  Pr(>F)
shape        1    12.000    12.000     1.8592   0.1797
color        1    12.000    12.000     1.8592   0.1797
shape:color  1 4.399e-29 4.399e-29 6.816e-30   1.0000
Residuals   44   284.000     6.455
```

Note about `Error()`   What goes inside the `Error()` statement, and the order in which they are arranged, are important in ensuring correct statistical tests. Suppose you replaced the asterisk inside `Error(subj/(shape * color))` with a plus sign, you got `Error(subj/(shape + color))` instead:

```
> summary(aov(rt ~ shape * color +
+     Error(subj/(shape + color)), data=Hays.df))

[same output as before ... skipped ]

Error: Within
            Df    Sum Sq    Mean Sq    F value  Pr(>F)
shape:color  1 1.185e-27 1.185e-27 4.272e-28        1
Residuals   11   30.5000    2.7727
```

Note that `Error()` lumps the `shape:color` and `subj:shape:color` sums of squares into a "Within" error stratum. The "Residuals" in the Within stratum is actually the last piece of sum of square in the previous output. This `Error(subj/(shape + color))` syntax gives you the wrong statistics when you have more than two within-subject variables. We will return to this point later.

There is a subtle detail in the `Error(subj/(shape * color))` syntax that is worth noticing. For reasons that will become clearer in the next section, the forward slash (the `/` in `subj/(shape * color)`) tells `aov()` that the shape and color of the buttons are actually *nested* within individual subjects. That is, the changes in response time due to shape and color should be considered within the subjects.

5.1.1 Unbalanced Designs

We will conclude the first example by introducing a common complication in repeated-measures ANOVA that involves uneven cell size. In the example above, there are four possible combinations of shape and color, each containing exactly 12 observations. We call this design *balanced* because an equal number of observations is found in every combination (or a cell) of the design. In a balanced design, the `aov()` syntax above produces exactly the same univariate test statistics as those obtained from other statistical packages. However, complications arise when the cell sizes are not even. Participants may drop out. A post-hoc grouping factor was not originally allotted the same number of participants. For example, the experimenter may have even numbers by gender, but later may decide to try analyzing the reaction time by years of professional experience.

When a design is unbalanced, its `aov()` test statistics may look very different from those obtained from other statistical packages. The reason is because statistical packages like the GLM procedure in SPSS adjust the default Type III Sums of Squares by the harmonic mean of the unbalanced cell sizes. The adjustment is discussed in Maxwell and Delaney (1990, pp. 271–297).

SPSS produces the same output as R if the user tells SPSS to calculate the Type I SS (`SSTYPE(1)`) or Type II SS (`SSTYPE(2)`) instead of the default `SSTYPE(3)`. As shown in Maxwell and Delaney (1990), the calculations of SS1 and SS2 do not involve the harmonic mean. Maxwell and Delaney discuss the pros and cons of each type of Sums of Squares. Apparently SPSS and SAS think that the harmonic mean SS3 is the right analysis. Afterall, the SS3 is in general what a behavioral scientist seeks. Readers who are interested in the distinctions between the different types of SS can find a discussion in Maxwell and Delaney (1990). The example `aov()` analysis below can be compared with the results of SPSS using `SSTYPE(2)`.

```
# add one unbalanced between-subject variable
# n=8 in grp 1; 4 in grp 2
> Hays.df$grp <-factor(rep(c(1,1,1,1,1,1,1,1,2,2,2,2),
+    4))
```

```
> summary(aov(rt ~ grp*color*shape +
+  Error(subj/(shape*color)), data = Hays.df))

Error: subj
          Df Sum Sq Mean Sq F value Pr(>F)
grp        1   37.5    37.5  1.9841 0.1893
Residuals 10  189.0    18.9

Error: subj:shape
          Df Sum Sq Mean Sq F value  Pr(>F)
shape      1   12.0    12.0  7.5000 0.02088
grp:shape  1    1.5     1.5  0.9375 0.35576
Residuals 10   16.0     1.6

Error: subj:color
          Df  Sum Sq Mean Sq F value  Pr(>F)
color      1 12.0000 12.0000  13.151 0.00464
grp:color  1  0.3750  0.3750   0.411 0.53590
Residuals 10  9.1250  0.9125

Error: subj:shape:color
                 Df     Sum Sq   Mean Sq   F value
color:shape       1 5.368e-29 5.368e-29 1.979e-29
grp:color:shape   1    3.3750    3.3750    1.2442
Residuals        10   27.1250    2.7125
                 Pr(>F)
color:shape      1.0000
grp:color:shape  0.2907
Residuals
```

Note that the between-subject grp effect has an F statistic of 1.984 with a p-value of 0.189. The SPSS code below shows a Type-III F statistic of 2.083 with a p-value of 0.179. The univariate within-subject tests are also different.

```
DATA LIST LIST / grp sh1col1 sh2col1 sh1col2 sh2col2.
BEGIN DATA
1 49 48 49 45
1 47 46 46 43
1 46 47 47 44
1 47 45 45 45
1 48 49 49 48
1 47 44 45 46
1 41 44 41 40
1 46 45 43 45
2 43 42 44 39
```

```
2 47 45 46 45
2 46 45 45 47
2 45 40 40 40
END DATA.

GLM sh1col1 sh1col2 sh2col1 sh2col2 BY grp
  /WSFACTOR=shape 2 Polynomial color 2 Polynomial
  /METHOD=SSTYPE(3)
  /CRITERIA=ALPHA(.05)
  /WSDESIGN=shape color shape*color
  /DESIGN=grp.
```

5.2   Example 2: Maxwell and Delaney

This example is found in Chap. 12 of Maxwell and Delaney (1990), on a laboratory experiment in which study subjects were asked to recognize letters presented visually on a tachistoscope. Each subject was given six trials in a 2 by 3 factorial design of visual interference by obscuring the letters with noise (noise present vs. noise absent) and by rotating the letters in 0, 4, and 8 degrees angles. The investigators wanted to examine the extent to which visual interference slows the recognition reaction time. The dependent variable was reaction time. The two independent variables were within-subject factors. We repeat the same R syntax, then we include the SAS GLM syntax for the same analysis. Here we have:

- *one dependent variable*: reaction time.
- *two independent variables*: visual stimuli are tilted at 0, 4, and 8 degrees; with noise absent or present. Each subject responded to 3 tilt by 2 noise = 6 trials.

The data are entered slightly differently; their format is like what you would usually do with SAS, SPSS, and Systat.

```
> MD497.dat <- matrix(c(
+ 420, 420, 480, 480, 600, 780,
+ 420, 480, 480, 360, 480, 600,
+ 480, 480, 540, 660, 780, 780,
+ 420, 540, 540, 480, 780, 900,
+ 540, 660, 540, 480, 660, 720,
+ 360, 420, 360, 360, 480, 540,
+ 480, 480, 600, 540, 720, 840,
+ 480, 600, 660, 540, 720, 900,
+ 540, 600, 540, 480, 720, 780,
+ 480, 420, 540, 540, 660, 780),
+ ncol = 6, byrow = T)
```

Next we transform the data matrix into a data frame.

```
> MD497.df <- data.frame(
+ rt    =as.vector(MD497.dat),
+ subj =factor(rep(paste("s", 1:10, sep=""), 6)),
+ deg  =factor(rep(rep(c(0,4,8), c(10, 10, 10)), 2)),
+ noise=factor(rep(c("no.noise","noise"),c(30, 30))))
```

Then we test the main effects and the interaction in one aov() model. The syntax is the same as in the Hays example:

```
> taov <- aov(rt ~ deg * noise +
+   Error(subj / (deg * noise)), data=MD497.df)
> summary(taov)

Error: subj
           Df Sum Sq Mean Sq F value Pr(>F)
Residuals  9 292140   32460

Error: subj:deg
           Df Sum Sq Mean Sq F value    Pr(>F)
deg         2 289920  144960  40.719 2.087e-07
Residuals 18  64080    3560

Error: subj:noise
           Df Sum Sq Mean Sq F value    Pr(>F)
noise       1 285660  285660  33.766 0.0002560
Residuals  9  76140    8460

Error: subj:deg:noise
            Df Sum Sq Mean Sq F value    Pr(>F)
deg:noise    2 105120   52560   45.31 9.424e-08
Residuals   18  20880    1160
```

The F values for deg, noise, and deg:noise are 40.72, 33.77, and 45.31, respectively. These statistics are identical to those produced by the SAS code below. These F statistics can be found in the "Univariate Tests of Hypotheses for Within Subject Effects" section in the SAS output.

```
data rt1;
input deg0NA deg4NA deg8NA deg0NP deg4NP deg8NP;
cards;
420 420 480 480 600 780
420 480 480 360 480 600
480 480 540 660 780 780
420 540 540 480 780 900
540 660 540 480 660 720
```

```
360 420 360 360 480 540
480 480 600 540 720 840
480 600 660 540 720 900
540 600 540 480 720 780
480 420 540 540 660 780
;

proc glm data=rt1;
model deg0NA deg4NA deg8NA deg0NP deg4NP deg8NP = ;
repeated noise 2 (0 1), degree 3 (0 4 8) / summary ;
run;
```

Maxwell and Delaney summarized how one weighs multivariate and univariate results. In SAS, each row contains the data from one subject, across 3 degrees of tilt and two levels of noise. The GLM syntax has a `class` option where the between-subject factors are listed (if any). SAS calculates the Pillai's Trace statistics. For the `degree` by `noise` interaction, it is 0.918.

Dalgaard (2007) showed that multivariate statistics such as the Pillai's Trace can be calculated by `lm()` and `anova.mlm()`. A brief summary of Dalgaard (2007) is provided here. First, the `mlmfit` object fits one intercept for each of the six columns in `MD497.dat`. Next, `mlmfit0` takes the intercepts away and fits a null model.

```
> mlmfit <- lm(MD497.dat ~ 1)
> mlmfit

Call:
lm(formula = MD497.dat ~ 1)

Coefficients:
              [,1]   [,2]   [,3]   [,4]   [,5]   [,6]
(Intercept)   462    510    528    492    660    762

> mlmfit0 <- update(mlmfit, ~ 0)
```

We already know that the columns of `MD497.dat` represent the six combinations of three tilt angles and two noise levels. These combinations can be represented in a data frame called `idata`, which can be passed on to `anova.mlm` to test the angle by noise interaction. Note that the `Pr(>F)` of `9.4e-08` is the same as the p-value found on page 86.

```
> idata <- expand.grid(deg=c("0", "4", "8"),
+                       noise=c("A", "P"))
idata
  deg noise
1   0     A
2   4     A
```

```
3    8     A
4    0     P
5    4     P
6    8     P
> anova(mlmfit, mlmfit0, X = ~ deg + noise,
+        idata = idata, test = "Spherical")
Analysis of Variance Table

Model 1: MD497.dat ~ 1
Model 2: MD497.dat ~ 1 - 1

Contrasts orthogonal to
~deg + noise

Greenhouse-Geisser epsilon: 0.904
Huynh-Feldt epsilon:        1.118

  Res.Df Df Gen.var.    F num Df den Df  Pr(>F)
1      9          317
2     10  1       996 45.3      2     18 9.4e-08
   G-G Pr  H-F Pr
1
2 3.5e-07 9.4e-08
```

Details on anova.mlm and the parameters X and M can be found on the open-access article by Dalgaard (2007) and are not discussed here.

5.3 Example 3: More Than Two Within-Subject Factors

Earlier we noted that Error(subj/(shape * color)), which uses an as-terisk to connect shape and color, produces detailed breakdown of the vari-ance components. The Error(subj/(shape + color)) statement prints out what you specifically ask for and lumps the remainder into a "Within" stratum. If you have more than two within-subject fixed effects, the latter will produce some undesirable side effects.

The next hypothetical example [1] shows this side effect.

```
> subj <- gl(10, 32, 320) # 10 subjects, each 32 times
> a   <- gl(2, 16, 320) # 16 trials w/ a1, next 16 a2
> b   <- gl(2,  8, 320) # 8 trials w/ b1, b2, etc.
> c   <- gl(2,  4, 320)
```

---

[1] contributed by Christophe Pallier.

```
> x   <- rnorm(320)
> d1 <- data.frame(subj, a, b, c, x)
> d2 <- aggregate(x, list(a = a, b = b, c = c,
+       subj = subj), mean)
> summary(a1 <- aov(x ~ a * b * c +
+              Error(subj/(a*b*c)), d2))
> summary(a2 <- aov(x ~ a * b * c +
+              Error(subj/(a+b+c)), d2))
> summary(a3 <- aov(x ~ a * b * c +
+              Error(subj/(a*b*c)), d1))
```

Note that `summary(a2)` does not give you the appropriate statistical tests for the two-way interactions among factors a, b, and c. The problem is because `Error()` lumps everything other than `Error: subj:a`, `Error: subj:b`, and `Error: subj:c` into a common entry of residuals. The S Model book by Chambers and Hastie contains some technical details that explains this behavior.

5.4   Example 4: A Simpler Design with Only One Within-Subject Variable

Data in this example are found in Stevens (1992, Sect. 13.2), with only one within-subject predictor.

```
> data <- c(
+ 30,14,24,38,26,
+ 28,18,20,34,28,
+ 16,10,18,20,14,
+ 34,22,30,44,30)
> Stv.df <- data.frame(rt=data,
+ subj = factor(rep(paste("subj", 1:5, sep=""), 4)),
+ drug = factor(rep(paste("drug", 1:4, sep=""),
+        c(5,5,5,5))))
> summary(aov(rt ~ drug + Error(subj/drug),
+        data = Stv.df))
```

5.5   Example 5: One Between, Two Within

Stevens (1992, Chap. 13) analyzed the effect of drug treatment effect by one between-subject factor: group (two groups of eight subjects each) and two within-subject factors: drug (2 drugs) and dose (3 doses).

```
> Ela.mat <- matrix(
+ c(19,22,28,16,26,22,
+ 11,19,30,12,18,28,
+ 20,24,24,24,22,29,
+ 21,25,25,15,10,26,
+ 18,24,29,19,26,28,
+ 17,23,28,15,23,22,
+ 20,23,23,26,21,28,
+ 14,20,29,25,29,29,
+ 16,20,24,30,34,36,
+ 26,26,26,24,30,32,
+ 22,27,23,33,36,45,
+ 16,18,29,27,26,34,
+ 19,21,20,22,22,21,
+ 20,25,25,29,29,33,
+ 21,22,23,27,26,35,
+ 17,20,22,23,26,28), nrow = 16, byrow = T)
```

We first put them in a multivariate format (the wide format), using the cbind.data.frame() function.

```
> Ela.mul <- cbind.data.frame(subj=1:16,
+           gp=factor(rep(1:2,rep(8,2))), Ela.mat)
> # d12 = drug 1, dose 2
> dimnames(Ela.mul)[[2]] <-
+ c("subj","gp","d11","d12","d13","d21","d22","d23")
```

Here is the command for transferring it to the univariate format (long format).

```
> Ela.uni <- data.frame(effect = as.vector(Ela.mat),
+ subj = factor(paste("s", rep(1:16, 6), sep="")),
+ gp = factor(paste("gp",rep(rep(c(1, 2),c(8,8)),6),
+           sep="")),
+ drug = factor(paste("dr",rep(c(1, 2),c(48, 48)),
+           sep="")),
+ dose=factor(paste("do", rep(rep(c(1,2,3),
+           rep(16, 3)), 2), sep="")),
+           row.names = NULL)
```

Next, we use Error(subj/(dose*drug)) to test the main effects and their interactions. It is worth noting that R knows that the gp effect goes with the subject error stratum.

```
> summary(aov(effect ~ gp * drug * dose +
+         Error(subj/(dose*drug)), data=Ela.uni))
```

5.6   Other Useful Functions for ANOVA

As we discussed earlier, we can use the `tapply()` function to calculate the means across various conditions. We can think of it as using one statement to run the `mean()` function 12 times. The output matrix is useful for plotting.

```
> tapply(Ela.uni$effect,
+   IND = list(Ela.uni$gp, Ela.uni$drug, Ela.uni$dose),
+   FUN = mean)
```

We can also easily custom design a function `se()` to calculate the standard error for the means. We can use one line of `tapply()` to get all standard errors. The `se()` makes it easy to find the confidence intervals for those means. Later we will demonstrate how to use the means and standard errors that we got from `tapply()` to plot the data.

```
> se <- function(x)
+ {
+   y <- x[!is.na(x)] # remove the missing values
+   sqrt(var(as.vector(y))/length(y))
+ }
```

In R, we not only can use the built-in functions such as `aov()` to do the analyses, we can but also take advantage of R's flexibility and do many analyses by hand. The following examples demonstrate that some of the ANOVA tests we did earlier with the `aov()` function can also be done manually with contrasts.

1. We can use the following contrast to test the group effect. On the left hand side of the `aov()` model, we use matrix multiplication (`%*%`) to apply the contrast (`contr`) to each person's six data points. As a result, each person's six data points become one number that is actually the person's total score summed across all conditions. The matrix multiplication is the same as doing `1 * d11 + 1 * d12 + 1 * d13 + 1 * d21 + 1 * d22 + 1 * d23` for each person.

   Then we use the `aov()` function to compare the total scores across the two groups. We can verify that in this output the F statistic for the `gp` marginal effect is exactly the same as the one in the previous `aov(... Error())` output, although the sums of squares are different because the contrast is not scaled to length 1.

```
> contr <- matrix(c(
+   1,
+   1,
+   1,
```

```
+   1,
+   1,
+   1), ncol = 1)

> taov <- aov(cbind(d11,d12,d13,d21,d22,d23)
+                 %*% contr ~ gp, data = Ela.mul)
> summary(taov, intercept = T)
```

2. The following contrast, when combined with the aov() function, will test the drug main effect and drug:group interaction. The contrast c(1, 1, 1, -1, -1, -1) applies positive 1's to columns 1:3 and negative 1's to columns 4:6. Columns 1:3 contain the data for drug 1 and 4:6 for drug 2, respectively. So the contrast and the matrix multiplication generates a difference score between drugs 1 and 2. When we use aov() to compare this difference between two groups, we actually test the drug:gp interaction.

```
> contr <- matrix(c(
+   1,
+   1,
+   1,
+  -1,
+  -1,
+  -1), ncol = 1)

> tmp <- aov(cbind(d11,d12,d13,d21,d22,d23)
+                 %*% contr ~ gp, Ela.mul)
> summary(tmp,intercept= T)
```

3. The next contrast, when combined with the manova() function, tests the dose main effect and the dose:group interaction. The first contrast c(1, 0, -1, 1, 0, -1) tests if the difference between dose 1 and dose 3 are statistically significant across groups; and the second contrast c(0, 1, -1, 0, 1, -1) tests the difference between dose 2 and dose 3 across two groups. When tested simultaneously with manova(), we get

```
> contr <- matrix(c(
+   1, 0,
+   0, 1,
+  -1,-1,
+   1, 0,
+   0, 1,
+  -1,-1), nrow = 6, byrow = T)
> tmp <- manova(cbind(d11,d12,d13,d21,d22,d23)
+                 %*% contr ~ gp, Ela.mul)
> summary(tmp, test="Wilks", intercept = T)
```

4. Another `manova()` contrast, which tests the `drug:dose` interaction and the three-way `drug:dose:group` interaction.

```
> contr <- matrix(c(
+   1,-1,
+   0, 2,
+  -1,-1,
+  -1, 1,
+   0,-2,
+   1, 1), nrow = 6, byrow = T)

> tmp <- manova(cbind(d11,d12,d13,d21,d22,d23)
+               %*% contr ~ gp, Ela.mul)
> summary(tmp, test="Wilks", intercept = T)
```

5.7   Graphics with Error Bars

Next we will demonstrate how to use R's powerful graphics functions to add error bars to a plot. The example uses the `Ela.uni` example discussed earlier. In this example we will briefly show how visual representations compliment the statistical tests. We use R's `jpg()` graphics driver to generate a graph that can be viewed by a web browser. The command syntax may appear intimidating for beginners, but it is worth for the increased efficiency in the long run.

Typically the graphs are first generated interactively with drivers like `X11()`, then the commands are saved and edited into a script file. A command syntax script eliminates the need to save bulky graphic files.

First we start the graphics driver `jpg()` and name the file where the graph(s) will be saved.

```
> attach(Ela.uni)
> jpeg(file = "ElasBar.jpg")
```

Then we find the means, the standard errors, and the 95% confidence bounds of the means.

```
> tmean <- tapply(effect,list(gp,drug,dose), mean)
> tse   <- tapply(effect,list(gp,drug,dose), se)
> tbarHeight <- matrix(tmean, ncol=3)
> dimnames(tbarHeight) <- list(c("gp1dr1","gp2dr1",
+   "gp1dr2","gp2dr2"), c("dose1","dose2" ,"dose3"))
> tn <- tapply(effect, list(gp, drug, dose), length)
> tu <- tmean + qt(.975, df=tn-1) * tse # upper 95%CI
> tl <- tmean + qt(.025, df=tn-1) * tse # lower
> tcol <- c("blue", "darkblue", "yellow", "orange")
```

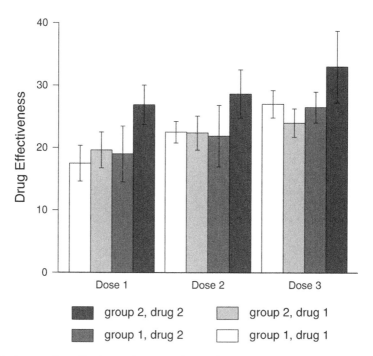

Fig. 5.1 Average drug effectiveness by group, drug, and dose

After all the numbers are computed, we start building the barplot. First we plot the bars without the confidence intervals, axes, labels, and tick marks. Note that the `barplot()` function returns the *x*-axis values at where the center of the bars are plotted. Later we will use the values in `tbars` to add additional pieces. Let us first take a look at the bar graph (Fig. 5.1).

The tallest bar shows that greatest drug effectiveness is attained by giving Group 2 subjects drug 2 at dose 3. This suggests a group by drug interaction, which is confirmed by the `aov()` results outlined earlier. It also indicates an increasing effectiveness from dose 1 to 3, which is also confirmed by the statistics. Below is how the rest of the barplot is done.

```
> tbars <- barplot(height=tbarHeight, beside=T,
+                  space=c(0, 0.5), axes=F,
+                  axisnames = F,
+                  ylim=c(-16, 40), col=tcol)
```

Then we add the 95% confidence intervals of the means to the bars.

```
> segments(x0=tbars, x1=tbars, y0=tl, y1=tu)
> segments(x0=tbars-.1, x1=tbars+0.1, y0=tl, y1=tl)
> segments(x0=tbars-.1, x1=tbars+0.1, y0=tu, y1=tu)
```

The axes labels are added.

```
> axis(2, at=seq(0, 40, by=10), labels=rep("", 5),
+        las=1)
> tx <- apply(tbars, 2, mean)  # 3 clusters of bars
```

We plot the horizontal axis manually so that we can ask R to put things at exactly where we want them.

```
> segments(x0=0, x1=max(tbars)+1.0,y0=0,y1=0, lty=1,
+        lwd = 2)
> text(c("Dose 1", "Dose 2", "Dose 3"), x = tx,
+      y = -1.5, cex =1)
> mtext(text=seq(0,40,by=10), side = 2,
+      at = seq(0,40,by=10), line = 1.5, cex =1,
+      las=1)
> mtext(text="Drug Effectiveness", side = 2,
+      line = 2.5, at = 20, cex =1.5)
```

We want to plot the legend of the graph manually. R also has a legend() function, although less flexible.

```
> tx1 <- c(0, 1, 1, 0)
> ty1 <- c(-15, -15, -13, -13)
> polygon(x=tx1, y=ty1, col=tcol[1])
> polygon(x=tx1, y=ty1 + 2.5, col=tcol[2])
> polygon(x=tx1, y=ty1 + 5, col=tcol[3])
> polygon(x=tx1, y=ty1 + 7.5, col=tcol[4])
```

We complete the graph by adding the legend labels.

```
> text(x = 2.0, y = -14, labels="group 1, drug 1",
+    cex = 1.2, adj = 0)
> text(x = 2.0, y = -11.5, labels="group 2, drug 1",
+    cex = 1.2, adj = 0)
> text(x = 2.0, y = -9, labels="group 1, drug 2",
+    cex = 1.2, adj = 0)
> text(x = 2.0, y = -6.5, labels="group 2, drug 2",
+    cex = 1.2, adj = 0)
```

5.8 Another Way to do Error Bars Using plotCI()

The gplots library has a function plotCI(), which does confidence intervals for plots. Here is an example, which is Fig. 1 in http://journal.sjdm.org /06137/jdm06137.htm. Note the use of a small horizontal offset (−0.01) so that the error bars do not overlap. The font "NimbusSan" is supposed to fit well with Times Roman.

```
> library("gplots")
> m.pg <- c(-2.64, 3.60, 6.00, 3.68, 5.44)
> se.pg <-c(1.71938, 1.86548, 1.74738, 1.94484, 1.83492)
> m.pl <-c(-4.9600, -3.7600, -2.3200, -.1600, 6.5600)
> se.pl <-c(1.47024, 1.72170, 1.79139, 1.36587, 1.56852)

> postscript(file="fig1.eps",family="NimbusSan",
+            width=8,height=8,horiz=F,pointsize=18,
+            paper="special")
> plotCI(y=c(m.pg,m.pl),x=c(c(1:5)-.01,c(1:5)+.01),
+        uiw=c(se.pg,se.pl),
+        ylim=c(-6,8),ylab="Net IGT score",
+        xlab="Block",lty=rep(c(1,2),c(5,5)))
> lines(y=m.pg,x=c(1:5)-.01,lty=1)
> lines(y=m.pl,x=c(1:5)+.01,lty=2)
> legend(3.6,-3.7,legend=c("Prior gain","Prior loss"),
+        lty=c(1,2))
> dev.off()
```

5.8.1   Use `Error()` *for Repeated-Measure ANOVA*

In this section we give an intuitive explanation to the use of the `Error()` statement for repeated-measure analysis of variance. These explanations are different than what are typically covered in advanced textbooks. The conventional method focuses on deriving the appropriate error terms for specific statistical tests. We use an intuitive method, which will show that using `Error()` inside an `aov()` function is actually the same as performing t-tests using contrasts.

The conventional explanation is computationally and theoretically equivalent to what we are about to summarize. Detailed theoretical explanations can be found in most advanced textbooks, including the book by Hoaglin et al. (1991). Explanations of the technical details can be found in the book by Chambers and Hastie (1993).

We first review Analysis of Variance using a method commonly seen in most of the introductory textbooks. This method uses an ANOVA table to describe how much of the total variability is accounted for by all the related variables. An ANOVA table is exactly what `aov()` does for you. We first apply this method to the `Hays.df` data described earlier (but repeated here), then we use the ANOVA table to explain why we must add the `Error()` statement in an `aov()` command in order to get the appropriate significance tests. Finally we draw a connection between `Error()` and specific t-tests tailored for repeated-measure data.

5.8.1.1   Basic ANOVA Table with `aov()`

The `aov()` function generates a basic ANOVA table if `Error()` is not inserted. Applying a simple `aov()` to the `Hays.df` data, you get an ANOVA table like the following:

```
> summary(aov(rt ~ subj*color*shape, data=Hays.df))
                    Df     Sum Sq     Mean Sq
subj                11    226.500      20.591
color                1     12.000      12.000
shape                1     12.000      12.000
subj:color          11      9.500       0.864
subj:shape          11     17.500       1.591
color:shape          1  1.493e-27   1.493e-27
subj:color:shape    11     30.500       2.773
```

R analyzes how reaction time differs depending on the subjects, color and the shape of the stimuli. Also, you can have R to explain how they interact with one another. A simple plot of the data may suggest an interaction between color and shape. A `color:shape` interaction occurs if, for example, the color yellow is easier to recognize than red when it comes in a particular shape. The subjects may recognize yellow squares much faster than any other color and shape combinations. Therefore the effect of color on reaction time is not the same for all shapes. We call this an interaction.

The above `aov()` statement divides the total sum of squares in the reaction time into pieces. By looking at the size of the sums of squares (`Sum Sq` in the table), you can get a rough idea that there is a lot of variability among subjects and negligible in the `color:shape` interaction.

So we are pretty sure that the effect of color does not depend on what shape it is. The sum of square for `color:shape` is negligible. Additionally, the `subj` variable has very high variability, although this is not very interesting because this happens all the time. We always know for sure that some subjects respond faster than others.

Obviously we want to know if different colors or shapes make a difference in the response time. One might naturally think that we do not need the `subj` variable in the `aov()` statement. Unfortunately doing so in a repeated design can cause misleading results:

```
> summary(aov(rt ~ color * shape, data = Hays.df))
              Df     Sum Sq     Mean Sq    F value   Pr(>F)
color          1     12.000      12.000     1.8592   0.1797
shape          1     12.000      12.000     1.8592   0.1797
color:shape    1  1.246e-27   1.246e-27  1.931e-28   1.0000
Residuals     44    284.000       6.455
```

This output can easily deceive you into thinking that there is nothing statistically significant. This is where `Error()` is needed to give you the appropriate test statistics.

5.8.1.2 Using `Error()` Within `aov()`

It is important to remember that `summary()` generates incorrect results if you give it the wrong model. Note that in the statement above the `summary()` function automatically compares each sum of square with the residual sum of square and prints out the F statistics accordingly. In addition, because the `aov()` function does not contain the `subj` variable, `aov()` lumps every sum of squares related to the `subj` variable into this big `Residuals` sum of squares. You can verify this by adding up those entries in our basic ANOVA table ($226.5 + 9.5 + 17.5 + 1.49E - 27 + 30 = 284$).

R does not complain about the above syntax, which assumes that you want to test each effect against the sum of residual errors related to the subjects. This leads to incorrect F statistics. The residual error related to the subjects is not the correct error term for all. Next we will explain how to find the correct error terms using the `Error()` statement. We will then use a simple t-test to show you why we want to do that.

5.8.1.3 The Appropriate Error Terms

In a repeated-measure design like that in Hays, the appropriate error term for the `color` effect is the `subj:color` sum of squares. Also the error term for the other within-subject, `shape` effect is the `subj:shape` sum of squares. The error term for the `color:shape` interaction is then the `subj:color:shape` sum of squares. A general discussion can be found in Hoaglin's book. In the next section we will examine in some detail the test of the `color` effect.

For now we will focus on the appropriate analyses using `Error()`. We must add an `Error(subj/(shape + color))` statement within `aov()`. This repeats an earlier analysis.

```
> summary(aov(rt ~ color * shape +
+        Error(subj/(color + shape)), data = Hays.df))

Error: subj
          Df Sum Sq Mean Sq F value Pr(>F)
Residuals 11  226.5    20.6

Error: subj:color
          Df Sum Sq Mean Sq F value Pr(>F)
color      1  12.00   12.00    13.9 0.0033
Residuals 11   9.50    0.86
```

```
Error: subj:shape
           Df Sum Sq Mean Sq F value Pr(>F)
shape       1  12.00   12.00    7.54  0.019
Residuals  11  17.50    1.59

Error: Within
              Df  Sum Sq Mean Sq F value Pr(>F)
color:shape  1 1.1e-27 1.1e-27 4.1e-28      1
Residuals   11   30.50    2.77
```

As we mentioned before, the `Error(subj/(color * shape))` statement is the short hand for dividing all the residual sums of squares – in this case all subject-related sums of squares – into three error strata.

The `Error()` statement says that we want three error terms separated in the ANOVA table: one for `subj`, `subj:color`, and `subj:shape`, respectively. The `summary()` and `aov()` functions are smart enough to do the rest for you. The effects are arranged according to where they belong. In the output the `color` effect is tested against the correct error term `subj:color`, etc. If you add up all the `Residuals` entries in the table, you will find that it is exactly 284, the sum of all subject-related sums of squares.

5.8.1.4 Sources of the Appropriate Error Terms

In this section we use simple examples of t-tests to demonstrate the need of the appropriate error terms. Rigorous explanations can be found in Edwards (1985) and Hoaglin et al. (1991). We will demonstrate that the appropriate error term for an effect in a repeated ANOVA is exactly identical to the standard error in a t statistic for testing the same effect.

We need the reaction time data in Hays (1988) in matrix form (`hays.mat` on page 80). In a repeated-measure experiment the four measurements of reaction time are correlated by design because they are from the same subject. A subject who responds quickly in one condition is likely to respond quickly in other conditions as well.

To take into consideration these differences, the comparisons of reaction time should be tested with differences across conditions. When we take the differences, we use each subject as his/her own control. So the difference in reaction time has the subject's baseline speed subtracted out. In the `hays.mat` data we test the `color` effect by a simple t-test comparing the differences between the columns of "Color1" and "Color2."

Using the `t.test()` function, this is done by

```
> t.test(x = hays.mat[, 1] + hays.mat[, 2],
+        y = hays.mat[, 3] + hays.mat[, 4], paired = T)
data:  hays.mat[, 1] + hays.mat[, 2] and
       hays.mat[, 3] + hays.mat[, 4]
```

```
t = 3.7276, df = 11, p-value = 0.003338
alternative hypothesis: true difference in means
is not equal to 0
95 percent confidence interval:
 0.81908 3.18092
sample estimates:
mean of the differences
                    2
```

An alternative is to test if a contrast is equal to zero, we talked about this in earlier sections:

```
> t.test(hays.mat %*% c(1, 1, -1, -1))
```

```
         One Sample t-test
```

```
data:   hays.mat %*% c(1, 1, -1, -1)
t = 3.7276, df = 11, $p$-value = 0.003338
alternative hypothesis: true mean is not equal to 0
95 percent confidence interval:
 0.819076 3.180924
sample estimates:
mean of x
        2
```

This $c(1, 1, -1, -1)$ contrast is identical to the first t-test. The matrix multiplication (the %*% operand) takes care of the arithmetic. It multiplies the first column by a constant 1, add column 2, then subtract from that columns 3 and 4. This tests the color effect. Note that the p-value of this t test is the same as the p-values for the first t test and the earlier F test.

It can be proven algebraically that the square of a t-statistic is identical to the F test for the same effect. So this fact can be used to double check the results. The square of our t-statistic for color is $3.7276^2 = 13.895$, which is identical to the F statistic for color.

Now we are ready to draw the connection between a t-statistic for the contrast and the F-statistic in an ANOVA table for repeated-measure aov(). The t statistic is a ratio between the effect size to be tested and the standard error of that effect. The larger the ratio, the stronger the effect size. The formula can be described as follows:

$$t = \frac{\bar{x}_1 - \bar{x}_2}{s/\sqrt{n}}, \tag{5.1}$$

where the numerator is the observed differences and the denominator can be interpreted as the expected differences due to chance. If the actual difference is substantially larger than what you would expect, then you tend to think that the difference is not due to random chance.

Similarly, an *F* test contrasts the observed variability with the expected variability. In a repeated design we must find an appropriate denominator by adding the `Error()` statement inside an `aov()` function.

The next two commands show that the error sum of squares of the contrast is exactly identical to the `Residual` sum of squares for the `subj:color` error stratum.

```
> tvec <- hays.mat %*% c(1, 1, -1, -1)/2
> sum((tvec - mean(tvec))^2)
[1] 9.5
```

The sum of squares of the contrast is exactly 9.5, identical to the residual sum of squares for the correct *F* test. The scaling factor $1/2$ is critical because it provides correct scaling for the numbers. By definition a statistical contrast should have a vector length of 1. This is done by dividing each element of the contrast vector by 2, turning it to `c(1/2, 1/2, -1/2, -1/2)`. The scaling does not affect the *t*-statistics. But it becomes important when we draw a connection between a *t*-test and an *F* test.

You get the standard error of the *t*-statistic if you do the following:

```
> sqrt(sum((tvec - mean(tvec))^2 / 11) / 12)
[1] 0.2682717
```

The first division of 11 is for calculating the variance; then you divide the variance by the sample size of 12, take the square root, you have the standard error for the t-test. You can verify it by running `se(hays.mat %*% c(1, 1, -1, -1)/2)`.

5.8.1.5 Verify the Calculations Manually

All the above calculations by `aov()` can be verified manually. This section summarizes some of the technical details. This also gives you a flavor of how Analysis Of Variance can be done by matrix algebra. First we re-arrange the raw data into a three-dimensional array. Each element of the array is one data point, and the three dimensions are for the subject, the shape, and the color, respectively.

```
> hays.A <- array(data1, dim=c(12, 2, 2))
> dimnames(hays.A) <- list(paste("subj",1:12,sep=""),
+    c("Shape1", "Shape2"), c("Color1", "Color2"))
```

Because at this point we want to solve for the effect of `color`, we use the `apply()` function to average the reaction time over the two shapes.

```
> Ss.color <- apply(hays.A, c(1, 3), mean)
```

Next we test a t-test contrast for the color effect.

```
> Contr <- c(1, -1)
> Ss.color.Contr <- Ss.color %*% Contr
> mean(Ss.color.Contr) / (sqrt(var(Ss.color.Contr) /
+     length(Ss.color.Contr)))
          [,1]
[1,] 3.727564
```

This is the same t-statistic as in `t.test(Ss.color %*% c(1, -1))`. Also note that the square of 3.73 equals the 13.9 F-statistic on page 99. The above t-test compares the mean of the contrast against the standard error of the contrast, which is `sqrt(var(Ss.color.Contr)/length(Ss.color.Contr))`.

Now we can verify that the sum of square of the contrast is exactly the same as the error term when we use `aov()` with the `Error(subj:color)` stratum.

```
> sum((Ss.color.Contr - mean(Ss.color.Contr))^2)
[1] 9.5
```

5.8.2   Sphericity

Sphericity is an assumption of repeated measure ANOVA. It means that the variance–covariance structure of the repeated measure ANOVA follows a certain pattern. In a repeated measure design, several measurements are made to the same groups of subjects under different conditions (and/or at different time). Sphericity is, in a nutshell, that the variances of the differences between the repeated measurements should be about the same. This is best explained with examples. We use an oversimplified example to explain what sphericity is, how to calculate and test it, and what alternative statistics can be used if the sphericity assumption is not met.

5.8.2.1   Why Is Sphericity Important?

Violations of the sphericity assumption lead to a biased p-values. The alpha error of a test may be set at 5%, but the test may be actually rejecting the null hypothesis 10% of the time. This raises doubts of the conclusions of the repeated measure ANOVA. Imagine a study about weight gains of new born babies at the Intensive Care Unit. The weight of the babies is measured every day for a critical period of three days. On the average the babies gain 100 grams between Days 1 and 2, and they gain 150 grams between Days 2 and 3. Sphericity says that the variance of the weight gain between Days 1 and 2 should be about the same as the variance of the weight gain between Days 2 and 3 (and also between Days 1 and 3). If not, the variance observed between different time periods are confounded with the correlation of the measurements made at different time. Suppose the variance of the first weight gain is 20 and the variance of the second weight gain is 100, then the measurements made at times 1 and 2 are likely to be correlated more closely than measurements made at times 2 and 3. As a result the variance over the whole 3-day period (what is often called the variance of the time effect in ANOVA jargon) fluctuates over time and is not reliable in describing the overall growth pattern in babies in the ICU.

In repeated measure experiments the same subjects are tested multiple times under different conditions. It is a good idea to check if the responses made under some conditions are correlated more closely than responses made under other conditions.

There is a statistic, the Greenhouse–Geisser epsilon ϵ, which measures by how much the sphericity assumption is violated. Epsilon is then used to adjust for the potential bias in the F statistic. Epsilon can be 1, which means that the sphericity assumption is met perfectly. An epsilon smaller than 1 means that the sphericity assumption is violated. The further it deviates from 1, the worse the violation. In real life epsilon is rarely exactly 1. If it is not much smaller than 1, then we feel comfortable with the results of repeated measure ANOVA. Thus the question is how small is too small. We will get to that below. Additionally, we will talk about two remedies when sphericity is violated: (1) correct for the p-value, and (2) use procedures that do not depend on sphericity, such as MANOVA.

5.9 How to Estimate the Greenhouse–Geisser Epsilon?

The Greenhouse–Geisser epsilon is derived from the variance–covariance matrix of the data. The `MD497.dat` example above involves a study where study subjects judged stimuli under three different angles of rotation, at 0, 4, and 8 degrees angle from the horizontal. In this subsection we estimate the Greenhouse–Geisser epsilon associated with the rotation of the stimuli. The three measurements of reaction time are stored in x0, x4, and x8, respectively.

```
> x0 <- apply(MD497.dat[, c(1, 4)], 1, mean)
> x4 <- apply(MD497.dat[, c(2, 5)], 1, mean)
> x8 <- apply(MD497.dat[, c(3, 6)], 1, mean)
```

We need to first calculate the variance–covariance matrix of the three variables. The `var()` function calculates the variance–covariance matrix if the data are arranged in a matrix, like `S <- var(cbind(x0, x4, x8))`:

```
> var(cbind(x0, x4, x8))
     x0   x4   x8
x0 4090 3950 4350
x4 3950 6850 6150
x8 4350 6150 8850
```

The diagonal entries are the variances and the off diagonal entries are the covariances. From this variance–covariance matrix the ϵ statistic can be estimated:

$$\hat{\epsilon} = \frac{k^2(\bar{s}_{ii} - \bar{s})^2}{(k-1)(\sum\sum s_{ij}^2 - 2k\sum \bar{s}_{i.}^2 + k^2\bar{s}^2)},$$

where $\bar{s}_{ii}$ is the mean of the entries on the main diagonal of S, which can be shown by mean (diag (S)) to equal 6596.667; $\bar{s}$ is the mean of all entries, $\bar{s}_{i.}$ is the mean of all entries in row i of S, and s_{ij} is the nine individual entries in the variance–covariance matrix.

```
> S   <- var(cbind(x0, x4, x8))
> k   <- 3
> D   <- k^2 * ( mean( diag(S) )  - mean(S) )^2
> N1 <- sum(S^2)
> N2 <- 2 * k * sum(apply(S, 1, mean)^2)
> N3 <- k^2 * mean(S)^2
> D / ((k - 1) * (N1 - N2 + N3))
```

Which returns [1] 0.9616 for the value of $\hat{\epsilon}$. This value rounds to the 0.9616 value calculated by SAS.

There are three important values of ϵ. It can be 1 when the sphericity is met perfectly. It can be as low as $\epsilon = 1/(k-1)$, which produces the lower bound of epsilon (the worst case scenario). The worst case scenario depends on k, the number of levels in the repeated-measure factor. In this example $k = 3$. Each subject is tested under three different levels of stimuli rotation. Epsilon can be as low as 0.50 when $k = 3$. Note that the sphericity assumption does not apply when $k = 2$. Another way to view it is that even the lowest epsilon is 1. Thus a repeated-measure design with only 2 levels does not involve violations of the sphericity assumption.

Adjustment of the F statistic can be made against either the estimated epsilon, in this case $\hat{\epsilon} = 0.962$; or against the worst case epsilon of 0.50. It depends on how conservative one wants to be. If the cost of falsely rejecting the null hypothesis is high, then one may want to adjust against the worst possible (and very conservative) epsilon. Both SPSS and SAS use the estimated value to make the Greenhouse–Geisser adjustment. The Greenhouse–Geisser adjustment made by SPSS and SAS is different from the adjustment originally proposed by Greenhouse and Geisser (1959). Although the adjustment made by SPSS and SAS is considered more reasonable (Stevens 1992).

The estimated epsilon is used to adjust the degrees of freedom associated with the F statistic from the unadjusted $(k-1)$ and $(k-1)(n-1)$ to $\epsilon(k-1)$ and $\epsilon(k-1)(n-1)$. Severe violations of the sphericity assumption (as $\hat{\epsilon} \rightarrow 0$) may decrease the degrees of freedom so much that the F statistic is no longer statistically significant. The p-value associated with the adjusted F can be obtained from the pf () function.

From the previous aov () output we get an F statistic of 40.719 for the variable deg. The numerator degree of freedom is $(k-1) = 2$ and the denominator degrees of freedom is $(k - 1)(n - 1) = (3 - 1)(10 - 1) = 18$. These can be verified with the output of the previous analysis. Suppose the value of epsilon is assigned to `epsi <- D / ((k - 1) * (N1 - N2 + N3))`. We can then use `epsi` to weigh down the degrees of freedom.

```
> 1 - pf(40.719, df1=2*epsi, df2=18*epsi)
[1] 3.401765e-07
```

The F statistic is still statistically significant below the 0.0001 level. The negligible violation of the sphericity assumption does not affect the conclusion we make.

5.9.1   Huynh–Feldt Correction

The Greenhouse–Geisser epsilon tends to underestimate epsilon when epsilon is greater than 0.70 (Stevens 1992). Huynh–Feldt correction is less conservative. The Huynh–Feldt epsilon is calculated from the Greenhouse–Geisser epsilon,

$$\bar{\epsilon} = \frac{n(k-1)\hat{\epsilon} - 2}{(k-1)[(n-1) - (k-1)\hat{\epsilon}]}.$$

The Huynh–Feldt epsilon can be easily calculated:

```
> epsiHF <- (10 * (k-1) * epsi - 2) /
+              ((k-1) * ((10-1) - (k-1)*epsi))
[1] 1.217564
> 1 - pf(40.719, df1=2*epsiHF, df2=18*epsiHF)
[1] 1.316553e-08
```

The Huynh–Feldt epsilon is 1.2176 with an adjusted p-value lower than 0.0001. Huynh-Feldt epsilon greater than 1.0 are set to 1.0 by some statistical computer packages because, for example, an estimated epsilon of 1.2176 makes the degrees of freedom greater than they should be. But we leave it as is here. Readers interested in this issue may consult Quintana and Maxwell (1994), which compares seven epsilon-adjustment procedures. Again, the Huynh–Feldt correction does not change the conclusion. In this example, the univariate results are preferred because an $\epsilon = 0.96$ is very close to 1.0. The sphericity corrections do not change the conclusions. MANOVA (and multivariate tests) may be better if the Greenhouse–Geisser and the Huynh–Feldt corrections do not agree, which may happen when epsilon drops below 0.70. When epsilon drops below 0.40, both the G–G and H–F corrections may indicate that the violation of sphericity is affecting the adjusted p-values. MANOVA is not always appropriate, though. MANOVA usually requires a larger sample size. Maxwell and Delaney (1990, p. 602) suggest a rough rule that the sample size n should be greater than $k + 10$. In the present example the sample size n is 10, which is smaller than $k + 10 = 13$. Fortunately we already have a strong univariate results.

Exercises

5.1. Sphericity

The Ela.uni data frame has one between-subject effect (variable gp) and two within-subject effect (variables drug and dose). Analyze it with aov() with appropriate Error() terms and answer the following questions.

(a) Is the sphericity assumption met for the variable dose?
(b) Is there evidence in support of a drug:dose interaction? That is, can we conclude that the effect of the drug is different depending on the dose?
(c) What about the results based on the G–G and H–F corrections (use the anova.mlm() method on page 87)
(d) What can you conclude about the effects associated with drug and dose?
(e) Is there an overall difference in effect across the two groups?

5.2. Repeated-measures ANOVA

Shoukri and Pause (1999, pp. 277–8) gave the following example of repeated-measures data. Twenty immunodeficient mice are divided into three groups. Group 1 is the control group (no inoculation). Group 2 is inoculated with live mycobacterium paratuberculosis (MPTB) and transplanted with leucocytes (PBL) from humans. Group 3 is inoculated with MPTB and transplanted with PBL from bovine. The mice are weighed at baseline (week 0), at week 2 and week 4.

mice	group	0	2	4
m1	g1	28	25	45
m2	g1	40	31	70
m3	g1	31	40	44
m4	g1	27	21	26
m5	g1	27	25	40
m6	g2	34	25	38
m7	g2	36	31	49
m8	g2	41	21	25
m9	g2	28	22	10
m10	g2	29	24	22
m11	g2	31	18	36
m12	g2	31	15	5
m13	g3	28	28	61
m14	g3	27	23	63
m15	g3	31	30	42
m16	g3	19	16	28
m17	g3	20	18	39
m18	g3	22	24	52
m19	g3	22	22	25
m20	g3	28	26	53

(a) What is the mean baseline weight in the control group?
(b) What are the mean baseline weights in Groups 2 and 3, respectively?
(c) Looking at the three mean baseline weights, do they appear different?
(d) How can this observation be tested more formally? (hint: aov(t0 ~ group).
(e) Do a reshape() to convert the data from wide format to long format.
(f) Run a repeated-measures ANOVA with a group effect, a time effect, and a group by time interaction.
(g) Is there a group by time interaction?
(h) Can you reject the null hypothesis that there is no time effect?
(i) Can you reject the null hypothesis that there is no overall group difference?
(j) Going back to the data in wide format, apply a contrast and manova() to test the hypothesis that the post-inoculation weight changes are difference across the three groups.

5.3. Repeated-measures ANOVA

Stevens (1992, p.491) gives the following example of a simple repeated-measures design with three treatments.

subj	y1	y2	y3
s1	5	6	1
s2	3	4	2
s3	3	7	1
s4	6	8	3
s5	6	9	3
s6	4	7	2
s7	5	9	2

(a) Do a reshape() to convert the data into a long format. Use varying = 3:5 or varying = c("y1", "y2", "y3").
(b) Is the sphericity assumption rejected?
(c) Do a univariate repeated-measures analysis using aov() with appropriate Error() terms. Can you reject the null hypothesis that all treatments are equal?
(d) Use a contrast and manova() to test the difference between y3 and the average of y1 and y2.

Chapter 6
Linear and Logistic Regression

6.1 Linear Regression

If you want to find whether `y1` depends on `x1` and `x2`, the basic thing you need is

```
> lm(y1 ~ x1 + x2)
```

If these variables are part of a data frame called `df1`, then you can say

```
> lm(y1 ~ x1 + x2, data=df1)
```

or you can say `attach(df1)` before you run the analysis.

Note that `lm()` by itself only fits the regression model. If you want a summary table, one way to get it is to say

```
> summary(lm(y ~ x1 + x2))
```

The coefficients are unstandardized. If you want standardized coefficients, use `summary(lm(scale(y) ~ scale(x1) + scale(x2)))`. The `scale()` function standardizes vectors by default (and it does many other things, which you can see from `help(scale)`).

Another way to get a summary is with `anova()`. The `anova()` command is most useful when you want to compare two models. For example, suppose that you want to ask whether `x3` and `x4` together account for additional variance after `x1` and `x2` are already included in the regression. You cannot tell this from the summary table that you get from

```
> summary(lm(y1 ~ x1 + x2 + x3 + x4))
```

That is because you get a test for each coefficient, but not the two together. So, you can do the following sequence:

```
> model1 <- lm(y1 ~ x1 + x2)
> model2 <- lm(y1 ~ x1 + x2 + x3 + x4)
> anova(model1,model2)
```

Y. Li and J. Baron, *Behavioral Research Data Analysis with R*, Use R,
DOI 10.1007/978-1-4614-1238-0_6, © Springer Science+Business Media, LLC 2012

As you might imagine, this is an extremely flexible mechanism, which allows you to compare two nested models, one with many predictors not contained in the other. Note that `anova` reports sums of squares sequentially, building up by adding the models successively. It is thus different from the usual report of a multiple regression, `summary(lm(...))`. Note also that you can add and drop variables from a model without retyping the model, using the functions `add()` and `drop()`.

6.2 An Application of Linear Regression on Diamond Pricing

In this section we describe a real-world example of pricing diamond stones from a tutorial paper by Chu (2001), designed to teach business school students how to analyze retail pricing of goods with multiple regression modeling. Chu (2001) collected actual trading information on 308 diamond stones sold in Singapore. We use Chu's data to examine how the 4 C's of the diamonds affect pricing. This example on diamond pricing makes a good illustration of linear regression modeling because the main attributes of diamond stones are widely covered in the mass media. (setting aside the economic, social, and human rights controversies) Consumers' spending on luxury goods is an interesting topic in marketing research. This example covers key aspects of how to model consumers' spending by regression modeling. Although this is not the typical survey dataset we analyze.

The main attributes are the four C's: carat, cut, clarity, and color. Chu's data contain price (in Singapore dollar), carat, color, and clarity. No information on the cut of the diamonds was available. But we can still compare the importance of the other three characteristics. As we will see, there is a roughly monotonic relationship between price and these attributes (although not perfectly linear). The departure from linearity leads to a few interesting discussion points below. Outliers in this dataset underscores the importance of checking linear regression assumptions. There are nevertheless patterns and regularities in this dataset.

R helps in discovering the regularities. First, we visualize the data with graphics. The graphs then generate several specific questions whose answers require the use of `lm()`.

The color of a diamond is graded from D (completely colorless), E, F, G, ..., to X (light yellow). The marketing of diamonds typically emphasizes that colorless diamonds are rare. Diamonds with a fancy color such as pink are rarer. Clarity refers to the diamond's internal and external imperfections. Clarity is graded on a scale from F (flawless), IF (internally flawless), ..., SI1–SI2 (slightly included), and I1–I2–I3 (inclusion; blemishes visible to the human eye). The grading of cut and color follows a set of formulae and color references and thus involves less subjectivity than the grading of clarity.

The raw data are in plain-text format. Instructions on how to download the raw data can be found in Chu (2001), Sect. 6. There is a web link to the raw data file named `4c1.dat`. Download the file and save it under your working directory. The commands below imports the data into a data frame called `dimd.df`.

```
> dimd.df <- read.table(file="./4c1.dat", header=FALSE,
+     row.names=NULL)
> names(dimd.df) <- c("Carat","D","E","F","G","H","IF",
+     "VVS1","VVS2","VS1", "GIA","IGI","med","lg",
+     "m_c","l_c","csq","Price","ln_price")
```

The raw data are in plain-text format.

```
> dimd.df[301:308, c(1:10, 18), ]
    Carat D E F G H IF VVS1 VVS2 VS1  Price
301  1.01 0 0 0 0 1  0    0    1   0   9433
302  1.01 0 0 0 0 1  0    0    0   1   9153
303  1.01 0 0 0 0 0  0    1    0   0   8873
304  1.01 0 0 0 0 0  0    0    0   1   8175
305  1.02 0 0 1 0 0  0    0    1   0  10796
306  1.06 0 0 0 0 1  0    0    1   0   9890
307  1.02 0 0 0 0 1  0    0    0   0   8959
308  1.09 0 0 0 0 0  0    0    1   0   9107
```

The first variable contains the carat weight of all 308 diamonds. The color of the diamonds are coded by 5 separate dummy variables, from the 2nd to the 6th column in the data frame. The color of a diamond is graded from D (completely colorless), E, F, G, ..., to X (light yellow). The marketing of diamonds typically emphasizes that colorless diamonds are rare. Diamonds with a fancy color such as pink are rarer. Clarity refers to the diamond's internal and external imperfections. Clarity is graded on a scale from F (flawless), IF (internally flawless), ..., SI1–SI2 (slightly included), and I1–I2–I3 (inclusion; blemishes visible to the human eye). The grading of cut and color follows a set of formulae and color references and thus involves less subjectivity.

Note that diamond 301 is a 1.01 carat stone with an H color. It is coded 1 (feature present) on H and 0 (feature absent) on all other color grades. Diamond stones 303, 304, and 308 are coded 0 on colors D through H, meaning that these stones have color I, the reference color grade (and the least valuable color grade in this data set). Diamond 307 is coded 0 on clarity IF through VS1. So it has the reference clarity grade, which is VS2 or worse.

6.2.1 Plotting Data Before Model Fitting

The initial steps in regression modeling often involve plotting the data according to the model of interest. Patterns and regularities are usually better revealed visually. Figure 6.1 shows how price increases by carat, separated by color grades. Each circle represents one diamond. Diamond stones with a D color are in the lower left panel and E in the lower middle, and so on, and diamonds with an I color are plotted in the upper right panel.

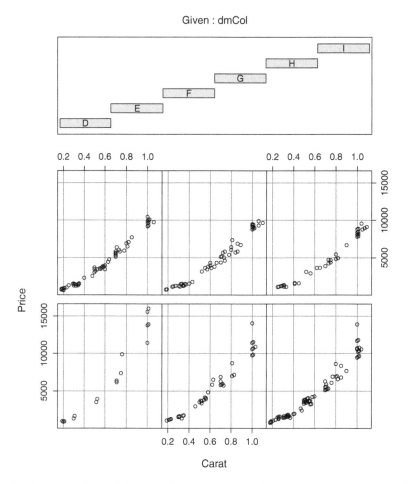

Fig. 6.1 A conditional plot of the price of diamond stones against carat weight, separated by color

```
> dmCol <- apply(dimd.df[, c("D","E","F","G","H")],
+    1, function(x)
+    {
+    ans <- which(x == 1);
+    if(length(ans) == 0) ans <- 6
+    return(ans)
+    } )
> dmCol <- unlist(dmCol, use.names = F)
> dmCol <- factor(dmCol, levels=1:6,
+    labels=c("D", "E", "F", "G", "H", "I"))
> coplot(Price ~ Carat | dmCol, data=dimd.df)
```

The `coplot()` function generates a conditional plot to visualize whether or not the relationship between price and carat weight changes across different colors. One obvious pattern in the graph is that price corresponds well with carat weight. Also, the rate of increase in price appears highest for diamonds with a D color ("colorless", the lower left panel). In this subplot, the relationship between price and carat appears curvilinear, thus a quadratic term on `Carat` may help in boosting model fit. The graph also shows some other characteristics of the data. For example, not many diamonds have a D color; the diamond stones are not big, the largest are slightly larger than 1.0 carat; and diamonds with some color do not seem to exceed $10,000 Singapore dollars (SGD), while large diamonds with a D or E color can be worth more than $15,000 SGD.[1]

We may begin by regressing `Price` on `Carat.c` (centered on the mean carat of all diamonds in the sample), a quadratic term for the centered carat, color (dummy variables D through H), clarity (dummy variables IF through VS1), and certifications (GIA and IGI). We first center the `Carat` and the square of carat by the average of the sample, which is 0.63. Centering improves the interpretability of a model.

```
> dimd.df$Carat.c <- dimd.df$Carat-mean(dimd.df$Carat)
> dimd.df$csq.c <- dimd.df$Carat.c^2
> lm1 <- lm(Price ~ Carat.c+csq.c+D+E+F+G+H+IF+
                VVS1+VVS2+VS1+GIA+IGI, data = dimd.df)
> summary(lm1)

Call:
lm(formula = Price ~ Carat.c + csq.c + D + E + F + G
    + H + IF + VVS1 + VVS2 + VS1 + GIA + IGI,
    data = dimd.df)

Residuals:
   Min      1Q  Median     3Q     Max
 -1381    -252     -36    172    3218

Coefficients:
              Estimate Std. Error t value Pr(>|t|)
(Intercept)    2553.11     146.94   17.37  < 2e-16
Carat.c       12207.61     157.31   77.60  < 2e-16
csq.c          7249.21     554.66   13.07  < 2e-16
D              3223.30     169.60   19.01  < 2e-16
E              1955.68     126.38   15.47  < 2e-16
F              1552.71     112.70   13.78  < 2e-16
G              1179.98     116.18   10.16  < 2e-16
H               652.73     116.99    5.58  5.5e-08
IF              915.10     120.38    7.60  3.9e-13
```

---

[1] According to x-rates.com, on Monday July 02, 2001, 1 SGD = 0.55 USD.

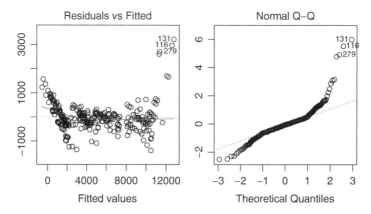

Fig. 6.2 Plots of model residuals. On the *left* is a residuals vs. fitted value plot to identify outliers of the model's prediction, plotted with the plot.lm(lm1, which = 1) command. On the *right* is a plot of observed quantiles of the residuals against the theoretical quantiles of a standard normal distribution, plotted with plot.lm(lm1, which = 2). A *dotted line* is added showing where the observed quantiles should be if they follow a standard normal distribution. The two plots identifies outliers of model assumptions

```
VVS1            1349.75      116.62     11.57   < 2e-16
VVS2             802.31      104.92      7.65   3.0e-13
VS1              389.48      102.19      3.81   0.00017
GIA               -6.15       85.44     -0.07   0.94266
IGI             -407.13      124.30     -3.28   0.00118

Residual standard error: 566 on 294 degrees of freedom
Multiple R-squared: 0.974, Adjusted R-squared: 0.972
F-statistic:  831 on 13 and 294 DF,  $p$-value: <2e-16
```

6.2.2   Checking Model Distributional Assumptions

A plot of model residuals against fitted values shows a problem in the model. Figure 6.2 shows that diamonds 116, 131, and 279 are outliers. They are identified automatically in a residual plot. The observed prices of these diamond stones greatly exceed the model's predicted prices.

The model underestimates the observed price of these larger stones with D and E color and VVS1 clarity (see the fitted column below). Diamonds of these characteristics are sold at a premium price, much higher than the fitted values of the model. The values of these residuals clearly depart from what are expected if they are normally-distributed.

```
> M <- dimd.df[c(116, 131, 279), c(1:10, 18)]
> cbind(M, fitted=fitted(lm1)[c(116, 131,279)])
     Carat D E F G H IF VVS1 VVS2 VS1 Price fitted
116  1.00 1 0 0 0 0  0    1    0   0 15582  12613
131  1.01 1 0 0 0 0  0    1    0   0 16008  12790
279  1.00 0 1 0 0 0  0    1    0   0 14051  11352
```

An important assumption of linear regression is that the residuals are normally distributed. These particular outliers and other unusual observations (e.g., prices lower than $2,000) contribute to a violation of this assumption. Chu (2001) fitted several alternative models including log-transformed price to make the normal residual assumption work better. However, these attempts would cause new problems, one being that the log-transformed price makes the model harder to explain than the straightforward lm1 model.

6.2.3 Assessing Model Fit

The Multiple R-squared of 0.974 summarizes the overall model fit in one number. For a Gausian model, the theoretical minimum is 0.0 and the maximum is 1.0. The 0.974 value indicates that the model fits the data nearly perfectly. The overall F statistic shows this model is significantly better than the null model (intercept only, as in lm(Price ~ 1). The (Intercept) term represents the estimated price of $2,553.11 SGD for a diamond that weighs 0.63 carat, has an I color, VS2 or lower clarity, and has no certification by either the GIA or the IGI. The coefficients for the linear term Carat.c and the quadratic term csq.c show that, other characteristics being equal, a diamond that weighs 1.63 carat is estimated to cost an additional $19,456.82 SGD. Both terms are statistically reliably different from zero. Although these coefficients being significant hardly surprises anyone. We also notice a somewhat monotonic decrease in estimated price from color D to H; whereas the relationship between price and clarity is not monotonic. What is unusual is the relatively small $915.10 price difference estimate between an "internally flawless," IF clarity and a VS2 or lower clarity. In comparison, the difference between a VVS1 and VS2 diamond is higher at an estimated $1,349.75. One plausible explanation is that low-clarity diamonds are greater in carat weight than IF diamonds, see below.

```
> ti <- apply(dimd.df[, c("IF","VVS1","VVS2","VS1")],
+     MARGIN = 1, FUN = function (x) { all(x == 0) })
> mean(dimd.df$Carat[dimd.df$IF == 0])
[1] 0.67409
> mean(dimd.df$Carat[ti])
[1] 0.7583
```

Part of assessing model fit involves reducing or simplifying the model. A simpler model is usually preferred unless there is significant loss in model fit. We may try to simplify the lm1 model by dropping the GIA variable.

```
> lm2 <- lm(Price ~ Carat.c+csq.c+D+E+F+G+H+IF+VVS1+
+           VVS2+VS1+IGI, data = dimd.df)
> anova(lm1, lm2)

Analysis of Variance Table

Model 1: Price ~ Carat.c + csq.c + D + E + F + G + H +
         IF + VVS1 + VVS2 + VS1 + GIA + IGI
Model 2: Price ~ Carat.c + csq.c + D + E + F + G + H +
         IF + VVS1 + VVS2 + VS1 + IGI
  Res.Df       RSS Df Sum of Sq    F Pr(>F)
1    294 94163607
2    295 94165266 -1     -1660 0.01   0.94
```

The anova() comparison of the two models shows that dropping GIA has a negligible effect. However, dropping IGI would cause significant loss in model fit.

```
> lm3 <- lm(Price ~ Carat.c+csq.c+D+E+F+G+H+IF+VVS1+
+           VVS2+VS1, data = dimd.df)

> anova(lm1, lm3)
Analysis of Variance Table

Model 1: Price ~ Carat.c + csq.c + D + E + F + G +
    H + IF + VVS1 + VVS2 + VS1 + GIA + IGI
Model 2: Price ~ Carat.c + csq.c + D + E + F + G +
    H + IF + VVS1 + VVS2 + VS1
  Res.Df       RSS Df Sum of Sq    F Pr(>F)
1    294 94163607
2    296 98638008 -2  -4474401 6.99 0.0011


> anova(lm2, lm3)
Analysis of Variance Table

Model 1: Price ~ Carat.c + csq.c + D + E + F + G +
    H + IF + VVS1 + VVS2 + VS1 + IGI
Model 2: Price ~ Carat.c + csq.c + D + E + F + G +
    H + IF + VVS1 + VVS2 + VS1
  Res.Df       RSS Df Sum of Sq  F   Pr(>F)
1    295 94165266
2    296 98638008 -1  -4472742 14 0.00022
```

The final lm2 model retains these covariates of price: carat weight, the square of carat weight, color, clarity, and the IGI certificate.

```
> summary(lm2)

Call:
lm(formula = Price ~ Carat.c + csq.c + D + E + F +
    G + H + IF + VVS1 + VVS2 + VS1 + IGI,
    data = dimd.df)

Residuals:
   Min     1Q Median     3Q    Max
 -1378   -253    -36    173   3215

Coefficients:
              Estimate Std. Error t value Pr(>|t|)
(Intercept)      2548         127   20.04  < 2e-16
Carat.c         12210         152   80.22  < 2e-16
csq.c            7250         554   13.09  < 2e-16
D                3223         169   19.04  < 2e-16
E                1956         126   15.53  < 2e-16
F                1553         112   13.84  < 2e-16
G                1181         116   10.22  < 2e-16
H                 654         116    5.62  4.3e-08
IF                915         120    7.62  3.4e-13
VVS1             1352         114   11.85  < 2e-16
VVS2              803         104    7.71  1.9e-13
VS1               389         102    3.82  0.00016
IGI              -403         108   -3.74  0.00022

Residual standard error: 565 on 295 degrees of
freedom
Multiple R-squared: 0.974,
Adjusted R-squared: 0.972
F-statistic:  904 on 12 and 295 DF,
p-value: <2e-16
```

Another approach to model simplification is to use a convenient function called
drop1(). It drops one predictor at a time and summarizes the resulting changes
in several goodness of fit indices. The test = "F" option prints out an *F*
statistic based changes in residual sums of squares. The top row (marked <none>)
represents the original lm1 model.

```
> drop1(lm1, test = "F")

Single term deletions

Model:
Price ~ Carat.c + csq.c + D + E + F + G + H + IF
        + VVS1 + VVS2 + VS1 + GIA + IGI
```

	Df	Sum of Sq	RSS	AIC	F value	Pr(F)
<none>			9.42e+07	3918		
Carat.c	1	1.93e+09	2.02e+09	4861	6022.42	< 2e-16
csq.c	1	5.47e+07	1.49e+08	4057	170.81	< 2e-16
D	1	1.16e+08	2.10e+08	4163	361.20	< 2e-16
E	1	7.67e+07	1.71e+08	4100	239.46	< 2e-16
F	1	6.08e+07	1.55e+08	4070	189.81	< 2e-16
G	1	3.30e+07	1.27e+08	4009	103.15	< 2e-16
H	1	9.97e+06	1.04e+08	3947	31.13	5.5e-08
IF	1	1.85e+07	1.13e+08	3971	57.79	3.9e-13
VVS1	1	4.29e+07	1.37e+08	4032	133.95	< 2e-16
VVS2	1	1.87e+07	1.13e+08	3972	58.47	3.0e-13
VS1	1	4.65e+06	9.88e+07	3931	14.53	0.00017
GIA	1	1.66e+03	9.42e+07	3916	0.01	0.94266
IGI	1	3.44e+06	9.76e+07	3927	10.73	0.00118

The AIC (Akaike 1974) column shows Akaike's information criterion, a goodness of fit index. It is used in model comparison. Among two alternative models, the one with a *smaller* AIC is preferred. For example, it is not advisable to drop Carat.c or csq.c because dropping them causes considerable increase in the AIC.

This concludes our introduction on linear regression. We have covered a few basics, including how to use coplot() in Fig. 6.1 and to inspect the data pattern before fitting the model. Figure 6.1 also suggests possible outliers if a linear model is fitted. These outliers are identified in the residual plot in Fig. 6.2. The final model has limitations. But the overall fit of the model is very good. There are many other aspects of linear regression that are not covered here. For interested readers, the book by Chambers and Hastie (1993) provides details on the lm() function. Model selection using anova() is also discussed in greater detail. There are numerous other texts on regression, for example, Fox (2002), Harrell (2001a), Venables and Ripley (2002), and Wonnacott and Wonnacott (1987).

6.3 Logistic Regression

Multiple regression is not appropriate when we regress a dichotomous (yes–no) variable on continuous predictors. The assumptions of normally distributed error are violated. So we use logistic regression instead. That is, we assume that the probability of a "yes" is certain function of a weighted sum of the predictors, the inverse logit. In other words, if Y is the probability of a "yes" for a given set of predictor values $X_1, X_2, \ldots$, the model says that

$$\log \frac{Y}{1-Y} = b_0 + b_1 X_1 + b_2 X_2 + \cdots + \text{error.}$$

The function $\log \frac{Y}{1-Y}$ is the logit function. This is the "link function" in logistic regression. Other link functions are possible in R. If we represent the right side of this equation as X, then the inverse function is

$$Y = \frac{e^X}{1 + e^X}.$$

In R, when using such transformations as this one, we use `glm` (the generalized linear model) instead of `lm`. We specify the "family" of the model to get the right distribution. Here the family is called `binomial`. Suppose the variable `y` has a value of 0 or 1 for each subject, and the predictors are `x1`, `x2`, and `x3`. We can thus say

```
> summary(glm(y ~ x1 + x2 + x3, family=binomial))
```

to get the basic analysis, including p values for each predictor. Psychologists often like to ask whether the overall regression is significant before looking at the individual predictors. Unfortunately, R does not report the overall significance as part of the `summary` command. To get a test of overall significance, you must compare two models. One way to do this is:

```
> glm1 <- glm(y ~ x1 + x2 + x3, family=binomial)
> glm0 <- glm(y ~ 1, family=binomial)
> anova(glm0,glm1,test="Chisq")
```

6.4   Log–Linear Models

Another use of `glm()` is log–linear analysis, where the family is `poisson` rather than `binomial`. Suppose we have a table called `t1.data` like the following (which you could generate with the help of `expand.grid()`). Each row represents the levels of the variables of interest. The last column represents the number of subjects with that combination of levels. The dependent measure is actually expens vs. notexpens. The classification of subjects into these categories depends on whether the subject chose the expensive treatment or not. The variable "cancer" has three values (cervic, colon, breast) corresponding to the three scenarios, so R makes two dummy variables, "cancercervic" and "cancercolon". The variable "cost" has the levels "expens" and "notexp." The variable "real" is "real" vs. "hyp" (hypothetical).

```
cancer cost real count
colon notexp real 37
colon expens real 20
colon notexp hyp  31
colon expens hyp  15
cervic notexp real 27
```

```
cervic expens real 28
cervic notexp hyp  52
cervic expens hyp   6
breast notexp real 22
breast expens real 32
breast notexp hyp  25
breast expens hyp  27
```

The following sequence of commands does one analysis:

```
> t1 <- read.table("t1.data",header=T)
> summary(glm(count ~ cancer + cost + real + cost*real,
+     family=poisson(), data=t1)
```

This analysis asks whether "cost" and "real" interact in determining "count," that is, whether the response is affected by "real." See the chapter on Generalized Linear Models in Venables and Ripley (2002) for more discussion on how this works.

6.5 Regression in Vector–Matrix Notation

Advanced statistics often require the use of matrix algebra. For example, in linear multiple regression, a model is typically written like this:

$$y_i = \beta_0 + \beta_1 x_{i1} + \beta_2 x_{i2} + \cdots + \beta_k x_{ik} + e_i, \tag{6.1}$$

where the subscript i refers to the ith observation and $1, 2, \cdots, k$ refers to the kth independent variable. Here we use the plant weight data in help(lm).

```
> ctl <- c(4.17,5.58,5.18,6.11,4.50,4.61,5.17,4.53,
+         5.33,5.14)
> trt <- c(4.81,4.17,4.41,3.59,5.87,3.83,6.03,4.89,
+         4.32,4.69)
> group <- gl(2,10,20, labels=c("Ctl","Trt"))
> weight <- c(ctl, trt)
> weight
 [1] 4.17 5.58 5.18 6.11 4.50 4.61 [.. snipped ..]
[16] 3.83 6.03 4.89 4.32 4.69
> group
 [1] Ctl Ctl Ctl Ctl Ctl [.. snipped ..]  Trt Trt Trt
[20] Trt
Levels: Ctl Trt
```

Here weight is y_i and group is x_{i1}. To compare the average weight difference between the two groups, we can run a simple lm() model.

```
> lm(weight ~ group)

Call:
lm(formula = weight ~ group)

Coefficients:
(Intercept)        groupTrt
      5.032          -0.371
```

The average weight of the `Ctrl` group is 5.032 and the `Trt` group weighs less than the `Ctl` group by −0.371. Most of us learn how to carry out multiple regression analysis this way.

We do not usually learn how the calculations are done behind the scene. However, the internal calculations are not prohibitively difficult to understand. R can help by turning the complicated mathematical notations into the more trackable R objects. A rudimentary understanding of the internal calculations can be useful, especially when you encounter error messages such as "matrix is singular." This can help a beginner to move on to more advanced texts. Here is an example.

In books on advanced statistics, Equation (6.1) is sometimes represented in vector notations:

$$
\begin{bmatrix} y_1 \\ y_2 \\ \vdots \\ y_i \end{bmatrix} = \begin{bmatrix} 1 & x_{11} & x_{12} & \cdots & x_{1k} \\ 1 & x_{21} & x_{22} & \cdots & x_{2k} \\ \vdots & & \vdots & \ddots & \vdots \\ 1 & x_{i1} & x_{i2} & \cdots & x_{ik} \end{bmatrix} \begin{bmatrix} \beta_0 \\ \beta_1 \\ \vdots \\ \beta_k \end{bmatrix} + \begin{bmatrix} e_1 \\ e_2 \\ \vdots \\ e_k \end{bmatrix},
$$

or by stacking all i observations into a column vector called $\mathbf{y}$ (note the bold face) and you get

$$\mathbf{y} = \mathbf{X_i}\beta + \mathbf{e}.$$

This notation can be intimidating to beginners. R makes it less intimidating. The R object of `weight` is $\mathbf{y}$ and `group` is x_{i1} in $\mathbf{X}$. R objects thus help to track the different pieces of this equation.

The vector notation can be further extended into matrix natation, transforming

$$\mathbf{y}_i \sim N(\mathbf{X}_i\,\beta, \theta^2), \quad \text{for } i = 1, \ldots, n, \quad \text{into matrix notation}$$

$$\mathbf{y} \sim N(\mathbf{X}\beta, \theta^2 I),$$

These different equations represent the same model. It can be shown (e.g., Wonnacott and Wonnacott 1987, Chap. 12) that the least-square estimate of the regression coefficients, $\hat{\beta}$, is

$$\hat{\beta} = (\mathbf{X}'\mathbf{X})^{-1}\mathbf{X}'\mathbf{y},$$

where **X'** is the transpose of the data matrix **X** and $(\mathbf{X'X})^{-1}$ refers to the matrix inverse of the product of $(\mathbf{X'X})$. This somewhat complicated matrix algebra can be made more accessible to students by working with R objects instead of the more abstract mathematical notations.

```
> X <- cbind(1, matrix(as.numeric(group == "Trt"),
         ncol = 1))
> solve(t(X) %*% X) %*% t(X) %*% weight
       [,1]
[1,]   5.032
[2,]  -0.371
```

Here **X** is the model matrix with 20 rows and two columns consisting of one column for the intercept (a vector of 1's) and the other column of the treatment effect (dummy coded 1 if in Trt and 0 otherwise). The t(X) function finds the transpose of the matrix **X**, the solve() function calculates the inverse of $(\mathbf{X'X})$. All objects are put together by the matrix multiplication function %*% and you get β = [5.032, -0.371], the same as what you get with lm(). Although lm() actually uses the orthogonal decomposition method, which is numerically more stable than solve().

6.6   Caution on Model Overfit and Classification Errors

Model overfit threatens the validity of research findings. Here is a somewhat extreme hypothetical example of model overfit.

```
> y <- c(10, 10.2, 9.7, 15, 14.8, 15.2)
> x <- c(0, 0.1, 0.2, 1, 1.2, 0.9))
> plot(x, y)
> lmOvfit <- lm(y ~ x)
> abline(lmOvfit)
```

The regression model in Fig. 6.3 is fitted to only six data points. The linear association is obviously not real because the empty area contains no data.

We get a misleading summary() *p*-value of 0.0023 for x.

```
> summary(lm(y ~ x))

Call:
lm(formula = y ~ x)

Residuals:
       1         2         3         4         5         6
  0.3871    0.0806   -0.9260    0.3216   -0.8915    1.0282

Coefficients:
```

Fig. 6.3 A hypothetical example of model overfit by fitting a regression line to six data points

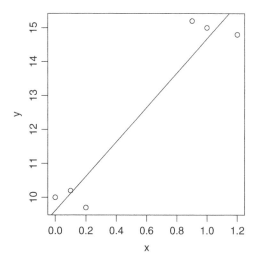

```
              Estimate Std. Error t value Pr(>|t|)
(Intercept)      9.613       0.545   17.63  6.1e-05
x                5.066       0.735    6.89   0.0023

Residual standard error: 0.862 on 4 degrees of
freedom
Multiple R-squared: 0.922, Adjusted R-squared: 0.903
F-statistic: 47.5 on 1 and 4 DF,  p-value: 0.00233
```

Model overfit happens when a relationship exists only in vacuum, with no actual observations to support the existence of a relationship. It happens easily, especially if p-values are sought indiscriminately and the number of predictors exceeds what can be supported by the sample size. Another scenario involves running a stepwise analysis and let the computer software program to decide what model is preferred.

For the first scenario, Peduzzi and colleagues recommend a 10-event per variable (EPV) rule (Peduzzi et al. 1996) in fitting logistic regression. For example, a logistic regression with up to three predictors has a low risk of overfitting if there are 35 events out of a sample of 97. This recommendation was challenged recently (Vittinghoff and McCulloch 2007). A relaxed rule of 5–9 events per variable was offered. Although the six observations in Fig. 6.3 are clearly not enough to support the model.

It is a good idea to visually inspect the data and the model (as we have done) before the model is fitted.

For the second scenario, it is a bad idea to let the computer determine the preferred model. In a stepwise analysis, the statistical computer program considers one predictor at a time (controlling for other predictors). The predictor is appended to the existing model if some test statistic exceeds a threshold. In the next iteration, the new model enters another test cycle, with or without the previous predictor.

The procedure iterates until all variables are considered. The main problem with a stepwise approach is that estimates of sampling variance in the stepwise selection process are conditional on the existing model as if there were no uncertainty about the variables already in the model. Breiman (1992) called this a "quiet scandal." There is uncertainty in the variables in the existing model that a new variable can cross that threshold purely by chance. Without explicitly modeling this chance and other related variabilities, the resulting model can be highly unreliable. Completely different sets of predictors will be selected under slightly different circumstances. Breiman (1992) offered a procedure called *little bootstrap*, although its routine application seems only available to researchers who have extensive statistical expertise.

Exercises

6.1. Modeling between-group difference by `lm()`.
The `sleep` data in Sect. 1.1 was analyzed in an independent-sample *t*-test by calling `t.test(extra ~ group, data = sleep)`. It can also be analyzed in a linear model by fitting each person's extra hours of sleep as a function of an intercept plus an estimated difference between the two groups:

$$y_i = \alpha_0 + \beta_1 x_i + \epsilon_i,$$

where y_i represents each person's `extra` hours of sleep and x_i represents each person's `group` assignment.

(a) Write the R command for this linear model.
(b) What is the estimated value of the intercept α_0?
(c) What does α_0 represent?
(d) Does α_0 represent the overall mean of `extra` hours of sleep averaged across the two groups?
(e) If not, then does it represent the average `extra` hours of sleep for Group 1?
(f) Verify your answers to (c), (d), and (e) above with the results of `with(sleep, tapply(extra, group, mean))`.
(g) What is the estimated value of β_1?
(h) What does β_1 represent? Does the value of β_1 map onto any number or difference between numbers in the result of `tapply()` above?
(i) Does the result by `lm()` on the between-group difference agree with the result by `t.test()`?

6.2. Hypothetical example on distress and depression.
Below is a hypothetical example on how changes in self-reported distress (d_distr) are associated with changes in depression (d_depr). The commands below are used to simulate the hypothetical data. Two groups of 20 participants each are assessed for changes in depression and distress. In group 1, the two

change scores have a correlation of 0.35. In group 2, the two changes scores have a correlation of 0.45. The rmvnorm() function is used to generate correlated variables.

```
> library(mvtnorm)
> set.seed(7)
> mean <- c(0, 0)
> sigma <- matrix(c(1, 0.35, 0.35, 1), ncol=2)
> y1 <- rmvnorm(n = 20, mean=mean, sigma=sigma)
> sigma <- matrix(c(1, 0.45, 0.45, 1), ncol=2)
> y2 <- rmvnorm(n = 20, mean=mean, sigma=sigma)
```

Next, the two sets of data for Groups 1 and 2 are stacked together. A grp variable is created to represent the group each participant is randomly assigned to.

```
> Y <- data.frame(rbind(y1, y2))
> names(Y) <- c("d_depr", "d_distr")
> Y$grp <- rep(c("grp1", "grp2"), each = 20)
```

(a) Apply the coplot() command below to plot the relationship between changes in distress and changes in depression for the two groups.

```
> coplot(d_depr ~ d_distr | grp, data = Y)
```

(b) Are there visible differences between the two scatterplots that would indicate different relationships of changes in depression and distress across the two groups?

(c) Often it is useful to use scatterplot smoothers to visualize the general patterns:

```
> coplot(d_depr ~ d_distr | grp,
+             panel = panel.smooth, data = Y)
```

Has this improved the ease with which you can interpret the two scatterplots?

(d) Fit a linear regression of changes in depression as a function of changes in distress, call the model m1.

(e) Use plot(m1) to check model distributional assumptions. Are there outliers? What are the values of changes in depression and distress?

(f) What is the Multiple R-squared statistic of model m1?

(g) Fit another regression model to changes in depression scores as a function of changes in distress as well as an interaction between changes in distress and group. Call this model m2.

(h) What is the value of the coefficient for the changes in distress and group interaction term?

(i) What does the value of this coefficient represent?

(j) Is there support for a statistically significant interaction between changes in distress and group?

(k) Make a model comparison between m1 and m2. Can the interaction term be dropped from model m2?

6.3. Simulate greater effects in a larger sample.

Rerun the simulation with a much larger sample size of 200 in each group instead of 20. Keep the all other parameters same the simulation.

(a) Does the 10-fold increase in sample size change the results of the simulation?
(b) Change the correlation in the variable y2 from 0.45 to 0.55 (keep the all other parameters same), again get a simulated sample of 200 in each group.
(c) Does the increase in correlation and sample size change the patterns of the plots? Is it easier to visualize a pattern without the aide of the scatterplot smoother?
(d) What is the Multiple R-squared statistic in the new model m1?
(e) Repeat the check for model distributional assumptions. Any improvement in the number of outliers?
(f) Does the increase of correlation from 0.45 to 0.55 change the statistical interaction term in the new regression model m2?

6.4. Sesame Street dataset.

Stevens (1992) describes the Sesame Street study in which young children were assessed before and after they had viewed a selected series of the television program Sesame Street. Here are the first few observations in that dataset. The two variables prebody and postbody represent respectively assessment scores of children's knowledge of body parts before and after having viewed a selected series of the television program Sesame Street. The third variable contains information on the children's gender (male = 1, female = 2).

```
> prebody <- c(16,30,22,23,32,29,23,32,28,30,25,21,
+      28,26,23,25,25,16,25,19,29,25,20,11,15)
> postbody <- c(18,30,21,21,32,27,22,31,32,32,26,17,
+      20,26,28,28,25,25,32,28,29,32,22,22,14)
> sex <- c(1,2,1,1,1,2,2,1,1,2,2,2,2,1,2,1,1,1,1,1,2,
+           1,2,1,2)
```

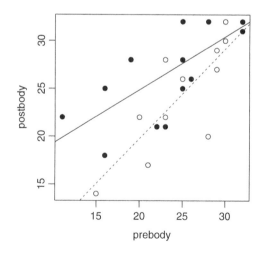

(a) Plot `postbody` against `prebody` scores. Make the plot look like the graph below. Data for boys are plotted with filled circles (e.g., `pch=19`) and data for girls with open circles. Add two regression lines to the plot for boys and girls, respectively. Use a different line type (e.g., `lty=2`) to plot the regression line for girls.

(b) Is there a significant change in knowledge after viewing Sesame Street?

(c) Do girls show more knowledge than boys *before* viewing Sesame Street?

(d) Do girls show more knowledge than boys *after* viewing Sesame Street?

(e) Is the association between pre- and post-viewing knowledge scores stronger in girls than in boys?

Chapter 7
Statistical Power and Sample Size Considerations

7.1 A Simple Example

Suppose a researcher wants to calculate the statistical power of an experiment comparing two parallel arms of behavioral interventions. Participants are randomized with equal probability into two intervention conditions. The experimenter wants to know the statistical power for a total sample size of 100 (50 in each intervention condition), assuming that the difference between the two sample means is half of the pooled standard deviation.

```
> power.t.test(n = 50, delta = 0.5, sd = 1,
               type="two.sample")

     Two-sample t test power calculation

              n = 50
          delta = 0.5
             sd = 1
      sig.level = 0.05
          power = 0.6968888
    alternative = two.sided

 NOTE: n is number in *each* group
```

The estimated statistical power is 70%, at a two-sided Type-I error rate of 0.05. The default of power.t.test() is a two-sided (alternative = "two.sided") Type-I error rate of 5% (sig.level = 0.05).

If the experimenter wants to know the sample size required to reach a desired level of statistical power (e.g., 80%), do power.t.test(delta = 0.5, power = 0.80, type = "two.sample"). A sample size of 64 in each group is needed to reach 80% power.

Y. Li and J. Baron, *Behavioral Research Data Analysis with R*, Use R,
DOI 10.1007/978-1-4614-1238-0_7, © Springer Science+Business Media, LLC 2012

7.2 Basic Concepts on Statistical Power Estimation

Figure 7.1 helps to explain the 70% power in the hypothetical t-test above with $n = 50$ in each of the two parallel intervention arms.[1]

Let μ_i and μ_c represent the population means of the primary post-intervention outcome for the intervention and control groups, respectively. The null and alternative hypotheses are:

$$H_0 : \mu_i = \mu_c \quad \text{versus} \quad H_a : \mu_i \neq \mu_c.$$

The null hypothesis states that the two population means are equal. The alternative hypothesis states that the two population means are not equal.

The pooled two-sample t-statistic for this comparison is

$$t = \frac{\bar{x}_i - \bar{x}_c}{s_p \sqrt{\frac{1}{n_i} + \frac{1}{n_c}}},$$

where $\bar{x}_i, \bar{x}_c$ represent the sample means; s_p represents the pooled estimator of population standard deviation, and s_p equals 1.0 because the two samples are assumed to have the same standard deviation of 1.0, thus

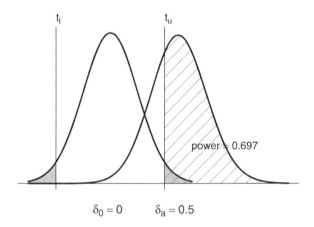

Fig. 7.1 The statistical power of this hypothetical two-sample t-test can be verified with `power.t.test(n = 50, delta = 0.5, sd = 1, type="two.sample")`

---

[1]The code to plot Fig. 7.1 is available upon request. R makes it easy to plot the shaded areas under a curve. Basically, filled histograms such as the ones in Fig. 4.1 are used to produce the shaded areas under the curves. The Greek letters are added, for example, for the null distribution at m0 `= 0` by `mtext(bquote(delta[0] == .(m0)), side = 1, at = m0, line=2, cex=2.0)`.

$$s_p^2 = \frac{(n_i - 1)s_i^2 + (n_c - 1)s_c^2}{n_i + n_c - 2} = \frac{(50 - 1)1^2 + (50 - 1)1^2}{50 + 50 - 2} = 1.$$

The two curves in Fig. 7.1 represent the population distributions of the two sample means. It helps to think of the two distributions on a scale of the *t*-statistics. The *t*-statistic for the null is 0.0. The upper critical *t*-statistic to reject the null hypothesis at a two-sided Type-I error rate of 5%, with the pooled 98 degrees of freedom, is qt(p = .975, df = 98) or 1.984467. It is marked as t_u. ($t_l = -1.984467$ marks the lower critical value)

The *t*-statistic for the mean of the alternative distribution is:

$$t_a = \frac{\delta}{s_p\sqrt{\frac{1}{n_i} + \frac{1}{n_c}}} = \frac{0.5}{1\sqrt{\frac{1}{50} + \frac{1}{50}}} = 2.5.$$

The numerator represents what the investigators' expected difference between the two group means: $\delta = \bar{x}_1 - \bar{x}_2 = 0.5$. The denominator, $1 \cdot \sqrt{\frac{1}{50} + \frac{1}{50}}$, represents the standard error of the expected group difference (Moore and McCabe 1993, their equation (7.3)). This t_a is also referred to as the **non-centrality parameter** (ncp). The ncp parameter of a *t*-distribution basically describes that (in this specific example) the distribution is shifted 2.5 standard error units greater than the null. It also affects the symmetry of the distribution. Unlike the Student's *t*-distribution, a noncentral *t* is not necessarily symmetrical (Cumming 2006, for a visual explanation). The standard Student's *t*-distribution is a special case of noncentral *t* with ncp = 0.0.

The statistical power is the probability of rejecting the null hypothesis when the alternative hypothesis is true. Taken altogether, the statistical power is the sum of the areas greater than t_u and less than t_l under the alternative δ_a distribution. The area greater than t_u gives

```
> 1 - pt(1.984467, df = 98, ncp = 2.5)
[1] 0.696889
```

and the combined two-sided statistical power is

```
> 1 - pt( 1.984467, df = 98, ncp = 2.5) +
      pt(-1.984467, df = 98, ncp = 2.5)
[1] 0.6968936
```

which agrees with the result of power.t.test() to within five decimal points.

7.3 *t*-Test with Unequal Sample Sizes

If for each participant randomized to the control condition, two participants are randomized to the intervention condition, then the statistical power for this 1:2 allocation ratio can be calculated by calling the pwr package by Stephane Champely.

```
> library(pwr)
> pwr.t2n.test(n1=85, n2=43, d = 0.50)

      t test power calculation

               n1 = 85
               n2 = 43
                d = 0.5
        sig.level = 0.05
            power = 0.75536
      alternative = two.sided
```

We show earlier that two groups of 64 each would yield 80% power. However, if the total sample of 128 is assigned to the intervention conditions in a 2:1 allocation ratio, then the power is down to 76%. The cost in power may be compensated by making the study more desirable to eligible participants because of the higher probability of getting into the intervention condition than the control condition.

7.4 Binomial Proportions

A smoking cessation intervention study may be expected to observe a 10% quit rate in the control group and a 20% quit rate in the intervention group. Such a study needs approximately 200 participants per treatment arm to reach a statistical power of 80%.

```
> power.prop.test(p1 = .10, p2 = .20, power = .80)

      Two-sample comparison of proportions power
      calculation

                n = 198.96
               p1 = 0.1
               p2 = 0.2
        sig.level = 0.05
            power = 0.8
      alternative = two.sided

   NOTE: n is number in *each* group
```

7.5 Power to Declare a Study Feasible

A researcher decides, based on published data from prior studies of similar designs, that a newly proposed study would be considered feasible if 65% of enrolled participants in the population complete the planned intervention(s) and provide post-intervention assessments. The study would be considered not feasible if the completion rate is 45% or lower in the population. How would one calculate the needed sample size to test the feasibility of this study?

We can approach it by setting up two alternative population proportions. The null and alternative hypotheses can be modeled as binomial distributions with means at 45% and 65%, respectively. These are hypothetical population proportions. The observed sample proportion may be lower than 45%, higher than 65%, or in-between 45% and 65%. If the researcher enrolls a sample of 50 participants and 30 or more of them complete the study, then the cumulative binomial probability of this observation is 0.023536 if the null hypothesis is true.

```
> sum(dbinom(30:50, size = 50, p = 0.45))
[1] 0.023536
```

So we would have a $2 \times 0.024 = 0.048$ tail probability (two-sided Type-I error) to reject the null hypothesis and a 0.81395 probability of rejecting the null hypothesis when the alternative hypothesis is true.

```
> sum(dbinom(30:50, size = 50, p = 0.65))
[1] 0.81395
```

Under this setting, if we observe a sample of 29 completers or less, then we would consider the study design not feasible. Thus the current study design may no longer be considered in future research. This manual calculation is inconvenient because it needs trial-and-error to find a workable combination of the parameters. However, it provides a more formal framework for a researcher to define precisely what he or she means by feasibility.

7.6 Repeated-Measures ANOVA

The calculation of statistical power by simulation is a relatively straightforward alternative to formulaic solutions, such as those used in the G*Power computer program (Faul et al. 2007). The example below can be used to calculate the statistical power of a repeated-measures ANOVA analysis with two within-subject factors (e.g., the Hays.df example in Sect. 5.1). Basically, we simulate the data from a repeated-measures ANOVA design with two within-subject factors and calculate as usual the p-value for the color effect. Repeat it a few hundred times and the resulting percentage of p-values rejecting the null is the statistical power for the within-subject color effect.

Lines 1–9 set up the simulation parameters based on the effects below:

	color1	color2	color effect
shape1	0.6	0.0	0.3
shape2	0.0	0.0	0.0
shape effect	0.3	0.0	

There is an assumed marginal color effect of 0.3 standard deviation units. The S matrix in line 7 assumes an average pairwise correlation of 0.35. From this design we draw a simulated sample of n = 50, calculate the color effect against the subj:color error using repeated-measures aov(), and check whether or not the *p*-value rejects the null hypothesis at the pre-specified sig.level. These steps are repeated nsim times in a for() loop between lines 14 and 28. Statistical power is the percentage of nsim simulations that the null hypothesis is rejected.

```
 1 require(MASS)    # multivariate normal by mvrnorm()
   set.seed(7)      # so that simulation is reproducible
   nsim <- 400      # run simulation 400 times
   n <- 50
 5 sig.level <- 0.05
   x <- c(0.6, 0, 0, 0)
   S <- matrix(NA, ncol = 4, nrow = 4)
   S[row(S) == col(S)] <- 1
   S[row(S) != col(S)] <- 0.35
10 pval <- rep(NA, nsim)
   # col.MS <- rep(NA, nsim)
   # res.MS <- rep(NA, nsim)

   for (i in 1:nsim)
15 {
   tdat <- mvrnorm(n = n, mu = x, Sigma = S)
   df <- data.frame(rt = as.vector(tdat),
   subj = rep(paste("subj", 1:n, sep=""), 4),
   shape = rep(rep(c("shape1", "shape2"), c(n, n)), 2),
20 color = rep(c("color1", "color2"), c(n*2, n*2)))

   av1 <- aov(rt ~ shape*color + Error(subj/
              (shape*color)), data = df)

   tlst <- unlist(summary(av1)["Error: subj:color"])
25 pval[i]    <- tlst[9]
   # col.MS[i] <- tlst[5]
   # res.MS[i] <- tlst[6]
   }
29 print(mean(pval < sig.level))
```

The output from line 29 is 71% power. The parameters x, S, and n can be modified. The user may need to run the simulation a few times with different values of n to find the required sample size to reach the 80% power. Lines 11, 12, 26, and 27 are commented out. They can be restored to extract the numerator and the denominator sums of squares for the `color` effect.

7.7   Cluster-Randomized Study Design

Cluster-randomized designs involve randomizing groups of individuals into intervention conditions (Murray 1998b). Donner and Klar (2000) showed how to estimate the statistical power for a two-arm design with m groups of n individual participants. They provided SAS code to carry out the calculation, which can be easily converted into a function in R. There is an 84% statistical power to detect a 0.20 treatment effect if 40 groups are randomized (20 groups in each of the two treatment conditions), and each group contains an average of 30 group members.

```
> dk.pow <- function(d, m, rho, n, alpha = 0.05)
{
# returns two-sided power at alpha error 0.05
# d <- 0.20      # effect size
# m <- 8         # number of clusters per Tx condition
# rho <- .01     # intraclass correlation
# n <- 30        # number of people in each cluster
df    <- 2 * (m - 1)
sigq <- qt(1 - alpha/2, df) # two-sided p = 0.05
inf   <- 2 * ( 1 + ((n-1)*rho) ) / (m * n)
nc    <- d / sqrt(inf)
pow   <- 1 - pt(sigq, df, nc) + pt(-sigq, df, nc)
return(pow)
}
dk.pow(d = .20, m = 20, rho = 0.01, n = 30)
[1]  0.8442535
```

Try running dk.pow() a few times with different values of m and n. If the value of m is too small, increasing the value of n does little to boost power. The statistical power in a cluster-randomized study is strongly influenced by the number of groups. If there is not enough number of groups, adding more participants per group would offer limited help in boosting power.

The dk.pow() function can also be used in a repeated-measures design. For example, 20 college students are randomized into each of two intervention conditions. Each student is asked to keep a diary on sleep quality for 30 days. The daily assessments are correlated, say at rho = 0.10. A call to dk.pow(d = 0.20, m = 20, n = 30, rho = 0.1) shows a 40% statistical power in this study. Doubling the number of longitudinal assessments per student provides only a small boost in power, as can be seen in the 44% power when n = 60.

The calculation involves a noncentral t-distribution with $2(m - 1)$ degrees of freedom and noncentrality parameter given by:

$$NC = \frac{d}{[2(1 + ((n - l)p))/(mn)]^{1/2}},$$

where d is the expected effect size in standardized units, m is the number of clusters per intervention condition, n is the expected average number of members within each cluster, and p is the expected intraless correlation. Note that m is the number of clusters *per treatment condition*. So the total number of clusters is $m \times 2$ in a two-arm randomized design. This method is one of several alternatives, including the power.grouped() function in the package grouped by Tsonaka, Rizopoulos and Lesaffre. In more complex designs, such as designs with uneven cluster sizes, the simulation method (Horton et al. 2004) is a better choice. We will cover that method in Sect. 11.9.1 on page 223, after we have gone over how to analyze cluster-randomized clinical trials.

Exercises

7.1. Power by simulation.

In Sect. 7.6 we see a repeated-measures ANOVA design with an average within-subject correlation of 0.35.

(a) Change the 0.35 correlation to 0.50, holding other parameters constant. Does a higher correlation of 0.50 increase or decrease the statistical power?
(b) Restore lines 11, 12, 26, and 27 in the R code to extract the numerator and the denominator sums of squares of the color effect when the correlation is set at 0.35.
(c) Change the correlation to 0.50, extract another set of sums of squares.
(d) Use the changes in sums of squares to explain the change in power when within subject correlation is increased.

7.2. Manual power calculation.

Figure 7.1 shows an estimated effect size of 0.50. The alternative distribution has a mean of 2.5 on the t-scale. Answer the questions below by assuming that the estimated effect size is changed to 0.75 (other assumptions remain the same).

(a) What is the mean of the alternative distribution?
(b) What are the lower and upper critical t-values?
(c) What is the statistical power for a sample of $n = 50$ per intervention condition?
(d) Can the researcher reduce the sample size to $n = 30$ per intervention condition and still maintain the 80% power?

7.3. A cluster-randomized design.

A physician colleague of yours is working with 20 community centers in a
metropolitan area to help adolescents with asthma. The community centers provide
after school programs for adolescents. Your colleague wants to randomize ten
community centers to the intervention condition (asthma self-management courses)
and the remaining ten to usual care (usual after school activities). Adolescents with
asthma are recruited into the study. The primary outcome is a summary score on
asthma symptoms.

(a) Assuming a 0.30 standardized difference in the asthma symptom scores between
    the two intervention groups, an average of 15 adolescents per community center,
    and a 0.01 intra-class correlation, what is the estimated statistical power to
    detect this level of difference at a two-sided Type-I error rate of 0.05?
(b) Would you recommend increasing the number of adolescent participants per
    community center to reach the 80% statistical power?
(c) Would you reach the 80% power target if you recruit 25 participants per
    community center?
(d) What would be the estimated statistical power if only 16 community centers can
    participate (eight community centers per intervention condition, 25 adolescents
    per center)?
(e) Can 35 adolescents per community center help restore the power to the 80%
    level?

Chapter 8
Item Response Theory

8.1 Overview

Several user-contributed packages can fit IRT models. The packages we use the most is the ltm package by Dimitris Rizopoulos and the MCMCpack packages by Andrew Martin, Kevin Quinn, and Jong Hee Park. The eRm package by Patrick Mair, Reinhold Hatzinger, and Marco Maier also has powerful features. But our experience with eRm is limited at this time. We also rely extensively on the Gibbs sampler approach to fit IRT models, using open-source computer programs such as JAGS and OpenBUGS on the Linux operational system, JAGS on Mac OS, and WinBUGS on the Windows platform. The Gibbs sampler is one of the popular Markov Chain Monte Carlo iterative simulation methods. R works seamlessly with these Gibbs sampler computer programs. The MCMCpack package on the 1-dimensional IRT model also uses the Gibbs sampler (see help(MCMCirt1d)). The ltm package uses a maximum-likelihood solution. The power of the Bayesian approach becomes apparent when we go over the latent regression Rasch model in Sect. 8.4.2. These methods are covered in this chapter. Additional resources can be found on the CRAN Task View on psychometric models and methods (CRAN 2011).

8.2 Rasch Model for Dichotomous Item Responses

One of the simplest IRT models is the Rasch Model (RM) (Rasch 1980) for dichotomized response data, developed by the Danish mathematician Georg Rasch. RM handles data coded as "correct"/"incorrect" or "yes"/"no" with a value of 1 coding a correct answer or a "yes" response. The log odds of answering an item correctly is a function of two parameters:

$$\ln\left[\frac{\Pr(x_{ij} = 1|\theta_i, \beta_j)}{1 - \Pr(x_{ij} = 1|\theta_i, \beta_j)}\right] = \theta_i - \beta_j, \tag{8.1}$$

Y. Li and J. Baron, *Behavioral Research Data Analysis with R*, Use R,
DOI 10.1007/978-1-4614-1238-0_8, © Springer Science+Business Media, LLC 2012

where $\Pr(x_{ij} = 1 \mid \theta_i, \beta_j)$ represents the probability of person i scoring a 1 versus 0 on item j. The interpretation of this model is made clearer if we let θ_i represent person i's innate "ability" and β_j represent item j's "difficulty." If a person's ability matches the difficulty of an item, then he/she has a 50–50 chance in answering the item correctly (assuming no guessing). This interpretation makes intuitive sense in an educational test setting. The equation can be unpacked by applying the inverse logit:

$$\Pr(x_{ij} = 1 \mid \theta_i, \beta_j) = \mathrm{logit}^{-1}(\theta_i - \beta_j) \tag{8.2}$$

$$= \frac{\exp(\theta_i - \beta_j)}{1 + \exp(\theta_i - \beta_j)} \tag{8.3}$$

$$= \frac{1}{1 + \exp(-(\theta_i - \beta_j))}. \tag{8.4}$$

Equation (8.3) is more commonly used in the literature for the classical RM. A more general form of the model includes an item discrimination parameter, α_j for each item.

$$\Pr(x_{ij} = 1 \mid \theta_i, \beta_j) = \frac{\exp(\alpha_j(\theta_i - \beta_j))}{1 + \exp(\alpha_j(\theta_i - \beta_j))}. \tag{8.5}$$

So the classical RM in (8.3) is a special case of the more general (8.5) with all α_j set to 1.0.

8.2.1 Fitting a `rasch()` Model

The `rasch()` function in `library(ltm)` can be used to fit this model. The commands below fit an RM to one of the most well-known datasets in the IRT literature, the `LSAT` data in   Bock and Lieberman (1970). A description of the dataset can be found by typing `help(LSAT)` (must load `library(ltm)` first).

```
> library(ltm)
> lsat.ltm <- rasch(LSAT,
+                   constraint=cbind(ncol(LSAT)+1, 1))
```

The `constraint = cbind(ncol(LSAT)+1, 1)` tells `rasch()` to set the item discrimination parameters to 1.0 for all 5 items. The `constraint` parameter takes a matrix with two columns. The first column specifies which model parameter(s) should be constrained, with a number 1 for item 1, number 2 for item 2, ..., and number 5 for item 5. Because the `LSAT` dataset contains 5 items, a number 6 refers to the item discrimination parameter. The second column of the `constraint` parameter specifies what the value of the constraint is. A value of 1 tells `rasch()` to fix the item discrimination parameters to 1.0 for all items.

```
> cbind(ncol(LSAT)+1, 1)
      [,1] [,2]
[1,]     6    1
```

The output shows the fitted item parameters:

```
> lsat.ltm

Call:
rasch(data = LSAT, constraint = cbind(ncol(LSAT) + 1,
      1))

Coefficients:
Dffclt.Item 1  Dffclt.Item 2  Dffclt.Item 3
       -2.872         -1.063         -0.258

Dffclt.Item 4  Dffclt.Item 5
       -1.388         -2.219

        Dscrmn
        1.000

Log.Lik: -2473.054
```

The parameters are scaled onto a latent norm, which is a standard normal z-scale of latent abilities (details see Bock and Aitkin (1981)). Thus, a -2.872 item difficulty for item 1 represents that item 1 is so easy that it can be answered correctly with a 50–50 chance by a person with an ability nearly 3 standard deviation below the norm; next is item 5 at a difficulty level of -2.219, item 4 at -1.388, item 2 at -1.063, and item 3 at -0.258. Note that the item discrimination parameter is set to 1.000 for all items.

For a two-parameter logistic model (2PL, Embretson and Reise (2000)), you can fit it with either the ltm or the MCMCirt1d packages. The two sets of parameter estimates do not necessarily agree because of the different scaling methods used in the functions.

```
> lsat.ltm <- ltm(LSAT ~ z1)
> lsat.ltm

Call:
ltm(formula = LSAT ~ z1)

Coefficients:
          Dffclt  Dscrmn
Item 1    -3.360   0.825
Item 2    -1.370   0.723
Item 3    -0.280   0.890
```

```
Item 4   -1.866     0.689
Item 5   -3.124     0.657


Log.Lik: -2466.7
```

The MCMCirt1d() function in library(MCMCpack) can be used to fit the same model. Note that the alpha parameters represent the item difficulty estimates and the beta parameters represent the item discrimination estimates. Also that store.ability is set to FALSE. This conserves space on storing the bulky MCMC chains for the theta estimates.

```
> lsat.mcmc <- MCMCirt1d(datamatrix = LSAT,
+     store.item = TRUE, store.ability = FALSE)
> summary(lsat.mcmc)

Iterations = 1001:21000
Thinning interval = 1
Number of chains = 1
Sample size per chain = 20000


1. Empirical mean and standard deviation for each
   variable, plus standard error of the mean:

                  Mean       SD Naive SE Time-series SE
alpha.Item 1 -1.549 0.1001 0.000708        0.00674
beta.Item 1   0.394 0.1482 0.001048        0.01232
alpha.Item 2 -0.594 0.0528 0.000373        0.00229
beta.Item 2   0.389 0.1421 0.001005        0.01257
alpha.Item 3 -0.305 0.3457 0.002445        0.04333
beta.Item 3   1.882 2.9364 0.020764        0.36375
alpha.Item 4 -0.767 0.0575 0.000406        0.00264
beta.Item 4   0.364 0.1332 0.000942        0.01048
alpha.Item 5 -1.190 0.0717 0.000507        0.00402
beta.Item 5   0.319 0.1417 0.001002        0.01208


2. Quantiles for each variable:

                  2.5%     25%     50%     75%    97.5%
alpha.Item 1 -1.7660 -1.608 -1.538 -1.479 -1.3837
beta.Item 1   0.1464  0.284  0.381  0.492  0.6979
alpha.Item 2 -0.7022 -0.628 -0.592 -0.558 -0.4963
beta.Item 2   0.1399  0.284  0.392  0.482  0.6646
alpha.Item 3 -1.3438 -0.229 -0.167 -0.129 -0.0676
beta.Item 3   0.3101  0.464  0.577  0.821 11.1881
alpha.Item 4 -0.8890 -0.802 -0.763 -0.728 -0.6627
beta.Item 4   0.1338  0.267  0.358  0.452  0.6438
```

Item Characteristic Curves

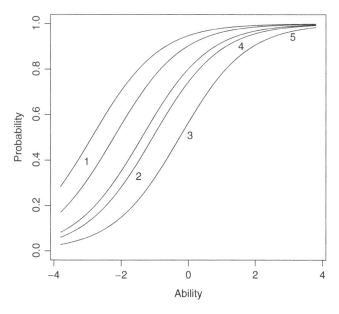

Fig. 8.1 Item characteristic curves for the Rasch model of the LSAT data

```
alpha.Item 5  -1.3424  -1.235  -1.185  -1.139  -1.0637
beta.Item 5    0.0641   0.210   0.320   0.418   0.5954

Warning message:
glm.fit: algorithm did not converge
```

8.2.2 Graphing Item Characteristics and Item Information

The plot(lsat.ltm, type = "ICC") command plots the item characteristics curves (ICC), shown in Fig. 8.1.

```
> plot(lsat.ltm, type = "ICC", col = "black")
```

The ICC curves are the probability of answering an item correctly across a range of hypothetical latent ability values. From left to right, the curves represent items 1, 5, 4, 2, and 3, respectively. The ICCs are plotted in color by default. They are easy to identify on the default graph window. The colors are suppressed in Fig. 8.1.

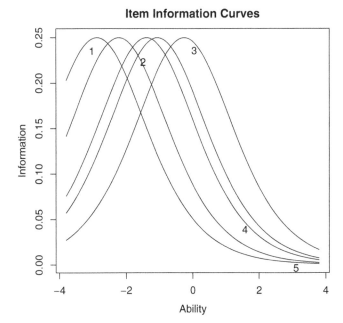

Fig. 8.2 Item information curves for the Rasch model of the LSAT data

A few dotted lines may be added in Fig. 8.1 (not shown) with these commands:

```
> abline(h = 0.50, lty = 2)
> xx <- coef(lsat.ltm)[1:5]
> segments(xx, 0, xx, 0.5, lty = 2)
```

The vertical dotted lines represent the item difficulty levels for all items – ability
levels for a 50–50 chance of answering the items correctly. The graph shows that
item 3 is the most difficult item and item 1 is the easiest. For the same latent ability
level, the probability of answering an item correctly is lowest for item 3.

Another useful graph to plot contains the item information curves, typing

```
> plot(lsat.ltm, type = "IIC", col = "black")
```

to produce Fig. 8.2.

Figure 8.2 plots the *Fisher information* of an item over a range of latent θ values.
Fisher information tells us how certain we are about a person's estimated level on
the latent θ continuum. A higher Fisher information means lower uncertainty for
the θ estimate (de Ayala 2009; Lord 1980) and vice versa.

Item 1 is the most informative item for examinees with very low latent ability
levels. We already know that item 1 is easy. Thus, if a person fails to answer item 1
correctly, then his/her latent ability level is likely to be low. In other words, failing
an item also provides information about a person's latent ability (Baker and Kim
2004). But item 1 is so easy that it provides limited information for latent ability

levels above 0.0. Item 3 is most informative for latent ability levels near the norm. It is also the most informative item among the 5 items for the above-norm latent ability levels.

8.2.3 Scoring New Item Response Data

The lsat.ltm object contains the Rasch Model calibrated by the sample of 1,000 examinees. The factor.scores() function in library(ltm) can use the already calibrated RM to score an independent sample of examinees. Suppose the same 5 items are given to two people. Their responses are entered as prsn1 and prsn2 below. A call to factor.scores returns the z1 scores, which are the estimated latent ability levels on a standard normal distribution.

```
> prsn1 <- c(1, 0, 1, 1, 1)
> prsn2 <- c(1, 1, 1, 0, 0)
> dat <- rbind(prsn1, prsn2)
> factor.scores(lsat.ltm, resp.pattern = dat)

Call:
rasch(data = LSAT, constraint = cbind(ncol(LSAT)+1,1))

Scoring Method: Empirical Bayes

Factor-Scores for specified response patterns:
        Item 1 Item 2 Item 3 Item 4 Item 5 Obs      Exp
prsn1       1      0      1      1      1   80   75.788
prsn2       1      1      1      0      0   11    7.340


           z1  se.z1
prsn1   0.025  0.761
prsn2  -0.526  0.726
```

8.2.4 Person Fit and Item Fit Statistics

The person fit and item fit statistics can also be calculated, using the person.fit() and item.fit() functions. Although by default these functions print out the test statistics and p-values, not the numeric values of the estimated fit statistics, such as the "infit" and "outfit" statistics (Masters and Wright 1996). These statistics can be calculated manually (Li 2006). There are limitations in these infit and outfit statistics. They are thoroughly examined in Karabatsos (2003). Alternative fit statistics and their advantages and disadvantages are also reviewed (Karabatsos 2003).

8.3 Generalized Partial Credit Model for Polytomous Item Responses

Masters (1982) proposed a Partial Credit Model (PCM) to handle polytomous items responses. The PCM extends the dichotomous RM to more than 2 response categories. Master's PCM assumes that the probability of selecting the kth response category over the $[k - 1]$th category is governed by the dichotomous RM. It is as though the person "passes through" each of the preceding response categories before finally stopping at a response (de Ayala 2009, p.165) that, presumably, most accurately reflects that person's standing on the latent variable continuum. The adjacent β_{jk} parameters represent the incremental item "difficulties" that the person has to step through in order to reach the next response category. Muraki (1992) further extended the PCM to include an item discrimination parameter in the Generalized Partial Credit Model (GPCM). In assessing health-related quality-of-life, the PCM and GPCM can be used to model responses on symptom severity such as responses of symptoms being "present" or "absent," or on a gradation such as "persistent/intermittent/none."

The PCM model in Masters (1982, p.158) has this form:

$$\Pr(x_j | \theta_i, \beta_{jh}) = \frac{\exp \sum_{h=0}^{x_j} (\theta_i - \beta_{jh})}{\sum_{k=0}^{m_j} \exp \sum_{h=0}^{k} (\theta_i - \beta_{jh})}, \tag{8.6}$$

where the numerator is the individual response outcomes and the denominator is the sum of all the possible outcomes. These characteristics led Thissen and Steinberg (1986) to classify the PCM as one of the "divide-by-total" models.

Muraki's GPCM (Muraki 1992) has a discrimination parameter α_j for each item:

$$\Pr(x_j | \theta_i, \alpha_j, \beta_{jh}) = \frac{\exp \sum_{h=0}^{x_j} \alpha_j (\theta_i - \beta_{jh})}{\sum_{k=0}^{m_j} \exp \sum_{h=0}^{k} \alpha_j (\theta_i - \beta_{jh})}. \tag{8.7}$$

These equations may appear intimidating for beginners. But they in fact follow a highly regular pattern. Later in Sect. 8.4, we will examines this highly regular pattern. There we will tackle Bayesian methods in fitting IRT models using iterative simulation. It will become clear that these complicated equations can be easily explained using the BUGS language (Lunn et al. 2000).

8.3.1   Neuroticism Data

The gpcm() function in library(ltm) can estimate the GPCM parameters. The dataset is the bfi dataset in the R package psych (Revelle 2010), which contains the responses of 2,800 subjects to 25 personality self-report items. We are analyzing a randomly selected subset of the 2,800 observations to save time. The 25 items map onto the "Big-Five" personality traits: Agreeableness, Conscientiousness, Extraversion, Neuroticism, and Openness. We analyze the 5 items assessing Neuroticism, which is a self-reported tendency to easily experience negative emotions, including anger ('item 1. Get angry easily'), unpleasant affect ('2. Get irritated easily' and '3. Have frequent mood swings'), depression ('4. Often feel blue'), and anxiety ('5. Panic easily').

Each item is rated on six response categories "1: Very Inaccurate," "2: Moderately Inaccurate," "3: Slightly Inaccurate," "4: Slightly Accurate," "5: Moderately Accurate," and "6: Very Accurate."

```
> library(psych)
> set.seed(7)   # for reproducibility
> data(bfi)
> neuroticism <- as.data.frame(bfi[,16:20 ])
> ti <- sample(1:nrow(bfi), size = 500)
> r <- matrix(unlist(neuroticism[ti,]), nrow = 500)
> neurot.gpcm <- gpcm(r)
> neurot.gpcm

Call:
gpcm(data = r)

Coefficients:
    Catgr.1 Catgr.2 Catgr.3 Catgr.4 Catgr.5  Dscrmn
V1   -0.889   0.045   0.189   0.949   1.699   2.106
V2   -1.478  -0.315  -0.479   0.799   1.328   1.819
V3   -1.171   0.247  -0.342   1.030   1.435   0.837
V4   -1.931   0.718  -1.006   1.754   2.203   0.437
V5   -0.518   1.769   0.081   1.077   1.873   0.367

Log.Lik: -3879.993
```

8.3.2   Category Response Curves and Item Information Curves

The category response curves for neurot.gpcm are plotted in Fig. 8.3. There is a visible overlap between response categories 2, 3, and 4 for all items. For example, in the second item (marked as 2. Irritated), the response category 3 is covered

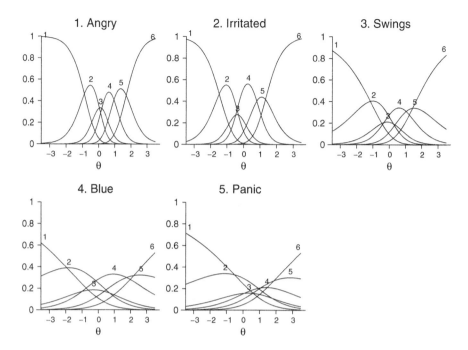

Fig. 8.3 Category response curves for the GPCM model of the `bfi` Neuroticism data

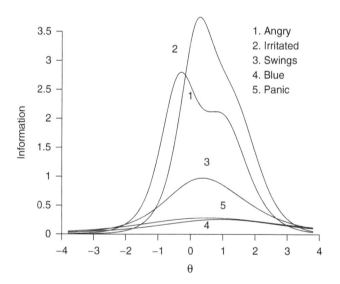

Fig. 8.4 Item information curves for the GPCM model of the `bfi` Neuroticism data

by the curves of categories 2 and 4. A similar pattern is also seen in items 1, 3, 4, and 5. If Fig. 8.3 is part of a scale validation study, then the overlapping response categories may be merged into one category. The probability of endorsing item 4 "feeling blue," an indication of depressive symptoms, is lower than in other items, due to low prevalence of depressive symptoms.

Figure 8.4 shows the item information curves for all items. Item 2 ('irritated') has the highest information profile. The next most informative items capture "anger" and "mood swings"; and "anger" tends to provide the most information at fairly intense levels of Neuroticism (i.e., $\theta > 1.5$). These three items do not appear to provide much information for θ values outside the $[-1.5, 2.5]$ range. Items 4 and 5 share a similar low information profile. They do not seem to provide as much information on Neuroticism as items 1, 2, and 3. They may be revised or replaced in a future version of the assessment if alternate items are available.

8.4 Bayesian Methods for Fitting IRT Models

Bayesian computation for IRT modeling is not new (see Baldwin et al. (2009); Gelman and Hill (2007); Albert (1992); Patz and Junker (1999); Torre et al. (2006)). More recently, Curtis (2010) published a collection of BUGS syntax codes for several IRT models, including the GPCM. Fox (2010) devotes a full volume to thoroughly cover the theory and applications of a Bayesian IRT modeling approach. The Bayesian approach provides flexible solutions to more sophisticated IRT models, such as, the latent regression Rasch model in Sect. 8.4.2 below. We hope that this section is most useful to researchers who are quite familiar with IRT and/or psychometrics but are new to a Bayesian analytic approach to IRT modeling. We only cover how to fit the polytomous GPCM model using the example in Curtis (2010) method. Bayesian solution to the dichotomous Rasch model is not covered here because it is well documented. It is part of the default WinBUGS version 1.4.3, under the menu "Help," "Examples Vol I," and "LSAT: latent variable models for item-response data." There is no need to repeat it.

8.4.1 GPCM

A random sample of 500 observations is taken from the `bfi` dataset. The `R2WinBUGS` package is loaded. The general workflow is as follows:

1. **Prepare data in R**: The first few lines of R code set up the raw item response matrix `Y` and its characteristics (number of persons `n`, the number of items `p`, and the number of response categories in the items `K`). A few assumptions are also made. The α_p item discrimination parameters are assumed to follow a fairly flat prior normal distribution with mean 1.0 and standard deviation of 2.5. The β_p item thresholds are assumed to follow a prior normal distribution with mean 0.0

and standard deviation 2.5. The lines commented out have already been done for
gpcm() on p. 147.

```
> library(R2WinBUGS)
## Already did these in gpcm(), no need to redo
# library(psych)
# set.seed(7)  # for reproducibility
# data(bfi)
# neuroticism <- as.data.frame(bfi[,16:20 ])
# ti <- sample(1:nrow(bfi), size = 500)
###########
> Y <- matrix(unlist(neuroticism[ti,]), nrow = 500)
> n <- nrow(Y)  # persons
> p <- ncol(Y)  # items
> K <- apply(Y, 2, max, na.rm = TRUE) # resp categ
> m.alpha <- 1.0
> s.alpha <- 2.5
> m.beta <- 0
> s.beta <- 2.5
```

2. **Prepare input for bugs()**: R uses the bugs() function to communicate
   with the WinBUGS computer program. We need to tell bugs() a few things,
   including a list of all data objects in step 1, the names of the parameters we are
   estimating, and how many simulations should be carried out.

```
> data <- list("Y", "n", "p", "K", "m.alpha",
+              "s.alpha", "m.beta", "s.beta")
> param <- c("alpha", "beta", "theta")
> n.burnin <- 100
> n.thin <- 10
> n.sim <- 5000 * n.thin + n.burnin
```

We want to discard the first 100 iterations (n.burnin) and save only 1 iteration
per every 10 (n.thin). This is because of the high autocorrelation typically
found in Markov Chain simulations. This "thinning" may help reduce the
autocorrelation between iterations. It certainly helps to save disk storage space by
keeping only 1 in 10 iterations. If we want to save 5,000 iterations, then we need
to run a total of 500 * n.thin + n.burnin iterative simulations. These
numbers are not arbitrary. We can calculate the Raftery and Lewis (1992) run-
length estimates to determine the minimum numbers of burn-ins and simulations
to achieve a prespecified precision of specific quantiles of a simulation. Details
on Markov Chain diagnostics can be found elsewhere (Jackman 2009; Ntzoufras
2009).

3. **Run the iterative simulations with bugs()**: proc.time() shows how long
   it takes to run the simulations. Then we call the bugs() function. The bugs()
   function tells WinBUGS to generate random initial values for the parameters
   because we set inits = NULL. The inits can be set manually. By setting

debug = FALSE, we ask bugs() to return everything back to R when the
simulation ends (debug = TRUE may be needed when WinBUGS fails).

```
> pr.time <- proc.time()[1:3]
> Neuro.Curtis.bugs <- bugs(data=data, inits=NULL,
+   parameters=param,
+   model.file="CurtisGPCM.bugs",
+   n.burnin=n.burnin, n.thin=n.thin, n.iter=n.sim,
+   n.chains=3, debug = FALSE)
> pr.time <- proc.time()[1:3] - pr.time
> print(pr.time)
> show(Neuro.Curtis.bugs)
```

The output of show(Neuro.Curtis.bugs) summarizes the parameter
estimates. They agree well with those obtained from gpcm() in package ltm.

The model.file="CurtisGPCM.bugs" input tells WinBUGS to fit the
model below. Line numbers are added to make them easier to track.

```
 1 model {
 2 for (i in 1:n) {
 3  for (j in 1:p) {
 4   Y[i, j] ~ dcat(prob[i, j, 1:K[j]])
 5   }
 6   theta[i] ~ dnorm(0.0, 1.0)
 7   }
 8 for (i in 1:n) {
 9  for (j in 1:p) {
10   for (k in 1:K[j]) {
11   eta[i,j,k] <- alpha[j] * (theta[i]-beta[j,k])
12   psum[i, j, k] <- sum(eta[i, j, 1:k])
13   exp.psum[i, j, k] <- exp(psum[i, j, k])
14   prob[i, j, k] <- exp.psum[i, j, k] /
15                       sum(exp.psum[i,j,1:K[j]])
16   } } }
17 for (j in 1:p) {
18  alpha[j] ~ dnorm(m.alpha, pr.alpha) I(0, )
19  beta[j, 1] <- 0.0
20  for (k in 2:K[j]) {
21    beta[j, k] ~ dnorm(m.beta, pr.beta)
22  }
23  }
24  pr.alpha <- pow(s.alpha, -2)
25  pr.beta  <- pow(s.beta, -2)
26 }
```

Line 4 shows that the item responses can be one of K[j] possible values, with the probability of each response separately specified in $\Pr(x_j|\theta_i, \alpha_j, \beta_{jh})$ (see (8.7)). Line 6 samples each person's latent characteristic from a standard normal distribution. Lines 11–13 calculate the numerators in the GPCM model in (8.7). Line 13 yields $\exp(\alpha_j(\theta_i - \beta_{j1}))$ when the response category is k = 1, $\exp(\alpha_j(\theta_i - \beta_{j1}) + \alpha_j(\theta_i - \beta_{j2})$ when k = 2, and so on for $\exp(\alpha_j(\theta_i - \beta_{j1}) + \alpha_j(\theta_i - \beta_{j2}) + \cdots + \alpha_j(\theta_i - \beta_{j6})$ when k = nK[j] (actually nK[i] is 6 for all items in the Neuroticism data). Lines 14–15 show the WinBUGS representation of (8.7). Line 15, sum(exp.psum[i, j, 1:K[j]]), is simply the sum of all numerators. Like Thissen and Steinberg (1986) said, the GPCM is one of the "divide-by-total" models. Lines 17–23 specify the prior distributions of the β and α parameters.

The GPCM model in (8.7) may appear complex, but the WinBUGS code shows that the complex summations can be reduced into three nested loops. This resemblance between mathematics and computer syntax is an important advantage of WinBUGS. The resemblance helps a beginner to develop a deeper understanding of the IRT theory as well as the statistical computation. WinBUGS, OpenBUGS, and JAGS force the learner to acquire a clear understanding of the statistical model, which hopefully discourages indiscriminately applying existing data analysis recipes.

8.4.2 Explanatory IRT

One might wonder why spend the time and effort to program the BUGS code in Sect. 8.4.1, while packages like ltm are much easier to use. The answer is that BUGS/WinBUGS/OpenBUGS can do much more – sophisticated models beyond the scope of any IRT package we know. De Boeck and Wilson (2004), in their book on Explantory IRT, describe a "latent regression Rasch model" (De Boeck and Wilson, 2004; Table 2.2). They provide SAS PROC NLMIXED syntax to carry out the analysis (Sect. 2.8, pp. 68–70). But it can also be done using JAGS. This subsection shows you how to fit such a model using De Boeck and Wilson's Verbal Aggression Assessment example (2004, p.9).

The Verbal Aggression Assessment is a 24-item survey on people's aggressive intentions and behaviors. The items are divided into different types. Some items describe a frustrating situation in which other people may be blamed for it. For example, a set of other-to-blame items say:

"A bus fails to stop for me. I would want to curse."
"A bus fails to stop for me. I would want to scold."
"A bus fails to stop for me. I would want to shout."

A second other-to-blame scenario involves missing a train because a clerk gave me the wrong information. So there are 6 other-to-blame items.

A second type of items describe a frustrating situation due to the subject's own fault:

"The grocery store closes just as I am about to enter. I would want to [curse | scold | shout]."

These are called "self-to-blame" items. A second self-to-blame scenario involves using up coins at a pay phone so the operator disconnects the phone call. There are also 6 self-to-blame items.

The 12 item stems are repeated to make up a total of 24 items. In the 12 repeated items the behavioral intention item stem "I would want to [curse | scold | shout]" is changed to the behavior "I will [curse | scold | shout]." Each person's Gender and Trait Anger are also known. The data file can be downloaded from the De Boeck and Wilson book website, which contains 7,584 entries and 28 variables.

De Boeck and Wilson fitted a *latent regression Rasch model* to the data:

$$\eta_{pi} = \mathrm{logit}^{-1}(\theta_p - \beta_i)$$

$$= \mathrm{logit}^{-1}\left(\left[\vartheta_1\,\mathrm{Anger}_p + \vartheta_2\,\mathrm{Gender}_p + \varepsilon_p\right] - \beta_i\right) \qquad (8.8)$$

$$= \mathrm{logit}^{-1}\left(\left[\sum_{j=1}^{J}\vartheta_j\mathbf{Z}_{pj} + \varepsilon_p\right] - \beta_i\right), \quad \varepsilon_p \sim N(0, \sigma_\varepsilon^2), \qquad (8.9)$$

where the first equation is the Rasch model, in which the item responses η_{pi} from person p on item i depend on the person's latent verbal aggression minus an outcome threshold for the ith item. In (8.8), the person's latent unobserved verbal aggression θ_i is regressed on the person's Trait Anger and Gender. The parameters ϑ_1 is an estimate of the impact of Trait Anger on latent verbal aggression controlling for Gender. Equation (8.9) is a general form of the model using matrix notation, $\mathbf{Z}_{pj}$ can include J explanatory variables.

The package rjags allows R to work with JAGS to fit the model. All the R commands are preceded by an > prompt to separate them from the output. We use R to set up the item response data, the explanatory covariates anger and gender, and the jags.model() function is called to specify the model. The jags.model() function is given the name of the JAGS syntax file ('lregRaschJAGS.bugs'), the data, and several Gibbs sampler parameters. The update() function carries out the burn-ins. The jags.samples() function takes the model and carries out a user-specified number of iterations to estimate the coefficients ang for Trait Anger (ϑ_1 above) and sex for gender (ϑ_2). A table(gender) shows that the sample consists of mostly female respondents. The β_i item thresholds are also calculated.

```
> library(rjags)
> agr.df <- data.frame(read.table(file =
+   "./data verbal aggression vector dichot.txt",
+   sep = "\t", header = TRUE))
> Y <- matrix(agr.df$Y, ncol = 24, byrow = T)
> anger <- matrix(agr.df$Anger, ncol=24, byrow=T)
> anger <- anger[, 1]
> gender <- matrix(agr.df$Gender, ncol=24, byrow=T)
> gender <- gender[, 1]
> table(gender)
gender
  0   1
243  73
> N <- nrow(Y)   # number of people
> I <- ncol(Y)   # number of items
> data <- list("Y"=Y, "N"=N, "I"=I, "anger"=anger,
        "gender"=gender)
> param <- c("b", "ang", "sex", "sigma")
> pr.time <- proc.time()[1:3]
> expirt.jags <- jags.model('lregRaschJAGS.bugs',
                data=data, n.chains=3, n.adapt=100)

Compiling model graph
   Resolving undeclared variables
   Allocating nodes
   Graph Size: 25342

   |++++++++++++++++++++++++++++++++++++++++++++++++++| 100%

> update(expirt.jags, 1000)
> jags.samples(expirt.jags, c('ang', 'sex', 'b'), 10000)

$ang
mcarray:
[1] 0.059

Marginalizing over: iteration(10000),chain(3)

$b
mcarray:
 [1] -1.394 -0.733 -0.246 -1.924 -0.877 -0.177
 [7] -0.698  0.523  1.369 -1.253  0.185  0.883
[13] -1.394 -0.556  0.709 -1.042 -0.109  1.322
[19]  0.046  1.346  2.831 -0.878  0.219  1.847

Marginalizing over: iteration(10000),chain(3)
```

```
$sex
mcarray:
[1] 0.3175268

Marginalizing over: iteration(10000),chain(3)

> pr.time <- proc.time()[1:3] - pr.time
> print(pr.time)
user.self   sys.self    elapsed
 3195.771      4.450   3202.037
```

The jags.samples() function prints out the parameter estimates averaged over iterations and chains. (Marginalizing over: iteration(10000), chain(3)) The ang and sex coefficient estimates agree well with the estimates of 0.056 and 0.292 obtained from SAS. The simulation took approximately 3,202 seconds (about 50 min) to run on a MacBook Pro laptop computer running MacOS X version 10.6.5 with a 2.66GHz Intel Core i7 CPU and 8GB of memory.

The JAGS model syntax is as follows. The JGAS syntax is stored separately in the file called lregRaschJAGS.bugs. The dichotomous response data Y are modeled after a Bernoulli distribution with response probabilities pr[p, i]. The logit of pr[p, i] follows the Rasch Model. Each person's latent verbal aggression theta[p] is regressed on his/her Trait Anger assessment and gender data, exactly as defined in (8.8). The prior distributions for the parameters are fairly flat and noninformative.

```
model
{
for (p in 1:N) {
  for (i in 1:I) {
  Y[p, i] ~ dbern( pr[p, i] )
  logit( pr[p, i] ) <- theta[p] - beta[i]
  }
  theta[p] <- ang * anger[p] + sex * gender[p]
  + eps[p]
  eps[p] ~ dnorm(0.0, tau)
  }
# Priors
for (i in 1:I) {
  beta[i] ~ dnorm(0.0, 0.001)
  b[i] <- beta[i] - mean(beta[])
  }
sigma ~ dunif(0, 10)
tau <- 1 / (sigma * sigma)
ang ~ dnorm(0.0, 0.01)
sex ~ dnorm(0.0, 0.01)
}
```

Our β_i estimates differ from those from SAS because we center them by the mean. Here we take the estimates from SAS and center them by the mean. The results agree well with the Bayesian estimates by JAGS.

```
> b <- c(-0.04423, 0.6114, 1.0957, -0.5715, 0.4686,
+ 1.1640, 0.6466, 1.8620, 2.7034, 0.09466, 1.5250,
+ 2.2199,-0.04423,0.7864,2.0469,0.3038,1.2323,
+ 2.6583,1.3867,2.6807,4.1548,0.4686,1.5598,3.1768)

> round(b - mean(b), 3)
 [1] -1.385 -0.730 -0.245 -1.913 -0.872 -0.177 -0.694
 [8]  0.521  1.362 -1.246  0.184  0.879 -1.385 -0.555
[15]  0.706 -1.037 -0.109  1.317  0.046  1.340  2.814
[22] -0.872  0.219  1.836
```

The coda.samples() function in package rjags is one way to get the 95% posterior interval estimates for the sex and ang coefficients. We carry out another 10,000 iterations with a thinning interval of 25. A sample of $10000/25 = 400$ is saved for each chain.

```
> expirt.coda <- coda.samples(expirt.jags,
+     variable.names=c('ang', 'sex', 'b'),
+     n.iter=10000, thin = 25)
> summary(expirt.coda)

Iterations = 11125:21100
Thinning interval = 25
Number of chains = 3
Sample size per chain = 400

1. Empirical mean and standard deviation for each
   variable, plus standard error of the mean:

          Mean      SD  Naive SE Time-series SE
ang    0.05901 0.01837 0.0005303       0.001441

[... snipped ...]

sex    0.33086 0.19272 0.0055633       0.007239

2. Quantiles for each variable:

          2.5%      25%      50%      75%     97.5%
ang    0.02324  0.04648  0.05986  0.07130  0.09514

[... snipped ...]

sex   -0.03735  0.19887  0.32963  0.46636  0.70768
```

The sex coefficient estimate is 0.318 without thinning. It gets a different value of 0.331 after thinning by every 25 iterations. Thinning changes the coefficient estimate for sex but not for ang. It is not always easy to find why only one coefficient estimate is affected by thinning. But it suggests that the coefficient sex is not stable. The 2.5% and 97.5% quantiles mark the 95% posterior intervals for the parameters. The posterior intervals for ang and sex are $(0.023, 0.095)$ and $(-0.037, 0.708)$, respectively.

Exercises

8.1. Rasch Model for the Knox Cube Test.

Wright and Stone (1979, Chap. 2) describe the Knox Cube Test for children's development in visual attention and memory. A child is asked to tap 4 cubes in specific orders, from the easiest sequence of '1–4' in item 1 to the most challenging sequence of '4–1–3–4–2–1–4' in the last and 18th item. Each item gets a score of 1 if the child taps the cubes in the correct order and 0 otherwise. The data from 35 children are presented below.

```
Richard  M 1 1 1 1 1 1 1 0 0 0 0 0 0 0 0 0 0 0
Tracie   F 1 1 1 1 1 1 1 1 1 1 0 0 0 0 0 0 0 0
Walter   M 1 1 1 1 1 1 1 1 1 0 0 1 0 0 0 0 0 0
Blaise   M 1 1 1 1 0 0 1 0 1 0 0 0 0 0 0 0 0 0
Ron      M 1 1 1 1 1 1 1 1 1 1 0 0 0 0 0 0 0 0
William  M 1 1 1 1 1 1 1 1 1 1 0 0 0 0 0 0 0 0
Susan    F 1 1 1 1 1 1 1 1 1 1 1 1 1 0 1 0 0 0
Linda    F 1 1 1 1 1 1 1 1 1 1 0 0 0 0 0 0 0 0
Kim      F 1 1 1 1 1 1 1 1 1 1 0 0 0 0 0 0 0 0
Carol    F 1 1 1 1 1 1 1 1 1 1 1 0 0 0 0 0 0 0
Pete     M 1 1 1 0 1 1 1 1 1 0 0 0 0 0 0 0 0 0
Brenda   F 1 1 1 1 1 0 1 0 1 1 0 0 0 0 0 0 0 0
Mike     M 1 1 1 1 1 0 0 1 1 1 1 0 0 0 0 0 0 0
Zula     F 1 1 1 1 1 1 1 1 1 1 1 0 0 0 0 0 0 0
Frank    M 1 1 1 1 1 1 1 1 1 1 1 1 0 0 0 0 0 0
Dorothy  F 1 1 1 1 1 1 1 1 0 1 0 0 0 0 0 0 0 0
Rod      M 1 1 1 1 0 1 1 1 1 1 0 0 0 0 0 0 0 0
Britton  F 1 1 1 1 1 1 1 1 1 1 0 0 1 0 0 0 0 0
Janet    F 1 1 1 1 1 1 1 1 1 0 0 0 0 0 0 0 0 0
David    M 1 1 1 1 1 1 1 1 1 1 0 0 1 0 0 0 0 0
Thomas   M 1 1 1 1 1 1 1 1 1 1 1 0 1 0 0 0 0 0
Betty    F 1 1 1 1 1 1 1 1 1 1 1 0 0 0 0 0 0 0
Bert     M 1 1 1 1 1 1 1 1 1 1 0 0 1 1 0 0 0 0
Rick     M 1 1 1 1 1 1 1 1 1 1 1 0 1 0 0 1 1 0
Don      M 1 1 1 0 1 1 0 0 0 0 0 0 0 0 0 0 0 0
Barbara  F 1 1 1 1 1 1 1 1 1 1 0 0 0 0 0 0 0 0
```

```
Adam     M 1 1 1 1 1 1 1 0 0 0 0 0 0 0 0 0 0 0
Audrey   F 1 1 1 1 1 1 1 1 1 0 1 0 0 0 0 0 0 0
Anne     F 1 1 1 1 1 1 0 0 1 1 1 0 0 1 0 0 0 0
Lisa     F 1 1 1 1 1 1 1 1 1 0 0 0 0 0 0 0 0 0
James    M 1 1 1 1 1 1 1 1 1 1 0 0 0 0 0 0 0 0
Joe      M 1 1 1 1 1 1 1 1 1 1 1 0 0 0 0 0 0 0
Martha   F 1 1 1 1 0 0 1 0 0 1 0 0 0 0 0 0 0 0
Elsie    F 1 1 1 1 1 1 1 1 1 1 0 1 0 1 0 0 0 0
Helen    F 1 1 1 0 0 0 0 0 0 0 0 0 0 0 0 0 0 0
```

(a) Enter the raw data into a text file and use `read.csv()` to read the data into R.
(b) Fit a Rasch Model to the 18 items using the `rasch()` function in the `ltm` package.
(c) Item 18 is designed to be the most challenging item. Is this supported by its item difficulty parameter estimate?
(d) Plot the item information curves of the 18 items.
(e) Which item provides the highest level of information for a child who has a latent ability of zero?
(f) Which item provides the highest level of information for a child who has a latent ability of 2 above the norm?
(g) Which item provides the highest level of information for a child who has a latent ability of 2 below the norm?

8.2. Bond's Logical Operations Test.
The `blot` dataset in `library(psych)` contains 35 items for 150 subjects from the Bond's Logical Operations Test. The BLOT is designed to measure the development of logical thinking. Details of the BLOT test are described in Bond and Fox (2001).

(a) Fit a `rasch()` model with all item discrimination parameters set to 1.
(b) Fit a 2PL model by `ltm()`, allowing a separate item discrimination parameter per item.
(c) Which item in the Rasch model is the most difficult item? (item V6, V12, or V21?)
(d) Which item in the 2PL model is the most difficult item? Does the 2PL agree with the Rasch model on this?
(e) Plot the "Item Characteristics Curves" for both models and put them side by side on a single plot. (hint, use `par(mfcol = c(1, 2))`)
(f) Does item 12, plotted as V12, have the same item characteristic curve across the two models?
(g) If not, what is the estimated item discrimination for item 12 in the 2PL model? Is it considerably different from the 1.0 value in the Rasch model?

8.3. Assessment of Openness.
The `bfi` dataset in `library(psych)` also contains 5 items assessing Openness. The `help(bfi)` documentation shows that they are O1: "Am full of ideas," O2: "Avoid difficult reading material," O3: "Carry the conversation to a higher

level," O4: "Spend time reflecting on things," and O5: "Will not probe deeply into a subject." The 6-point response scale is described in Sect. 8.3.1. Note that items 2 and 5 are usually reverse-coded before being analyzed. Let us not apply reverse coding for now and see what the model does to the raw data.

(a) Run a Graded Response Model using the grm() function in library(ltm).
(b) Plot the item response category characteristic curves.
(c) Take item O1 as an example, what is the most likely response for a person with a latent score of −2? Is it "2: Moderately Inaccurate," "3: Slightly Inaccurate," or "4: Slightly Accurate"?
(d) There may be overlaps between the response category characteristics curves. An example is presented in Fig. 8.3 on page 148. Are there indications of overlapping curves among the 5 items of openness assessment to justify the reduction of the 6 response categories?
(e) Note how the order of the curves is reversed for items 2 and 5. Does this imply that reverse coding would not have affected the model's predictions?
(f) Is there a way to check your answer above? (e.g., a call to factor.scores() with two sets of data, one original and the other reverse-coded)

8.4. Continue with the Openness assessment.
Plot the item information curves of the grm() model above. Use the plot to guide your answers to the following questions.

(a) Which item provides the greatest amount of overall item information for latent scores between the $[−3, 3]$ range?
(b) Which item provides the least amount of overall item information for latent scores between the $[−3, 3]$ range.
(c) Which item provides the greatest information for a latent score of $+3$? Is the item you identify a strong winner over the other items?

8.5. Is latent Neuroticism associated with age and gender?
Fit an explanatory Rasch model to the 5 Neuroticism items in data(bfi). First, a copy of the Neuroticism data can be obtained from the psych package, along with the age and gender variables. Next, dichtomize the Neuroticism item responses into $0 = 1$ through 3 and $1 = 4$ through 6. Recode the gender variable into $0 = $ Male and $1 = $ Female. Follow the example in Sect. 8.4.2 and fit an explanatory Rasch model predicting the latent Neurotism scores by age and gender. Run 10,000 iterations. Use a thinning interval of 10 in coda.samples().

(a) Is there a gender difference in the latent Neurotism scores?
(b) What is the coefficient associated with gender?
(c) What is the 95% posterior interval for the gender coefficient?
(d) Is latent Neurotism associated with age (controlling for gender)?
(e) What is the estimated coefficient for age?
(f) What is the 95% posterior interval of the age coefficient?

Chapter 9
Imputation of Missing Data

9.1 Missing Data in Smoking Cessation Study

Below is a subset of data from a smoking cessation study for smokers newly diagnosed with cancer.[1] Patients were assessed for anxiety and depression at baseline using the Hospital Anxiety and Depression Scale (Zigmond and Snaith 1983), at least 7 days before they were hospitalized for surgery. The baseline assessments of anxiety and depression were scored and saved into variables ANX.ba and DPR.ba, respectively. The scores were centered (average ANX.ba of 8.9 and average DPR.ba of 4.2). A team of clinicians provided smoking cessation counseling and pharmacotherapy for enrolled patients. On the day of hospital admission, each patient's 24-hour point abstinence status was determined by biochemical verification (variable abst, coded 1 if abstinence from smoking was verified and 0 otherwise).

```
> hads.df
   abst    ANX.ba DPR.ba
1     1 -3.913333  -4.24
2     0 -0.746667  -4.24
3     0  2.086667  -4.24
4    NA -8.913333  -3.24
5     0 -7.913333  -3.24
6     0  2.086667  -3.24
7     0  0.086667  -1.24
8     0  0.086667  -1.24
9     1  2.753333  -1.24
10    1  7.086667  -1.24
11    0  9.086667  -1.24
12    1 -5.913333  -0.24
```

---

[1]NCI grant R01CA90514 to Jamie Ostroff, PhD.

Y. Li and J. Baron, *Behavioral Research Data Analysis with R*, Use R,
DOI 10.1007/978-1-4614-1238-0_9, © Springer Science+Business Media, LLC 2012

```
13    0 -5.913333    -0.24
14    0 -0.913333    -0.24
15    1  0.086667    -0.24
16    1  1.086667    -0.24
17    1 -4.913333     0.76
18    0 -2.913333     0.76
19    1 -1.913333     0.76
20    0 -5.913333     2.76
21    1  3.086667     2.76
22    0  0.086667     3.76
23    0  9.086667     3.76
24    1  9.086667     5.76
25    1  4.086667     8.76
26    1        NA       NA
27    0        NA       NA
28    0        NA       NA
29    0        NA       NA
30    0        NA       NA
```

The data frame above is a small subset of the total sample of approximately 200 participants enrolled in the study. Missing data were observed in only 6 of the 200 participants. This simple illustrative example is based on data from these 6 participants and another 24 participants randomly selected from the rest of the full dataset. Five participants did not provide baseline assessments of anxiety and depression. One participant's smoking abstinence status at hospital admission could not be verified because the person was ill.

This example lends itself to a logistic regression analysis predicting smoking abstinence at hospital admission by baseline assessments of anxiety and depression. The standard complete-data methods would carry out a casewise deletion by default.

```
> glm1 <- glm(abst == 1 ~ ANX.ba + DPR.ba,
              family = "binomial", data = hads.df)
> summary(glm1)

Call:
glm(formula = abst == 1 ~ ANX.ba + DPR.ba,
    family = "binomial", data = hads.df)

Deviance Residuals:
   Min      1Q  Median      3Q     Max
  -1.43   -1.05   -0.82    1.25    1.61

Coefficients:
              Estimate Std. Error z value Pr(>|z|)
(Intercept)    -0.1968     0.4257   -0.46     0.64
ANX.ba          0.0149     0.0919    0.16     0.87
```

```
DPR.ba          0.1723      0.1514     1.14       0.26
```

```
(Dispersion parameter for binomial family taken to be 1)

    Null deviance: 33.104  on 23  degrees of freedom
Residual deviance: 31.374  on 21  degrees of freedom
  (6 observations deleted due to missingness)
AIC: 37.37
```

```
Number of Fisher Scoring iterations: 4
```

A message in the output shows that (six observations deleted due to missingness). The parameter estimates for baseline anxiety and depression assessments suggest that, other covariate being equal, higher anxiety and depression scores are associated with a higher probability of smoking abstinence. However, none of the parameter estimates is statistically significantly different from zero.

Across all 29 available outcomes on smoking abstinence, the average abstinence rate is 0.414. The casewise deletion of the six observations causes the abstinence rate to go up slightly to 0.458.

```
> mean(hads.df$abst, na.rm=T)
[1] 0.41379
> mean(hads.df$abst[1:25], na.rm=T)
[1] 0.45833
```

From the output of the glm1 model above we can calculate the fitted probability of abstinence for a patient whose anxiety and depression scores are at the sample averages. It is exp(-0.1968) / (1 + exp(-0.1968)) or 0.451, a value closer to the 0.458 average from casewise deletion of six cases than to 0.414 (only one case deleted). We would expect a predicted probability nearer to 0.414 if we had complete anxiety and depression scores on the six deleted cases. This makes intuitive sense. As will become clearer later in this chapter, the predicted probability from imputed data is indeed closer to 0.410 than to 0.458. An imputed logistic regression model is build in Sect. 9.3. The prediction made by the imputed model is 0.421. The remainder of this chapter focuses on how to impute missing data in this example so that the imputed datasets can be used to carry out data analysis as usual, using standard complete-data methods.

9.2 Multiple Imputation with aregImpute()

The aregImpute() function below carries out 5 imputed datasets using predictive mean matching (type = "pmm") by the closest match in the nonmissing values. Details can be found in the help files, other documentations of the Hmisc package and in Harrell (2001b, Sect. 8.10).

```
library(Hmisc)
Loading required package: survival
Loading required package: splines
> set.seed(7)
> imp <- aregImpute(~ abst + ANX.ba + DPR.ba,
    data = hads.df, n.impute = 5, type = "pmm",
    match = "closest")
Iteration 8
```

In `aregImpute()`, missing values for any variable are estimated from other variables. For example, the formula $\sim$ `abst + ANX.ba + DPR.ba` specifies that missing `abst` values are estimated from variables `ANX.ba` and `DPR.ba`; missing `ANX.ba` values are estimated from variables `abst` and `DPR.ba`, etc. Missing values are then substituted by these estimates, or "imputed values" to yield a complete dataset, or an "imputed dataset." The imputation process is carried out several times (e.g., `n.impute = 5`) to produce multiple imputed datasets. Each newly imputed value of the same variable would not necessarily be the same as the previous because the imputation processes needs to account for variability between imputed datasets. The multiply imputed datasets are stored in `imp`. Next, the `fit.mult.impute()` function is called to apply the standard complete-data logistic regression (`fitter = glm` with `family = "binomial"`) to all the imputed datasets. Each logistic regression would be different because of the variability across multiply imputed datasets. Finally, the `fit.mult.impute()` function combines the results from the multiple complete-data analyses to produce an overall analysis.

A crude example may help give an intuitive explanation on multiple imputation by predictive mean matching. The actual implementation in `aregImpute()` is much more sophisticated than the crude explanation below. Details on predictive mean matching can be found in Little (1988).

Let us begin with participant number 4 whose abstinence outcome is missing. To impute this missing value, we may use a logistic regression model like `glm1` above to calculate a predictive value of `abst` for this participant. It is $-0.197 + 0.015 \times (-8.913) + 0.172 \times (-3.24) = -0.888$. By taking the inverse logit of -0.888, we get a predicted probability of abstinence of 0.292 for this participant. Then we look into other participants with complete data. We find that participant 3 has a predicted value of 0.290, participant 5 a 0.294, and participant 2 a 0.281, and so on. The top five closest matches are:

```
> ty <- fitted(glm1)
> YY <- sort(abs(ty - TT))[1:5]
> ty[names(YY)[1:5]]
        3        5        2        1        6
  0.28985  0.29465  0.28124  0.27179  0.32655
```

We call participants 3, 5, 2, 1, and 6 the donors of potential imputed `abst` value for participant number 4 whose `abst` outcome is missing. We know that participants 3, 5, 2, and 6 continue to smoke and participant 1 abstains.

```
> hads.df[names(YY), "abst"]
[1] 0 0 0 1 0
```

Let us assume that, for the sake of simplicity, we fill in participant number 4's missing outcome by the outcome of one randomly selected donor, e.g., donor number 3 who smokes. Little (1988, Equation (2)) describes the details of predictive mean matching. A similar regression-like model may be used to impute the missing values for the `DPR.ba` and `ANX.ba` predictors. The whole process is repeated `n.impute` times to generate the specified number of imputed datasets.

9.2.1 Imputed Data

The imputed datasets are stored in the `imp` object. In the first imputed dataset, the missing abstinence outcome is filled in with a 1, the missing baseline anxiety scores for participants 26 through 30 are filled in with 2.75, 9.09, ..., 9.09, and so on. The imputation is repeated five times, each time with a set of imputed values.

```
> imp$imputed
$abst
  [,1] [,2] [,3] [,4] [,5]
4    1    0    0    0    0

$ANX.ba
        [,1]       [,2]       [,3]       [,4]     [,5]
26    2.7533   7.086667   7.086667   2.753333   2.7533
27    9.0867   0.086667   0.086667   0.086667   9.0867
28   -7.9133  -8.913333  -7.913333  -8.913333  -8.9133
29    9.0867   0.086667   0.086667   0.086667   9.0867
30    9.0867   0.086667   0.086667   0.086667   9.0867

$DPR.ba
       [,1]   [,2]   [,3]   [,4]   [,5]
26    -1.24  -1.24  -1.24  -1.24  -1.24
27    -1.24  -1.24  -1.24   3.76  -1.24
28    -3.24  -3.24  -3.24  -3.24  -3.24
29    -1.24  -1.24  -1.24   3.76  -1.24
30    -1.24  -1.24  -1.24   3.76  -1.24
```

This output shows an obvious problem. Respondent 26 has the same imputed depression score across multiple imputations. Several other imputed values also lack variability. This occurs more easily when the sample size is small. Default options in aregImpute() can be modified to introduce variability in the imputation process. However, Lazzeroni et al. (1990) found that, generally, predictive mean matching works better when the sample size is large. It makes sense intuitively because a larger sample offers more potential donors for the imputed values.

9.2.2   Pooling Results Over Imputed Datasets

The fit.mult.impute() function carries out the complete-data logistic regression analysis over the imputed datasets and combine the results into an overall summary. The user specifies the model formula, the fitter = glm function used to carry out the logistic regression with family = "binomial", the imputed data object imp, and the raw data.

```
> abst.mi <- fit.mult.impute(abst ~ ANX.ba + DPR.ba,
    glm, imp, family = "binomial", data = hads.df)

Variance Inflation Factors Due to Imputation:

(Intercept)        ANX.ba        DPR.ba
       1.07          1.66          1.25

Rate of Missing Information:

(Intercept)        ANX.ba        DPR.ba
       0.06          0.40          0.20

d.f. for t-distribution for Tests of Single Coefficients:

(Intercept)        ANX.ba        DPR.ba
    1068.58         25.38         98.98

The following fit components were averaged over the 5
model fits:

    fitted.values linear.predictors

Warning message:
In fit.mult.impute(abst ~ DPR.ba + ANX.ba, glm, imp,
    family = "binomial",  : Not using a Design fitting
    function; summary(fit) will use standard errors,
    t, P from last imputation only.  Use vcov(fit)
    to get the correct covariance matrix,
    sqrt(diag(vcov(fit))) to get s.e.
```

The warning message seems alarming. It suggests that a `summary(abst.mi)` output only uses the results from the last imputation, rather than the combined results pooled over the multiply imputed data. A detailed investigation was recently made available online by Paul Johnson at `http://pj.freefaculty.org/ guides/Rcourse/multipleImputation/multipleImputation-1- lecture.pdf`. Johonson's recommendation was to check with another imputation tool when you get this error.

```
> summary(abst.mi)

Call:
fitter(formula = formula, family = "binomial",
       data = completed.data)

Deviance Residuals:
   Min     1Q  Median      3Q     Max
-1.431  -0.951  -0.756   1.315   1.706

Coefficients:
              Estimate Std. Error z value Pr(>|z|)
(Intercept)   -0.3445     0.3970   -0.87    0.39
ANX.ba         0.0307     0.0718    0.43    0.67
DPR.ba         0.1753     0.1494    1.17    0.24

(Dispersion parameter for binomial family taken to
   be 1)

    Null deviance: 40.381  on 29  degrees of freedom
Residual deviance: 37.442  on 27  degrees of freedom
AIC: 43.44

Number of Fisher Scoring iterations: 4
```

The `summary(abst.mi)` command shows that higher baseline scores of anxiety and depression are associated with a higher probability to abstain from smoking at hospital admission. However, the coefficients associated with the anxiety and depression scores are not statistically reliably different from zero.

The example shows several advantages of predictive mean matching. It works with binary, categorical, and continuous variables. Imputation from observed values in the donors' data ensures that, for example, the binary outcome of smoking abstinence is either 0 or 1.

9.3 Multiple Imputation with the `mi` Package

The `mi` package by Su et al. (in press) uses an algorithm different from that of predictive mean matching. It uses what is known as a chained equation approach. Su et al. (in press) describes the algorithm in more detail. The `mi` package contains several useful features in data transformation, data imputation, and model diagnostics. Here we only cover some of the basic options to illustrate how to impute missing data in the smoking cessation study above.

```
> library(mi)
Loading required package: MASS
Loading required package: nnet
Loading required package: car
Loading required package: lme4
mi (Version 0.09-13, built: 2011-2-15)
> set.seed(7)
> info <- mi.info( hads.df )
> info
    names include order number.mis all.mis       type
1    abst     Yes     1          1      No     binary
2  ANX.ba     Yes     2          5      No continuous
3  DPR.ba     Yes     3          5      No continuous
  collinear
1        No
2        No
3        No
```

The `mi.info()` function extracts information from the dataset, including the names of the variables, the number of missed observations in each variable, and the type of each variable. Usually, the variable types are ascertained correctly. If not, then the variable types can be set manually by, e.g., `update(info, "type", list("abst" = "binary"))`.

Next the information is entered into `mi.preprocess()` to prepare the variables for multiple imputation. Skewed variables may be log-transformed and returned into the processed dataset called `dat.proc`.

```
> dat.proc <- mi.preprocess(hads.df, info = info)
```

Next, imputation is done through the `mi()` function. The default options are three imputed datasets by the chained equation algorithm (`n.imp = 3`) and 20 iterations per chain. Here we increase `n.iter` to 50 to help the chains to converge.

```
> imp.mi <- mi(dat.proc, n.imp = 5, n.iter = 50,
+    check.coef.convergence = TRUE,
+    add.noise = noise.control( post.run.iter = 50))
```

```
Beginning Multiple Imputation
( Thu Apr  7 11:10:10 2011 ):
Iteration 1
 Chain 1 : abst*   ANX.ba*   DPR.ba*
 Chain 2 : abst*   ANX.ba*   DPR.ba*
 Chain 3 : abst*   ANX.ba*   DPR.ba*
 Chain 4 : abst*   ANX.ba*   DPR.ba*
 Chain 5 : abst*   ANX.ba*   DPR.ba*
 ....
Iteration 50
 Chain 1 : abst    ANX.ba    DPR.ba
 Chain 2 : abst    ANX.ba    DPR.ba
 Chain 3 : abst    ANX.ba    DPR.ba
 Chain 4 : abst    ANX.ba    DPR.ba*
 Chain 5 : abst    ANX.ba    DPR.ba
mi converged ( Thu Apr  7 11:10:32 2011 )
Run 50 more iterations to mitigate the influence of
the noise...
Beginning Multiple Imputation
( Thu Apr  7 11:10:32 2011 ):
Iteration 1
 ....
Iteration 50
mi converged ( Thu Apr  7 11:11:02 2011 )
```

The check.coef.convergence option checks the convergence of the chained equation approach using the Gelman and Rubin (1992) convergence diagnostic. The add.noise = noise.control(post.run.iter = 50) option runs another 50 iterations after the first 50 iterations are done.

To show the imputed data, type:

```
> mi.completed(imp.mi)
[[1]]
    abst    ANX.ba    DPR.ba
 ....
4     0 -8.913333 -3.24000
 ....
26    1  1.086856  1.45733
27    0  2.280348 -0.37503
28    0  6.353274  0.82913
29    0 -4.852233 -4.40118
30    0  4.972868 -4.65457

[[2]]
    abst    ANX.ba    DPR.ba
4     1 -8.913333 -3.24000
```

```
. . . .

26    1 -1.779520 -3.91537
27    0  3.928673  2.63901
28    0 -0.648088 -3.75788
29    0  1.584324  4.05128
30    0 -2.517066  0.18439

[[3]]
    abst    ANX.ba    DPR.ba
4      0 -8.913333 -3.24000
. . . .
26    1  6.373419 -0.01220
27    0  0.781545 -3.78449
28    0 13.099146  0.01708
29    0  2.485995 -2.27167
30    0 -0.665939 -2.47556
```

The pooled estimates can be calculated by glm.mi().

```
> glm.fit <- glm.mi(abst ~ ANX.ba + DPR.ba,
      mi.object = imp.mi, family = binomial)
> display(glm.fit, digits = 4)


. . . .


=========================================
Pooled Estimates
=========================================
glm.mi(formula = abst ~ ANX.ba + DPR.ba,
    mi.object = imp.mi, family = binomial)
            coef.est coef.se
(Intercept) -0.3294    0.4029
ANX.ba       0.0052    0.0885
DPR.ba       0.1946    0.1635
---
```

Another method for pooled logistic regression is the bayesglm.mi() function.

```
> bayesglm.fit <- bayesglm.mi(abst ~ ANX.ba + DPR.ba,
      mi.object = imp.mi, family = binomial)
> display(bayesglm.fit, digits = 4)
. . . .
=========================================
Pooled Estimates
=========================================
bayesglm.mi(formula = abst ~ ANX.ba + DPR.ba,
```

```
         mi.object = imp.mi, family = binomial)
                   coef.est coef.se
 (Intercept) -0.3177    0.3880
 ANX.ba        0.0088    0.0788
 DPR.ba        0.1632    0.1426
 ---
```

According to the pooled logistic regression model by bayesglm.mi(), a patient with average anxiety and depression scores has a predicted probability of abstinence of exp(-0.3177) / (1 + exp(-0.3177)) or 0.421, a value closer to the average 0.414 from all 29 nonmissing outcomes than the average 0.458 from casewise deletion (see Sect. 9.1). This is only a crude way to check the imputed model. Horton and Kleinman (2007) describe a more formal way to compare the performance of multiple imputation methods.

Additional details on visual diagnostics of imputed results can be found in Su et al. (in press). The paper also uses a large dataset to demonstrate the many other features in the mi package.

Introduction of variability into the multiple imputation process appears to be useful when the sample size is small. Our experiences show that multiple imputation works best when the dataset is large, such as in publicly available databases with several hundred observations or more. After all, multiple imputation was originally designed to handle such datasets (Rubin 1996).

9.4 Multiple Imputation with the Amelia and Zelig Packages

The Amelia II package uses a powerful and fast algorithm to carry out multiple imputation for cross-sectional and longitudinal data. The bootstrapping-based EM algorithm is described in King et al. (2001) and Honaker and King (2010). Both articles can be found at the Amelia II website.[2] For Windows users who are not familiar with R, a self-install package can be used to install Amelia without directly working with R.

A call to the AmeliaView() function brings up a graphical user interface shown in Fig. 9.1. There the user specifies the names of the input raw data file and output imputed datasets, with options to transform the variables and add priors to missing values. The saved imputed datasets can later be used by Zelig or other statistical packages for analysis.

---

[2]http://gking.harvard.edu/amelia/, last accessed April, 2011.

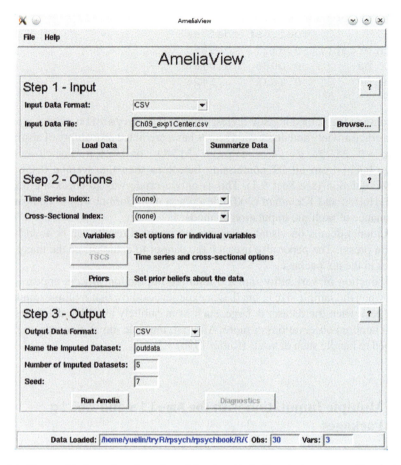

Fig. 9.1 The graphical user interface of `AmeliaView()`. In Step 1, the user specifies the input data. In Step 2, the user can transform raw data and to add priors to the missing values. In Step 3, the user saves the imputed datasets as `outdata1`, `outdata2`, ..., `outdata5` for further analyses

The `zelig()` function by Kosuke Imai, Gary King, and Olivia Lau can be used to fit an overall logistic regression model based on the imputed datasets.

```
> dat1 <- read.csv("outdata1.csv")
> dat2 <- read.csv("outdata2.csv")
> dat3 <- read.csv("outdata3.csv")
> dat4 <- read.csv("outdata4.csv")
> dat5 <- read.csv("outdata5.csv")
> glmAm.fit <- zelig(abst == 1 ~ ANX.ba + DPR.ba,
+ data = mi(dat1, dat2, dat3, dat4, dat5),
+ model = "logit")
> summary(glmAm.fit)
```

```
   Model: logit
   Number of multiply imputed data sets: 5

Combined results:

Call:
zelig(formula = abst == 1 ~ ANX.ba + DPR.ba,
      model = "logit",
      data = mi(dat1, dat2, dat3, dat4, dat5))

Coefficients:
                  Value Std. Error      t-stat $p$-value
(Intercept) -0.4293496    0.394132 -1.089354 0.27602
ANX.ba       0.0085301    0.086268  0.098879 0.92126
DPR.ba       0.1751224    0.153711  1.139295 0.25620

For combined results from datasets i to j, use
summary(x, subset = i:j).
For separate results, use
print(summary(x), subset = i:j).
```

The overall parameter estimates are similar to those obtained using `glm.mi()` and `bayesglm.mi()` functions in the `mi` package.

9.5 Further Reading

This chapter only covers some of the basic steps in carrying out multiple imputation in a logistic regression model using cross-sectional data. Not covered here are theoretical concepts such as the nature of missing data (e.g., *missing completely at random*, *missing at random*, and *missing not at random*). Theoretical foundations on multiple imputation are described in Rubin (1987). Chapter 1 of Rubin (1987) contains an example on how to manually pool data over the imputed datasets. It is worth spending the time carefully tracking the manual calculations to understand the basics in multiple imputation. Gelman and Hill (2007, Chap. 25) also summarizes the theory of multiple imputation. Gelman and Hill (2007) discuss why it is generally impossible to determine if data missingness is missing at random. The same point is discussed in Schafer and Graham (2002, p. 152).

Imputation techniques are constantly evolving. Open access journals are good sources for new analytic techniques and hands-on tutorials (e.g., Su et al. (in press)). Horton and colleagues (Horton and Kleinman 2007; Horton and Lipsitz 2001) have written tutorials on many new techniques on multiple imputation. They can be immediately applied. We have also learned from Allison (2002) and from the extensive works by Schafer, Graham and colleagues (Graham 2009; Schafer 1997;

Schafer and Olsen 1998; Graham et al. 1997). Their papers are widely cited by behavioral scientists. We have consulted other sources not covered above (e.g., Little and Rubin (2002)).

We have not covered analytic strategies for missing longitudinal data. Interested readers may begin with Hedeker and Gibbons (1997) who describe the pattern mixture model framework by Little (1993).

Exercises

9.1. Logistic regression on children who had corrective spinal surgery.
There is a kyphosis dataset in the rpart package. A summary of the dataset is found by calling help(kyphosis). A logistic regression can be fitted to model Kyphosis caseness as a function of the patients' characteristics:

```
> data(kyphosis, package = "rpart")
> glm1 <- glm(Kyphosis=="present" ~ Age+Number+Start,
+     data = kyphosis, family = binomial)
```

(a) What are the regression coefficients for Age, Number, and Start?
(b) What is the estimated probability of Kyphosis caseness for a 6-year-old child who has four vertebrae involved in the surgical procedure and the topmost vertebrae operated on is the 9th?

9.2. Logistic regression with missing data.
The commands below introduce random missing data into the kyphosis dataset.

```
> dat <- data(kyphosis, package = "rpart")
> kp <- lapply(kyphosis, function(x)
+    { is.na(x) <- sample(1:length(x), size=10); x })
> kp <- data.frame(kp)
> kp$kyp <- kp$Kyphosis == "present"
```

Fit a logistic regression with the kp dataset predicting kyp by Age, Number, and Start.

(a) What are the regression coefficient estimates for the covariates? Do they agree well with the coefficient estimates using the complete kyphosis data?
(b) What is the estimated probability of Kyphosis caseness for a 6-year-old child who has 4 vertebrae involved in the surgical procedure and the topmost vertebrae operated on is the 9th?

Next, following the commands below to carry out multiple imputation with the aregImpute() function. Then fit a logistic regression with the imputed data, by Age, Number, and Start.

```
> set.seed(7)
> imp <- aregImpute( ~ kyp + Age + Start + Number,
```

```
+          dat = kp, n.impute = 10, type = "pmm",
+          match = "closest")
> f <- fit.mult.impute(kyp ~ Age + Start + Number,
+          fitter=glm, xtrans=imp,
+          family = "binomial", data = kp)
```

(c) What are the imputed regression coefficient estimates for the covariates Age, Number, and Start?

(d) What is the estimated probability of Kyphosis caseness for a 6-year-old child who has 4 vertebrae involved in the surgical procedure and the topmost vertebrae operated on is the 9th?

(e) Does the estimated probability based on the imputed logistic regression agree well with that of the complete kyphosis logistic regression?

9.3. Multiple Imputation with the Amelia and Zelig Packages.

Follow the instructions in Sect. 9.4 to use the packages Amelia and Zelig to impute the missing data in kyp. Fit a logistic regression with the imputed data.

(a) What are the imputed logistic regression coefficient estimates for Age, Number, and Start?

(b) What is the estimated probability of Kyphosis caseness for a 6-year-old child whose Number and Start are 4 and 9, respectively?

(c) Does the estimated probability based on the imputed logistic regression agree well with that of the complete kyphosis logistic regression?

9.4. Multiple imputation with the mi packages.

Follow the instructions in Sect. 9.3 to use the mi package to impute the missing data in kyp and fit a logistic regression with the imputed data.

(a) What are the imputed logistic regression coefficient estimates for Age, Number, and Start?

(b) What is the estimated probability of Kyphosis caseness for a 6-year-old child whose Number and Start are 4 and 9, respectively?

(c) Does the estimated probability based on the imputed logistic regression agree well with that of the complete kyphosis logistic regression?

Chapter 10
Linear Mixed-Effects Models in Analyzing Repeated-Measures Data

10.1   The "Language-as-Fixed-Effect Fallacy"

Clark (1973) wrote a highly influential paper on the problems of treating experimental stimuli as a fixed effect (e.g., words in a psycholinguistics experiment, visual stimuli in a memory study, hypothetical scenarios in a judgment and decision-making experiment). The gist of the problem is that the dependent variable could depend systematically on the particular choice of stimuli. With a small number of stimuli, the average of the dependent variable could be higher in one condition than in another just by chance. So we must consider the variation due to stimuli, just as we consider the variance due to subjects. This is illustrated in the hypothetical data in Raaijmakers et al. (1999, Table 2). A sample of eight study participants are presented with eight items each. Items 1–4 are presented under a short stimulus-onset asynchrony (SOA) and items 5–8 are presented under a long SOA. The hypothetical data are simulated from a model with no SOA effect. Thus an SOA effect is not expected.

```
> rt <- c(546,566,567,556,595,569,527,551,
+ 567,556,598,565,609,578,554,575,
+ 547,538,568,536,585,560,535,558,
+ 566,566,584,550,588,583,527,556,
+ 554,512,536,516,578,501,480,588,
+ 545,523,539,522,540,535,467,563,
+ 594,569,589,560,615,568,540,631,
+ 522,524,521,486,546,514,473,558)
> subj <- rep(paste("s", 1:8, sep=""), 8)
> item <- rep(paste("i", 1:8, sep=""), each=8)
> SOA <- rep(c("short", "long"), each = 32)
> rsg.df <- data.frame(rt, subj, item, SOA)
```

Incorrect F statistics are obtained if, for example, data points in an analysis are collapsed over items. Raaijmakers et al. (1999) show that the $F(1,7) = 7.41$ for the SOA effect below would lead to a false inference.

Y. Li and J. Baron, *Behavioral Research Data Analysis with R*, Use R,
DOI 10.1007/978-1-4614-1238-0_10, © Springer Science+Business Media, LLC 2012

```
> summary(aov(rt ˜ SOA + item + Error(subj/SOA),
+     data = rsg.df))

Error: subj
          Df Sum Sq Mean Sq F value Pr(>F)
Residuals  7  26252    3750

Error: subj:SOA
          Df Sum Sq Mean Sq F value Pr(>F)
SOA        1   8033    8033    7.41   0.03
Residuals  7   7587    1084

Error: Within
          Df Sum Sq Mean Sq F value  Pr(>F)
item       6  22174    3696    36.9 3.3e-15
Residuals 42   4209     100
```

The *F* value of 7.41 is incorrect, so is the *p* value of 0.03. Additional details on how to avoid the problems can be found in Raaijmakers et al. (1999). An appropriate statistic can be calculated. A better study design helps, too.

Baayen et al. (2008) provide complete solutions to the problems identified by Clark (1973). Their step-by-step guide may be the most cited recent article in psycholinguistics in the last few years. The linear mixed model below treats item as a random effect. The statistic for the SOAshort effect is considerably reduced.

```
> library(lme4)
> rsg.lmer1 <- lmer(rt ˜ SOA + (1 | item) +
+       (1 | subj), data = rsg.df)
> summary(rsg.lmer1)
Linear mixed model fit by REML
Formula: rt ˜ SOA + (1 | item) + (1 | subj)
   Data: rsg.df
 AIC BIC logLik deviance REMLdev
 568 579   -279      572     558
Random effects:
 Groups   Name         Variance Std.Dev.
 item     (Intercept)  432        20.8
 subj     (Intercept)  439        20.9
 Residual              241        15.5
Number of obs: 64, groups: item, 8; subj, 8

Fixed effects:
            Estimate Std. Error t value
(Intercept)    540.9       13.1    41.4
SOAshort        22.4       15.2     1.5
```

```
Correlation of Fixed Effects:
          (Intr)
SOAshort -0.582
```

We can use the `HPDinterval()` function to show that there is no `SOA` effect. We can also use the `pvals.fun()` in the `languageR` package or the `MCMCglmm` package, or by building the model directly using WinBUGS or OpenBUGS.

```
> set.seed(101)
> rsg.mcmc <- mcmcsamp(rsg.lmer1, n = 10000)
> HPDinterval(rsg.mcmc)
$fixef
                lower upper
(Intercept) 522.984 559.7
SOAshort     -0.803  42.9
attr(,"Probability")
[1] 0.95

$ST
     lower upper
[1,] 0.407  1.12
[2,] 0.417  1.11
attr(,"Probability")
[1] 0.95

$sigma
     lower upper
[1,]    15  22.9
attr(,"Probability")
[1] 0.95

> # languageR
> library(languageR)
> rsg.mcmc <- pvals.fnc(rsg.lmer1, nsim=10000)
> rsg.mcmc$fixed
            Estimate MCMCmean HPD95lower HPD95upper
(Intercept)   540.91   540.89   522.8301     559.37
SOAshort       22.41    22.47     0.8401      44.42

              pMCMC    Pr(>|t|)
(Intercept) 0.0001    0.0000
SOAshort    0.0456    0.1455
```

10.2   Recall Scores Example: One Between and One Within Factor

We now take up the discussion of modeling correlation pattern and heteroscedasticity in repeated outcome assessments. We use the recall scores example in Stevens (1992, Sect. 13.10). Sixteen subjects are randomized into one of two groups of learning methods. The investigator collects recall scores on verbal materials after 1, 2, 3, 4, and 5 days post intervention. Thus, this example has one between-subject factor (the randomized treatment interventions) and one within-subject factor (number of days post intervention). The raw data are found in Table 13.7 of Stevens (1992). In the context of repeated-measures ANOVA, Stevens (1992) treats the days variable as a categorical variable. But it can be treated as a continuous variable in a linear mixed-effects model. In this section we will go over both, using lme() and gls().

10.2.1   Data Preparations

The raw data are organized into a data frame. The data frame is then converted into a groupedData() object.

```
> library(nlme)
> stevens.mat <- c(26, 34, 41, 29, 35, 28, 38, 43,
+ 42, 31,45,29,39,33,34,37,20,35,37,28,34,22,34,
+ 37,38,27,40,25,32,30,30,31,18,29,25,22,27,17,
+ 28,30,26,21,33,17,28,24,25,25,11,22,18,15,21,
+ 14,25,27,20,18,25,13,22,18,24,22,10,23,15,13,
+ 17,10,22,25,15,13,18,8,18,7,23,20)
> stevens.mat <- matrix(stevens.mat, ncol = 5)
> tx <- c(1,1,1,1,1,1,1,1,2,2,2,2,2,2,2,2)
> stevens.df <- data.frame(subj=paste("s",1:16,
  sep=""),
+   stevens.mat, tx = tx)
> names(stevens.df) <- c("subj","y1","y2","y3","y4",
+    "y5","tx")
> stevens.df <- reshape(stevens.df,
+   varying = paste("y",1:5, sep=""), idvar = "subj",
+   timevar = "days", sep = "", direction = "long")
> rownames(stevens.df) <- NULL
> stevens.df <- groupedData(y ~ days | subj,
+    data = stevens.df)
```

The groupedData() function specifies how the data entries are structured in a mixed model analysis. The y ˜ days | subj formula specifies that recall

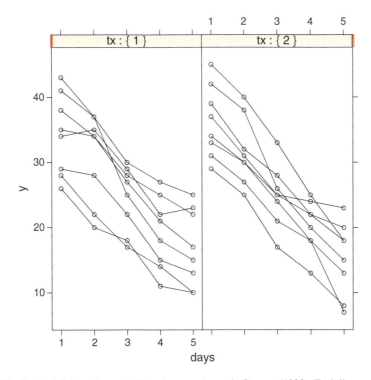

Fig. 10.1 Original data on the verbal learning experiment in Stevens (1992). Each line represents data from one study participant

scores y is the dependent variable measured across days. The vertical bar specifies that the data entries are grouped by subject ids. For reasons that will be discussed later, the variable days is kept as continuous variables, not as a categorical factor.

10.2.2   Data Visualizations

The first steps of lme () modeling often involve plotting the original data to help understand the scope of modeling if the size of the dataset is not large. Figure 10.1 is an example; the recall scores data are stratified by tx and grouped by subj so that it is easier to compare each subject's data profile across treatment groups. The strip.levels = TRUE plots the values of tx on top of each panel. The panel.superpose option tells xyplot () to overlay all the individual lines.

```
> library(lattice)
> xyplot(y ~ days | tx, groups = subj, type = "o",
+     stevens.df,
+     strip = strip.custom(strip.levels = TRUE),
+     panel = panel.superpose)
```

Figure 10.1 shows that recall scores decline steadily over the course of 5 days. The decline appears to be linear. Figure 10.1 shows no sign of an interaction between days and tx on y. Another way to visually inspect a potential interaction is through an interaction plot (not shown).

```
> with(stevens.df, interaction.plot(response = y,
+      x.factor = days, trace.factor = tx, fun = mean,
+      xlab = "Days",
+      ylab = "Recall Scores", lwd = 2, type = "b"))
```

The plot indicates no interaction either. The two treatment groups show a similar pattern of decline in recall scores over time.

10.2.3   Initial Modeling

The model below includes the fix effects of the treatment, the days, and the interaction of the two. Also included is a random effect term allowing each subject to have his/her unique intercept. The fixed effects are entered into lme() like an ordinary regression formula. The model contains only one random effect, specified in the formula as random = ˜ 1 | subj to represent one random intercept for each subject. The number 1 represents an intercept term in the formula.

```
> lme1 <- lme(y ˜ factor(tx)*factor(days),
+      random = ˜ 1 | subj, data = stevens.df)
> anova(lme1)
                          numDF denDF F-value p-value
(Intercept)                   1    56  409.07  <.0001
factor(tx)                    1    14    0.04  0.8374
factor(days)                  4    56  166.38  <.0001
factor(tx):factor(days)       4    56    1.20  0.3229
```

The anova() output shows statistically reliable fixed effect in days but no treatment effect. The F-value statistics are identical to those obtained by Stevens (1992, Table 13.9) using repeated-measures ANOVA.

10.2.4   Model Interpretation

10.2.4.1   Fixed Effects

A summary(lme1) command prints the parameter estimates. By default the (Intercept) term represents the estimated recall score for treatment Group 1 on Day 1 because both tx and days are treated as a categorical factor. The value of 34.250 can be easily verified with a simple with(stevens.df, tapply (y, list(tx, days), mean)). The coefficient of 2.0 for factor(tx)2 represents the recall score difference between 36.25 (treatment Group 2 on Day 1) and 34.25 (treatment Group 1 on Day 1). The coefficient of −17.375 for factor(days)5 represents the recall score difference between 16.875 (treatment Group 1 on Day 5) and 34.25, and so on.

```
> summary(lme1)
Linear mixed-effects model fit by REML
 Data: stevens.df
      AIC     BIC   logLik
  411.95 438.93 -193.97

Random effects:
 Formula: ~1 | subj
         (Intercept) Residual
StdDev:       4.899   2.4593

Fixed effects: y ~ factor(tx) * factor(days)
                              Value Std.Error DF
(Intercept)                  34.250    1.9381 56
factor(tx)2                   2.000    2.7408 14
factor(days)2                -3.375    1.2297 56
factor(days)3                -9.750    1.2297 56
factor(days)4               -15.125    1.2297 56
factor(days)5               -17.375    1.2297 56
factor(tx)2:factor(days)2    -1.250    1.7390 56
factor(tx)2:factor(days)3    -1.625    1.7390 56
factor(tx)2:factor(days)4    -0.875    1.7390 56
factor(tx)2:factor(days)5    -3.625    1.7390 56
                            t-value p-value
(Intercept)                 17.6724  0.0000
factor(tx)2                  0.7297  0.4776
factor(days)2               -2.7447  0.0081
factor(days)3               -7.9290  0.0000
factor(days)4              -12.3002  0.0000
factor(days)5              -14.1300  0.0000
factor(tx)2:factor(days)2   -0.7188  0.4752
factor(tx)2:factor(days)3   -0.9344  0.3541
factor(tx)2:factor(days)4   -0.5032  0.6168
factor(tx)2:factor(days)5   -2.0845  0.0417
 ...
```

The values of parameter estimates are affected by how the model is internally coded. R uses the treatment coding by default. The model.matrix() function can be used to extract the internal coding of a model (some manual editing is made to align the entries).

```
> model.matrix(lme1, data = stevens.df[
+      which(stevens.df$subj %in% c("s1", "s16")), ])
> model.matrix(lme1, data = tmp.df)
   (Int) tx2 d2 d3 d4 d5 tx2:d2 tx2:d3 tx2:d4 tx2:d5
1      1   0  0  0  0  0      0      0      0      0
16     1   1  0  0  0  0      0      0      0      0
17     1   0  1  0  0  0      0      0      0      0
32     1   1  1  0  0  0      1      0      0      0
33     1   0  0  1  0  0      0      0      0      0
48     1   1  0  1  0  0      0      1      0      0
49     1   0  0  0  1  0      0      0      0      0
64     1   1  0  0  1  0      0      0      1      0
65     1   0  0  0  0  1      0      0      0      0
80     1   1  0  0  0  1      0      0      0      1
attr(,"assign")
 [1] 0 1 2 2 2 2 3 3 3 3
attr(,"contrasts")
attr(,"contrasts")$`factor(tx)`
[1] "contr.treatment"

attr(,"contrasts")$`factor(days)`
[1] "contr.treatment"
```

The first two columns of the matrix above show how the coefficient for tx2 is coded. The coding of 1 for the (Int) term alone represents treatment Group 1 on Day 1. The 1's for both (Int) and tx2 represent Group 2 on Day 1. Thus, tx2 represents the mean difference in reaction time between the two conditions on Day 1.

The internal coding can be changed. For example, the default treatment coding can be changed to the helmert coding by saying options(contrasts = c("contr.helmert", "contr.poly")). The helmert coding causes the resulting (Intercept) term to represent the grand mean of 25.387. The coefficient of 0.262 for factor(tx)2 represents half of the marginal difference between treatment groups 2 and 1 (collapsing over days). More details on the coding of factors can be found in Chambers and Hastie (1993) and in Pinheiro and Bates (2000). The point of showing this is that R and other statistical packages may yield different parameter estimates because they do not necessarily use the same internal coding schemes.

The confidence intervals of the parameter estimates can be obtained through intervals(lme1).

```
> intervals(lme1)
Approximate 95% confidence intervals

  Fixed effects:
                         lower      est.       upper
(Intercept)            30.3676    34.250    38.13237
```

```
factor(tx)2                         -3.8785    2.000    7.87846
factor(days)2                       -5.8383   -3.375   -0.91170
factor(days)3                      -12.2133   -9.750   -7.28670
factor(days)4                      -17.5883  -15.125  -12.66170
factor(days)5                      -19.8383  -17.375  -14.91170
factor(tx)2:factor(days)2   -4.7336   -1.250    2.23363
factor(tx)2:factor(days)3   -5.1086   -1.625    1.85863
factor(tx)2:factor(days)4   -4.3586   -0.875    2.60863
factor(tx)2:factor(days)5   -7.1086   -3.625   -0.14137
attr(,"label")
[1] "Fixed effects:"

 Random Effects:
  Level: subj
                   lower   est.   upper
sd((Intercept))  3.3196  4.899  7.2298

 Within-group standard error:
  lower    est.   upper
2.0435  2.4593  2.9597
```

10.2.4.2   Random Effects

The `summary(lme1)` command also prints out estimates of random effects. The random effect of 4.899 for `(Intercept)` represents the estimated population standard deviation of the subjects' recall scores on the reference `factor(day)`, which is Day 1. We are not usually interested in the individual subject-specific random effects estimates. They can nevertheless be obtained through `ranef(lme1)`.

```
> ranef(lme1)
     (Intercept)
s1      -7.7351
s6      -6.5927
s12     -6.9021
s4      -3.5463
...
```

The `VarCorr()` function prints the estimated random effect(s) and within-subject standard deviation which are already part of `summary()` and `intervals()`.

```
> VarCorr(lme1)
subj = pdLogChol(1)
             Variance  StdDev
(Intercept) 24.0000   4.8990
Residual     6.0482   2.4593
```

The Residual variance of 6.0482 represents the within-subject error variance. The within-subject errors follow a normal distribution with a variance–covariance matrix

$$
\begin{array}{c}
\begin{array}{ccccc} \text{day1} & \text{day2} & \text{day3} & \text{day4} & \text{day5} \end{array} \\
\begin{array}{c} \text{day1} \\ \text{day2} \\ \text{day3} \\ \text{day4} \\ \text{day5} \end{array}
\begin{pmatrix}
6.05 & 0 & 0 & 0 & 0 \\
0 & 6.05 & 0 & 0 & 0 \\
0 & 0 & 6.05 & 0 & 0 \\
0 & 0 & 0 & 6.05 & 0 \\
0 & 0 & 0 & 0 & 6.05
\end{pmatrix},
\end{array}
$$

which is estimated based on the assumption of independence between the within-subject errors in recall scores over time. This independence assumption fixes the off-diagonal entries at zero. We can build alternative models that allow dependence – nonzero correlations in within-subject errors. Some of these alternative models are explored next.

10.2.5 Alternative Models

Our first model lme1 treats the days variable as a discrete time variable so that the results can be more easily compared with those obtained through repeated-measures ANOVA. However, Fig. 10.1 clearly shows a linear pattern of declining recall scores over 5 days. Therefore, it is sensible to model the days variable as a continuous variable to better model this linear pattern. Two alternative models to lme1 are sought:

1. lmeN1: continuous days and one intercept per person.
2. lmeN2: continuous days, one intercept and one slope per person.

We first center the days by Day 3 so that the Intercept term represents the estimated recall score at Day 3. The lmeN1 model below models days as a continuous variable. Like the first model lme1, lmeN1 contains a subject-specific intercept as its random effect. This random intercept is expanded in the alternative lmeN2 model to include both a random intercept and a slope per subject.

```
> stevens.df$days <- stevens.df$days - 3
> lmeN1 <- lme(y ~ factor(tx)*days,
+      random = ~ 1 | subj, data = stevens.df)
> lmeN2 <- lme(y ~ factor(tx)*days,
+      random = ~ 1 + days | subj, data = stevens.df)
```

The lmeN2 model is preferred over lmeN1 because of its smaller AIC and BIC values.

```
> anova(lmeN1, lmeN2)
      Model df    AIC     BIC  logLik    Test L.Ratio
```

```
lmeN1      1  6 424.57 438.56 -206.29
lmeN2      2  8 409.39 428.03 -196.69 1 vs 2   19.187
        p-value
lmeN1
lmeN2   1e-04
```

The `lmeN2` model equation is:

$$r_{ijk} = \beta_0 + \beta_1 \text{tx}_j + \beta_2 \text{days}_k + \beta_3 \text{tx}_j : \text{days}_k + b_{0i} + b_{1i} \text{days}_k + \epsilon_{ijk},$$

$$i = 1, \ldots, n, \quad j = 1, 2, \quad k = 1, 2, \ldots, 5; \tag{10.1}$$

$$\mathbf{b}_i = \begin{bmatrix} b_{0i} \\ b_{1i} \end{bmatrix} \sim \mathcal{N}(0, \boldsymbol{\Psi}), \quad \epsilon_{ijk} \sim \mathcal{N}(0, \sigma^2).$$

where r_{ijk} represents person i's recall scores on the kth day after treatment j.

The first few terms represent the fixed effects of the model. Specifically, the terms $r_{ijk} = \beta_0 + \beta_1 \text{tx}_j + \beta_2 \text{days}_k + \beta_3 \text{tx}_j : \text{days}_k$ are entered into `lme ()` like an ordinary regression formula. The random effects, $b_{0i} + b_{1i} \text{days}_k$, can be viewed as fitting one intercept (b_{0i}) and one linear slope (b_{1i}) for each person. The random effects are entered as `random = ~ 1 + days | subj`. The random intercepts and slopes in the vector $\mathbf{b}_i$ follow a multivariate normal distribution with a variance–covariance matrix $\boldsymbol{\Psi}$. These assumptions can be checked visually, for example, as in Fig. 10.3. This equation is a simplified version of the generic linear mixed-effects model described in Laird and Ware (1982) and in Pinheiro and Bates (2000, Sect. 2.1.1). Next we link the results of `lme ()` to model parameters.

A `summary(lmeN2)` shows an estimated average recall score of 25.125 on Day 3 ($\beta_0 = 25.125$), a non-significant treatment effect of $\beta_1 = 0.525$, an overall daily decline in recall by $\beta_2 = -4.650$, and a small difference in the daily decline between the two treatment conditions ($\beta_3 = -0.6875$). Additionally, the variance–covariance matrix $\boldsymbol{\Psi}$ yields a correlation between the random slopes and intercepts. The estimated correlation of -0.174 shows that subjects with high intercepts on Day 3 have a slightly more rapid decline of recall scores over 5 days.

```
> summary(lmeN2)
Linear mixed-effects model fit by REML
 Data: stevens.df
      AIC     BIC   logLik
   409.39 428.03 -196.69

Random effects:
 Formula: ~1 + days | subj
 Structure: General positive-definite, Log-Cholesky
            parameterization

            StdDev Corr
(Intercept) 4.9582 (Intr)
```

```
days          1.1642 -0.174
Residual      1.7695

Fixed effects: y ~ factor(tx) * days
                    Value Std.Error DF   t-value
(Intercept)        25.1250   1.77516 62   14.1536
factor(tx)2         0.5250   2.51046 14    0.2091
days               -4.6500   0.45668 62  -10.1821
factor(tx)2:days   -0.6875   0.64585 62   -1.0645
                    p-value
(Intercept)         0.0000
factor(tx)2         0.8374
days                0.0000
factor(tx)2:days    0.2912
 Correlation:
                    (Intr) fct()2 days
factor(tx)2         -0.707
days                -0.155  0.109
factor(tx)2:days     0.109 -0.155 -0.707

Standardized Within-Group Residuals:
      Min         Q1        Med         Q3         Max
-1.784284 -0.570531   0.084398   0.488157   1.791706

Number of Observations: 80
Number of Groups: 16
```

In an attempt to simplify lmeN2, we constrain this fitted correlation of −0.174 to zero. The resulting lmeNdiag model shows nearly no difference in the AIC and BIC goodness of fit.

```
> lmeNdiag <- lme(y ~ factor(tx)*days,
+     random = list(subj = pdDiag(~ days)),
+     data = stevens.df)
> anova(lmeN2, lmeNdiag)
         Model df    AIC      BIC  logLik     Test
lmeN2        1  8 409.39 428.03 -196.69
lmeNdiag     2  7 407.73 424.04 -196.86 1 vs 2
         L.Ratio p-value
lmeN2
lmeNdiag 0.33955  0.5601
```

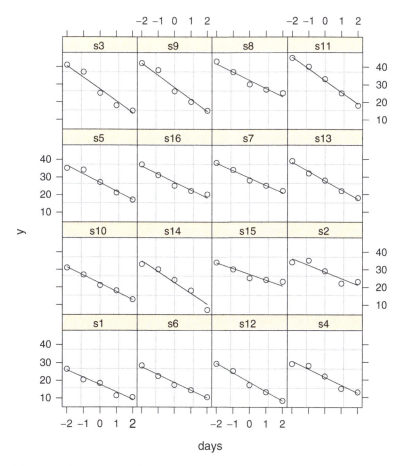

days

Fig. 10.2 A plot of observed and fitted values of model `lmeN2` by the `augPred()` function

10.2.6   Checking Model Fit Visually

Figure 10.2 shows that `lmeN2` closely fits the observed recall scores.

```
> plot(augPred(lmeN2), aspect = "4", grid = T)
```

Figure 10.3 checks the multivariate normal assumption in the random effects (see (10.1)) against the quantiles of a standard normal.

```
> qqnorm(lmeN2, ~ ranef(.), id = 0.10, cex = 0.7)
```

The `id` option is used to identify outliers in the normal quantile plot. The value of `id` sets the significance level of a two-sided test. An `id` = `0.10` sets the significance level at a two-sided 95% (the tail probability being 1 minus the value

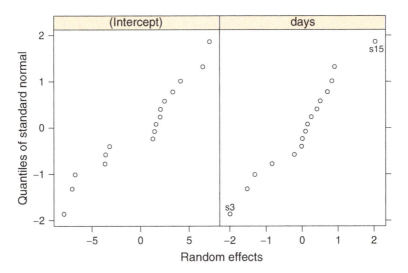

Fig. 10.3 Visual examination of the random effects assumptions in the lmeN2 model

of id divided by 2). The slopes of subjects 3 and 15 are identified as outliers. Other than these, both random effects appear to be within the normality assumption. Mild asymmetry exists, but they do not visibly deviate from normality.

There is a useful function comparePred() that visually compares the fit of two models. It works like superimposing two augPred() curves on the same plot. Figure 10.4 shows the difference between the fit of the lmeN1 and the lmeN2 models. The difference is that lmeN2 allows each subject to have his/her own growth slope over days, while lmeN1 fits one common slope for all subjects.

```
> plot(comparePred(lmeN1, lmeN2))
```

The dotted lines for lmeN2 appear to fit the observed values slightly better than the solid lines for lmeN1.

Visual evaluations of model assumptions and model fit are not usually reported in journal articles. They may be useful in methodology papers or in teaching, especially in helping visual learners to appreciate the main difference between fixed and random growth curves. There is a frequently asked question on when to use fixed and when to use random effects. Gelman and Hill (2007, Sect. 11.4) contains an informative overview of relevant issues.

10.2.7 Modeling Dependence

Figure 10.2 shows that lmeN2 fits the recall scores very well. Perhaps the model can be further improved by incorporating correlated within-subject errors. The first model we try has a symmetric but *unstructured* correlation pattern and heteroscedasticity.

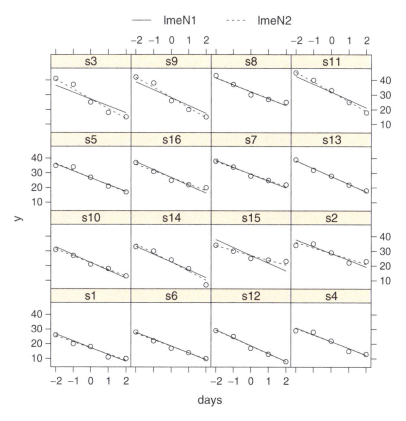

Fig. 10.4 A visual comparison of model fit between lmeN1 and lmeN2 using the comparePred() function

1. lmeN.UN: *unstructured* correlation. Two other simpler models are also tried.
2. lmeN.ARh: auto-correlation.
3. lmeN.CS: compound symmetry.

An *unstructured* variance/correlation matrix follows the pattern:

$$
\begin{array}{ccccc}
 & \texttt{day1} & \texttt{day2} & \texttt{day3} & \texttt{day4} & \texttt{day5} \\
\begin{array}{c} \texttt{day1} \\ \texttt{day2} \\ \texttt{day3} \\ \texttt{day4} \\ \texttt{day5} \end{array} &
\left(
\begin{array}{ccccc}
\sigma_{11}^{2} & & & & \\
\rho_{21} & \sigma_{22}^{2} & & & \\
\rho_{31} & \rho_{32} & \sigma_{33}^{2} & & \\
\rho_{41} & \rho_{42} & \rho_{43} & \sigma_{44}^{2} & \\
\rho_{51} & \rho_{52} & \rho_{53} & \rho_{54} & \sigma_{55}^{2}
\end{array}
\right),
\end{array}
$$

where the entries along the main diagonal $(\sigma_{11}^{2}, \ldots, \sigma_{55}^{2})$ represent heteroscedastic variances and the below-diagonal entries $(\rho_{11}, \rho_{21}, \ldots, \rho_{54})$ represent the pairwise correlations among the five assessments. The above-diagonal entries are left blank because they are symmetric to the below-diagonal entries.

We use the weight option in lme() to control the variances $\sigma_{11}^2, \ldots, \sigma_{55}^2$. The option weight = varIdent(form = ˜ 1 | days) says that we want one variance estimate per day. We also want all the pairwise correlations, which can be calcualted by saying corr = corSymm(form = ˜ 1 | subj).

```
> lmeN.UN <- lme(y ˜ factor(tx)*days,
+    random = ˜ 1 + days | subj, data = stevens.df,
+    corr = corSymm(form = ˜ 1 | subj),
+    weight = varIdent(form = ˜ 1 | days)  )
> lmeN.UN
Linear mixed-effects model fit by REML
  Data: stevens.df
  Log-restricted-likelihood: -189.89
  Fixed: y ˜ factor(tx) * days
     (Intercept)          factor(tx)2                 days
        22.67127              1.80523            -4.48012
factor(tx)2:days
        -0.58455


Random effects:
 Formula: ˜1 + days | subj
 Structure: General positive-definite, Log-Cholesky
 parameterization
            StdDev Corr
(Intercept) 4.5790 (Intr)
days        1.0291 -0.152
Residual    3.2591

Correlation Structure: General
 Formula: ˜1 | subj
 Parameter estimate(s):
 Correlation:
  1     2     3     4
2 0.918
3 0.725 0.872
4 0.768 0.638 0.503
5 0.724 0.582 0.621 0.826
Variance function:
 Structure: Different standard deviations per stratum
 Formula: ˜1 | days
 Parameter estimates:
      -2        -1         0        1        2
1.00000 1.36528 0.61444 0.54311 1.19586
Number of Observations: 80
Number of Groups: 16
```

The variances are printed in the output labeled as `Variance function`. The pairwise within-subject correlations are in the `Correlation Structure`. The first variance is constrained to 1.0 and the other variance entries are scaled relatively (Pinheiro and Bates 2000, explained in Sect. 5.1.3). The `Variance function` and the `Correlation Structure` can be put together in one place to make them easier to track:

$$
\begin{array}{c}
 \\
day1 \\
day2 \\
day3 \\
day4 \\
day5
\end{array}
\begin{array}{ccccc}
day1 & day2 & day3 & day4 & day5 \\
\left(1.000 \right. & & & & \\
.918 & 1.365 & & & \\
.725 & .872 & 0.614 & & \\
.768 & .638 & .503 & .543 & \\
.724 & .582 & .621 & .826 & \left. 1.196 \right)
\end{array}
$$

Note that the entries below the main diagonal are estimated correlation coefficients, not covariance estimates.

The first column (labeled day1) shows higher correlations for assessments made closer in time than assessments made further apart in time. This prompts the consideration of a first-order auto-regressive correlation pattern:

$$
\begin{array}{c}
 \\
day1 \\
day2 \\
day3 \\
day4 \\
day5
\end{array}
\begin{array}{ccccc}
day1 & day2 & day3 & day4 & day5 \\
\left(\sigma_{11}^2 \right. & & & & \\
\rho & \sigma_{22}^2 & & & \\
\rho^2 & \rho & \sigma_{33}^2 & & \\
\rho^3 & \rho^2 & \rho & \sigma_{44}^2 & \\
\rho^4 & \rho^3 & \rho^2 & \rho & \left. \sigma_{55}^2 \right)
\end{array}
$$

The result below shows the estimated value of $\rho = 0.887$.

```
> lmeN.ARh <- lme(y ~ factor(tx)*days,
    random = ~ 1 + days | subj, data = stevens.df,
    corr = corAR1(form=~1|subj),
    weight = varIdent(form = ~ 1 | days))
> lmeN.ARh
Linear mixed-effects model fit by REML
...
Correlation Structure: AR(1)
 Formula: ~1 | subj
 Parameter estimate(s):
   Phi
0.8871
Variance function:
 Structure: Different standard deviations per stratum
 Formula: ~1 | days
```

```
Parameter estimates:
     -2         -1          0          1          2
1.00000 1.19351 0.86062 0.84469 1.24869
```

A model comparison shows that the more complex unstructured correlation pattern has worse AIC and BIC values than the independence correlation in lmeN2.

```
> anova(lmeN2, lmeN.UN)
         Model df    AIC     BIC   logLik     Test L.Ratio
lmeN2        1  8 409.39 428.03 -196.69
lmeN.UN      2 22 423.77 475.05 -189.88 1 vs 2   13.616
         p-value
lmeN2
lmeN.UN  0.4787
```

The AR1 model shows a marginal improvement over lmeN2. However, this more complex model has comparable AIC and BIC statistics. There is no strong reason to consider this more complex model.

```
> anova(lmeN2, lmeN.ARh)
         Model df    AIC     BIC   logLik    Test
lmeN2        1  8 409.39 428.03 -196.69
lmeN.ARh     2 13 408.34 438.64 -191.17 1 vs 2
         L.Ratio p-value
lmeN2
lmeN.ARh  11.050   0.0504
```

The last correlation pattern we try is a compound symmetry pattern (all off-diagonal entries are the same). It yields no improvement.

```
> lmeN.CS <- lme(y ~ factor(tx)*days,
+     random = ~ 1 + days | subj, data = stevens.df,
+     corr = corCompSymm(form = ~ 1 | subj) )
> anova(lmeN2, lmeN.CS)
         Model df    AIC     BIC   logLik     Test L.Ratio
lmeN2        1  8 409.39 428.03 -196.69
lmeN.CS      2  9 411.39 432.36 -196.69 1 vs 2          0
         p-value
lmeN2
lmeN.CS         1
```

The lmeN2 model with independent within-subject errors remains the most promising model. Additional correlations in the within-subject errors provide no improvement. Perhaps by allowing subject-specific slopes and intercepts, lmeN2 has already captured aspects of dependence in the within-subject recall score changes over time.

Details on the varIdent() function and a list of available correlation functions can be found in Pinheiro and Bates (2000, Sects. 5.2.1, 5.3.3), respectively.

10.3   Generalized Least Squares Using gls()

Now we approach repeated-measures data using Generalized Least Squares (GLS), implemented in the gls() function. The gls() function can be viewed as the lme() function without the option random (Pinheiro and Bates 2000, Sect. 5.4). We cannot use gls() to estimate the correlation between the random slopes and intercepts. Dependence and heteroscedasticity in within-subject errors can still be estimated, using the correlation option to address the correlated errors and the weights option to address the heteroscedastic variance.

The first model is similar to the lmeN.UN model earlier. No specific structure is assumed in the within-subject errors. All entries in the matrix are allowed to be different.

```
> st.glsUN <- gls(y ~ factor(tx)*days,
+      data = stevens.df,
+      corr = corSymm(form = ~ 1 | subj),
+      weight = varIdent(form = ~ 1 | days))
> anova(st.glsUN)
Denom. DF: 76
                numDF F-value p-value
(Intercept)         1  340.06  <.0001
factor(tx)          1    0.43  0.5128
days                1  298.19  <.0001
factor(tx):days     1    1.12  0.2936
> st.glsUN
Generalized least squares fit by REML
  Model: y ~ factor(tx) * days
  Data: stevens.df
  Log-restricted-likelihood: -189.89

  Coefficients:
      (Intercept)        factor(tx)2            days
         22.67130            1.80522        -4.48011
factor(tx)2:days
         -0.58455

  Correlation Structure: General
  Formula: ~1 | subj
  Parameter estimate(s):
  Correlation:
   1     2     3     4
2 0.942
3 0.873 0.896
4 0.792 0.778 0.905
5 0.680 0.700 0.796 0.893
```

```
Variance function:
 Structure: Different standard deviations per stratum
 Formula: ~1 | days
 Parameter estimates:
      -2        -1        0        1        2
 1.00000 1.05742 0.80353 0.78321 0.98501
 Degrees of freedom: 80 total; 76 residual
 Residual standard error: 6.2197
```

Note that the fixed effects estimates and the anova() results are identical to those in lmeN.UN. Similar but not identical are the estimates in Variance function and Correlation:

$$
\begin{array}{c}
\begin{array}{ccccc} \text{day1} & \text{day2} & \text{day3} & \text{day4} & \text{day5} \end{array} \\
\begin{array}{c} \text{day1} \\ \text{day2} \\ \text{day3} \\ \text{day4} \\ \text{day5} \end{array}
\left(
\begin{array}{ccccc}
1.000 & & & & \\
.942 & 1.057 & & & \\
.873 & .896 & .803 & & \\
.792 & .778 & .905 & .783 & \\
.680 & .700 & .796 & .893 & .985
\end{array}
\right).
\end{array}
$$

Next we try AR1 and Compound Symmetry correlation patterns. The AR1 correlation estimate is 0.92435.

```
> st.glsAR1 <- gls(y ~ factor(tx)*days,
+      data = stevens.df,
+      corr = corAR1(form = ~ 1 | subj),
+      weight = varIdent(form = ~ 1 | days))
> st.glsAR1
Generalized least squares fit by REML
  Model: y ~ factor(tx) * days
  Data: stevens.df
  Log-restricted-likelihood: -191.72

 . . .

Correlation Structure: AR(1)
 Formula: ~1 | subj
 Parameter estimate(s):
    Phi
0.92435
Variance function:
 Structure: Different standard deviations per stratum
 Formula: ~1 | days
 Parameter estimates:
      -2        -1        0        1        2
 1.00000 1.09373 0.85613 0.84247 1.09187
```

```
Degrees of freedom: 80 total; 76 residual
Residual standard error: 6.2869
```

The estimated Compound Symmetry variance/correlation pattern is:

$$
\begin{array}{l}
 \quad \text{day1} \quad \text{day2} \quad \text{day3} \quad \text{day4} \quad \text{day5} \\
\begin{array}{l}
\text{day1} \\
\text{day2} \\
\text{day3} \\
\text{day4} \\
\text{day5}
\end{array}
\left(
\begin{array}{ccccc}
1.000 & & & & \\
.825 & 1.058 & & & \\
.825 & .825 & .802 & & \\
.825 & .825 & .825 & .800 & \\
.825 & .825 & .825 & .825 & 1.075
\end{array}
\right).
\end{array}
$$

```
> st.glsCS <- gls(y ~ factor(tx)*days,
+     data = stevens.df,
+     corr = corCompSymm(form = ~ 1 | subj),
+     weight = varIdent(form = ~ 1 | days))
> st.glsCS
Generalized least squares fit by REML
  Model: y ~ factor(tx) * days
  Data: stevens.df
  Log-restricted-likelihood: -202.99

Coefficients:
    (Intercept)           factor(tx)2               days
       23.02523               1.72293           -4.69308
factor(tx)2:days
       -0.62704

Correlation Structure: Compound symmetry
 Formula: ~1 | subj
 Parameter estimate(s):
    Rho
0.82521
Variance function:
 Structure: Different standard deviations per stratum
 Formula: ~1 | days
 Parameter estimates:
     -2        -1         0         1         2
1.00000 1.05777 0.80196 0.80018 1.07542
Degrees of freedom: 80 total; 76 residual
Residual standard error: 5.9462
```

The next task is model selection. The more complex unstructured model (st.glsUN) may be simplified to either an AR1 (st.glsAR1) or a compound symmetry (st.glsCS) pattern. However, the comparisons below show potentially confusing results. The compound symmetry pattern has a lower BIC but a higher

`AIC` than those in the unstructured model. The AR1 pattern has a lower `AIC` and `BIC` than those in the unstructured correlation model but the likelihood test shows no reliable difference. There are no clear indications that any of the simplified models is preferred over the unstructured model.

```
> anova(st.glsUN, st.glsCS)
          Model df    AIC     BIC   logLik    Test
st.glsUN      1 19 417.77 462.05 -189.88
st.glsCS      2 10 425.98 449.29 -202.99 1 vs 2
          L.Ratio p-value
st.glsUN
st.glsCS  26.209  0.0019
> anova(st.glsUN, st.glsAR1)
          Model df    AIC     BIC   logLik    Test
st.glsUN      1 19 417.77 462.05 -189.88
st.glsAR1     2 10 403.43 426.74 -191.72 1 vs 2
          L.Ratio p-value
st.glsUN
st.glsAR1 3.6604  0.9323
```

The AR1 model has a lower `AIC` and `BIC` than those in the compound symmetry model. A formal log likelihood test is not available because the two models are not nested.

```
> anova(st.glsCS, st.glsAR1)
          Model df    AIC     BIC   logLik
st.glsCS      1 10 425.98 449.29 -202.99
st.glsAR1     2 10 403.43 426.74 -191.72
```

The choice between `AIC` and `BIC` involves technical details beyond the scope of this book. So far as this example is concerned, there are no clear indications by either fit statistic that a simplified within-subject error pattern is preferred over the unstructured pattern. Interested readers are referred to a few recent developments (Vaida and Blanchard 2005; Liang et al. 2008; Acquah 2010).

10.4   Example on Random and Nested Effects

Maxwell and Delaney (1990, Chap. 10) describe a hypothetical study involving a random effect nested within a fixed effect. A sample of 24 clients undergo a psychological evaluation by six psychologist trainees (each trainee sees four clients). Each client receives a rating from a psychologist. The rating represents the psychologist's overall impression on the client's psychological well-being. Higher scores represent better well-being. Among the six psychologist trainees, three are female and three are male. We enter the ratings from Maxwell and Delaney (1990, p. 439) into a data frame.

```
> y <- c(49,40,31,40,42,48,52,58,42,46,50,54,54,60,
+         64,70,44,54,54,64,57,62,66,71)
> y <- array(y, dim = c(4, 3, 2))
> dimnames(y) <- list(paste("i", 1:4, sep=""),
+   paste("k", 1:3, sep=""), paste("j", 1:2, sep=""))
> nested.df <- data.frame(y = as.vector(y),
+     sex = factor(rep(c("male", "female"), c(12,12))),
+     trainee = factor(paste("tr", rep(1:6, each = 4),
+       sep="")))
> nested.df <- groupedData(y ~ sex | trainee,
+     nested.df)
```

The training director of the institution wants to know two things: (1) whether or not ratings given by psychologist trainees differ by gender and (2) whether or not there is considerable heterogeneity attributable to psychologist trainees. The heterogeneity associated with psychologists is nested within the gender effect.

Next we estimate the sex effect and the variability attributable to the trainees.

```
> lmeNested <- lme(y ~ sex, random = ~ 1 | trainee,
+                  nested.df)
```

The model equation is

$$y_{ijk} = \beta_0 + \beta_1 \text{sex}_j + b_k + \epsilon_{ijk}, \quad i = 1,\dots,4, \quad j = 1,2, \quad k = 1,\dots,6,$$

where the i's represent the clients, j's represent the gender of the kth psychologist trainee. Male trainees assign a significantly lower average rating by 14 points. The estimated standard deviation of the trainee variability is 4.0757.

```
> summary(lmeNested)
Linear mixed-effects model fit by REML
 Data: nested.df
      AIC    BIC   logLik
   163.02 167.38 -77.509

Random effects:
 Formula: ~1 | trainee
         (Intercept) Residual
StdDev:       4.0757   6.7495

Fixed effects: y ~ sex
             Value Std.Error DF t-value p-value
(Intercept)     60    3.0550 18 19.6396  0.0000
sexmale        -14    4.3205  4 -3.2404  0.0317
 Correlation:
         (Intr)
sexmale -0.707
```

```
Standardized Within-Group Residuals:
      Min         Q1        Med         Q3        Max
-1.84317 -0.46329 -0.11553   0.64599   1.42633
```

```
Number of Observations: 24
Number of Groups: 6
> anova(lmeNested)
            numDF denDF F-value p-value
(Intercept)     1    18  601.93  <.0001
sex             1     4   10.50  0.0317
```

The RLRsim package by Scheipl (2010) provides a way to test whether or not the trainee variability is statistically reliable.

```
> library(RLRsim)
> exactRLRT(lmeNested, seed = 13)

       simulated finite sample distribution of RLRT.
       (p-value based on 10000 simulated values)

data:
RLRT = 1.5766, p-value = 0.0841
```

The exactRLRT() function carries out an exact restricted likelihood ratio test of a random effect based on simulations (default is 10,000 simulations). Setting the seed ensures the same sequence of simulation and thus identical p-value = 0.0841. This exact test indicates no significant effect associated with therapist trainees. Maxwell and Delaney (1990, p.441) reach the same conclusion with a different statistical approach.

10.4.1 Treatment by Therapist Interaction

Maxwell and Delaney (1990, p.450) describe a more advanced analysis in testing a treatment by therapist interaction. A hypothetical sample of 45 individuals are randomly assigned to three treatment methods. Three therapists are involved in the delivery of all three treatment methods. Each therapist treats 5 persons with a treatment method called RET, another 5 persons with the CCT treatment, and the last 5 persons with the BMOD treatment.

```
> y<-c(40,42,36,35,37, 42,39,38,44,42, 48,44,43,48,47,
+      40,44,46,41,39, 41,45,40,48,46, 41,40,48,47,44,
+      36,40,41,38,45, 41,39,37,44,44, 39,44,40,44,43)
> method <- rep(rep(c("RET","CCT","BMOD"), each=5), 3)
> therapist <- rep(c("ther1","ther2","ther3"),each=15)
> MD450.df <- data.frame(y = y, method = method,
+            therapist = therapist)
```

In this hypothetical example, the researcher wants to know whether or not the psychotherapists have an equal affinity to all therapy methods. To get exactRLRT() to test the methods by therapists variability, we need to set up an alternative model and a null model. The alternative model contains two variance components: (1) the within-therapist variance and (2) the variance for psychotherapy methods nested within therapists. The null model contains only the therapist variance component.

```
# under alternative: therapist and ''method:therapist''
> th.mA <- lmer(y ~ method + (1 | therapist) +
+                   (1 | method:therapist), data = MD450.df)
> ranef(th.mA)
$'method:therapist'
            (Intercept)
BMOD:ther1      0.98305
BMOD:ther2     -0.14554
BMOD:ther3     -0.83751
CCT:ther1      -0.43695
CCT:ther2       0.80113
CCT:ther3      -0.36418
RET:ther1      -0.91028
RET:ther2       0.80113
RET:ther3       0.10916

$therapist
       (Intercept)
ther1    -0.076905
ther2     0.307619
ther3    -0.230714
# under null: only therapist effect
> th.m0 <- update(th.mA, . ~ . - (1 | method:therapist))
```

The effect of interest is a model between the null and the alternative, a model with only the method:therapist variance component:

```
# test single random effect of ''method:therapist''
> th.m <- update(th.mA, . ~ . - (1 | therapist))
> th.m
Linear mixed model fit by REML
Formula: y ~ method + (1 | method:therapist)
   Data: MD450.df
 AIC BIC logLik deviance REMLdev
 233 242   -111      229     223
Random effects:
 Groups            Name        Variance Std.Dev.
 method:therapist (Intercept) 1.91      1.38
 Residual                     8.78      2.96
Number of obs: 45, groups: method:therapist, 9
```

```
Fixed effects:
            Estimate Std. Error t value
(Intercept)     44.00        1.11    39.8
methodCCT       -2.00        1.56    -1.3
methodRET       -4.00        1.56    -2.6

Correlation of Fixed Effects:
            (Intr) mthCCT
methodCCT -0.707
methodRET -0.707  0.500
```

We enter all three models into exactRLRT() to test the method:therapist effect. No reliable effect is found.

```
> exactRLRT(th.m, m0 = th.m0, mA = th.mA)

    simulated finite sample distribution of RLRT.
    (p-value based on 10000 simulated values)

data:
RLRT = 0.8777, p-value = 0.1363
```

The comparisons between psychotherapy methods can be done by simulations.

```
> set.seed(101)
> th.mcmc <- mcmcsamp(th.mA, n = 1000)
> HPDinterval(th.mcmc)$fixef
                lower      upper
(Intercept) 40.9754 46.85780
methodCCT    -4.5005  0.79591
methodRET    -6.7266 -1.29033
attr(,"Probability")
[1] 0.95
```

The highest posterior density intervals indicate no reliable difference between the CCT therapy method and the BMOD (the reference condition), and the RET method has a significantly lower score than BMOD.

Exercises

10.1. Orthdontic measurement data.
The library(nlme) includes a dataset called Orthodont which contains the longitudinal orthodontic measurements for several children.

(a) Type help(Orthodont) to learn more about the dataset.
(b) Use the xyplot() command to visualize the pattern of orthodontic measurements over time. Are girls and boys grow at a different pattern?
(c) Fit a lme model of the distance measurements with fixed effects of age and Sex, and one random intercept per child.
(d) Is there a significant overall difference between girls and boys?
(e) Add to the model a random age effect per child.
(f) Is there support for adding a random age effect per child? Use compare Pred() to compare the two models visually, and use anova() to compare them statistically. Which of the two models above is preferred?
(g) Take the model with a random age effect and fit an unstructured correlation pattern with heteroscedastic variances. Does it improve the model?
(h) Fit an AR1 correlation pattern with heteroscedastic variances. Does the AR1 correlation pattern improve the model?
(i) Overall, which model is the preferred model? Why?

10.2. Ergonomic experiment.
The ergoStool dataset in library(nlme) contains repeated-measured data. Each of the nine study participants is assessed four times. At each assessment, the study participant is asked to arise from one type of ergonomic stool. The amount of effort to arise from the ergonomic stool is recorded in the variable effort. The four types of ergonomic stools are labeled in the variable Type.

(a) Analyze the ergoStool data with repeated-measures ANOVA using aov() and Error(Subject/Type) to handle the within-subject error terms. Is there a significant effect associated with ergonomic stool Type?
(b) Analyze the data with lme(). How would you use lme() to handle the within-subject errors?
(c) Does lme() show a significant effect associated with stool Type? Is it consistent with the result from repeated-measures aov()?
(d) Treating the first stool type as the reference (type T1), which other stool type requires the most effort?

10.3. Hypothetical psychotherapy study: no clustering.
In Sect. 10.4.1, we analyze the hypothetical psychotherapy example, taking into consideration the clustering of patients within therapists and psychotherapy methods. It makes sense to consider patient clusters because, for example, patients seeing the same psychotherapists under the same treatment method tend to have correlated outcomes.

Problems arise if these clusters are ignored. Here is an example. Suppose the researcher fitted an aov(y ~ method, data=MD450.df). This model ignores the patients clusters. An aov() model assumes that the outcomes of individual patients are independent of one another.

(a) Does the assumption of independent outcomes make sense to you?
(b) Run the `aov()` above. Feed the result into `summary()` to get the test statistic for the effect for psychotherapy `method`. Is there a significant `method` effect?
(c) If there is a significant `method` effect, would it still hold if the independent outcomes assumption is known to be violated?

10.4. Hypothetical psychotherapy study: `therapist` as a fixed factor.
Another problematic analytic approach is to treat `therapist` as a fixed factor, in `aov(y ~ method*therapist, data=MD450.df)`. Here the model takes into consideration the clustering effect. However, if the `method` effect is significant, it is limited to these specific therapists; the significant finding cannot be generalized beyond these three therapists.

(a) Run the fixed effects model and obtain the test statistics.
(b) Is there a significant fixed effect interaction between method and therapist?
(c) Is there a significant effect of `method`?
(d) Is it problematic to only limit a treatment effect, if significant, to within these three specific psychotherapists?

10.5. Hypothetical psychotherapy study: `therapist` variance components.
The `th.mA` model in Sect. 10.4.1 is better than the two previous models because it takes into account the psychotherapy methods nested within therapists. Effects associated with the three therapists are assumed to be a part of a population distribution. So any significant findings for psychotherapy methods can be generalized to other therapists.

   An `anova(th.mA)` prints an F-statistic of 3.6, which is lower than the 6.84 F-statistic above. A two-sided p-value can be calculated from the F-statistic, by using a numerator 2 degrees of freedom and a denominator 42 degrees of freedom. It yields a p-value of `2*(1-pf(3.6, df1=2, df2=24))` `= 0.435`.

(a) How would you interpret an F-statistic of 3.6 with a two-sided p-value of 0.435? Is there an overall difference between the three psychotherapy methods?
(b) How would you compare the effects of specific treatment methods? For example, how would you interpret the results from the highest posterior intervals in Sect. 10.4.1?
(c) What would be the overall conclusions based on these results?

Chapter 11
Linear Mixed-Effects Models in Cluster-Randomized Studies

11.1 The Television, School, and Family Smoking Prevention and Cessation Project

This example is based on the smoking cessation and prevention study reported in Flay et al. (1995) and discussed in Fitzmaurice et al. (2004b, pp. 453–455). The data file can be downloaded from the website for the Fitzmaurice et al. (2004b) book. The data file contains 1,600 observations of 7th-grade students in 135 classes nested within 28 schools in Los Angeles. Each school was randomized into one of four intervention conditions. The four intervention conditions were in a factorial design between intervention delivery method (by television or not by television in variable TV: coded 1 = Yes, 0 = No) and setting (with or without a school-based social resistance program, variable CC: coded 1 = Yes, 0 = No). Therefore, the four intervention conditions were TV+CC, TV-Only, CC-Only, and Neither. Individual students were in classes nested within schools and nested within intervention conditions.

The primary outcome variable was the tobacco and health knowledge survey summary scores assessed before and after the intervention. The total number of correct answers was recorded in a variable we call THKS. The researchers were interested in comparing postintervention THKS scores across the intervention conditions, adjusting for a covariate of preintervention THKS scores.

Studies like this are known as "group-randomized trials" or "cluster-randomized trials" (Murray 1998a; 1998b; Murray et al. 2004; Donner and Klar 2000; Janega et al. 2004) because randomization into intervention conditions is done by groups, in this example by schools. Children in the same classrooms receive the intervention together. Interactions between children and between children and teachers are likely to influence the effect of the intervention. Children in the same classes are likely to attain similar levels of knowledge on tobacco and health. Children in the same classrooms are likely to show *cluster-correlated* outcomes. Children from different classrooms within the same schools are also likely to show correlated outcomes, perhaps to a lesser extent. Correlation between members of the same group or cluster

Y. Li and J. Baron, *Behavioral Research Data Analysis with R*, Use R, DOI 10.1007/978-1-4614-1238-0_11, © Springer Science+Business Media, LLC 2012

is called the intraclass correlation (ICC) which will be defined later. In this example, the ICC can be at the class level (correlation between classmates in the same school) and at the school level (correlation among children from different classrooms within the same school). We need an analytic strategy that accounts for the ICCs.

11.2   Data Import and Preparations

The data can be directly imported into R from the URL of the data file.

```
> url <- paste("http://www.biostat.harvard.edu/",
+              "~fitzmaur/ala/tvsfp.txt", sep = "")
> tvsfp.df <- read.table(url, header = FALSE,
+ skip = 44, col.names = c("school", "class",
+ "schtx", "tvtx", "prethks", "postthks"))
```

The `skip = 44` option skips the first 44 lines because they are notes describing the data. The notes tell us that the first column is the school id, the second the class id, the third an indicator variable for the school-based intervention, and so on. The variable names are specified by `col.names`. The variables `prethks` and `postthks` contain the pre- and postintervention THKS scores. It is often useful to add documentations into the raw data files. There is no need to save the data documentation in a separate file.

Categorical variables have to be converted into factors. The pre-THKS scores are centered by the average pre-THKS score of each school.

```
> tvsfp.df$school <- factor(tvsfp.df$school)
> tvsfp.df$class  <- factor(tvsfp.df$class)
> tvsfp.df$schtx  <- factor(tvsfp.df$schtx,
+    levels=c(0,1),labels=c("sr.n", "sr.y"))
> tvsfp.df$tvtx   <- factor(tvsfp.df$tvtx,
+    levels=c(0,1),labels=c("tv.n", "tv.y"))
> pre.avg <- tapply(tvsfp.df$prethks, tvsfp.df$school,
+ mean)
> pre.len <- tapply(tvsfp.df$prethks, tvsfp.df$school,
+ length)
> pre.avg <- rep(pre.avg, times = pre.len)
# centering by school average
> tvsfp.df$prethksC <- tvsfp.df$prethks - pre.avg
```

The `tvsfp.df` data frame is now ready for analysis by the `lme4` and/or the `nlme` package. It can also be converted into a `groupedData()` object for the `nlme` package. The main advantage of a `groupedData()` object is that functions in the `nlme` package can use the hierarchical data structure to aid data visualization and analysis.

```
> library(nlme)
> tvsfp.df <-
+ groupedData(postthks ~ prethksC | school/class,
+ data = tvsfp.df, outer= list(~ schtx, ~ tvtx),
+ labels = list(x = "Pre-intervention THNKS scores",
+                y = "Post-intervention THNKS scores"),
+ units = list(x = "(-4 to +5)", y = "(0 to 6)"))
```

The postthks ~ prethksC part of a grouped data specifies the dependent and
the primary independent variables. The | school/class part specifies how the
data are grouped into clusters. Classes are nested within schools (school/class
is a shorthand for school + class %in% school). The outer option states
that the intervention conditions for ~ schtx and ~ tvtx are assigned to the
schools. The parameters outer, labels, and units are optional. They are used,
for example, when plot(tvsfp.df) is called to graph the data. These options
help determine the appearance of the graph.

11.2.1 Exploratory Analyses

Figure 11.1 summarizes the tvsfp.df data frame. Post intervention THKS scores
are plotted on the y-axis, against on the x-axis the centered preintervention THKS
scores. Each panel represents data from one school; nested within the schools are
the classes plotted with different symbols. Each symbol represents one student. The
school id numbers are plotted on top of each panel in a "strip." The schools plotted
in light grey strips were randomized to the school-based intervention, while schools
in dark grey were not. Least-squares regression lines are plotted for each school.

Figure 11.1 shows that classes nested within schools are not very different from
one another. For example, there are no obvious pattern of clusters of squares or
triangles that deviate from the overall pattern. Figure 11.1 is produced with the
commands below.

```
> library(lattice)
> # grey90 means 90% lighter than black
> tcol <- c("grey50", "grey90")
> bg.col <- rep(tcol[1],
+     length(levels(tvsfp.df$school)))
> tt <- tapply(as.character(tvsfp.df$schtx),
+     tvsfp.df$school, function(x) {x[1]})
> # light grey if schtx, dark grey if no schtx
> bg.col[tt == "sr.y"] <- tcol[2]
> xyplot(jitter(postthks) ~ prethksC | school,
+   data = tvsfp.df,
+   groups = class, outer= TRUE,
+   panel = function(x, y, ...)
```

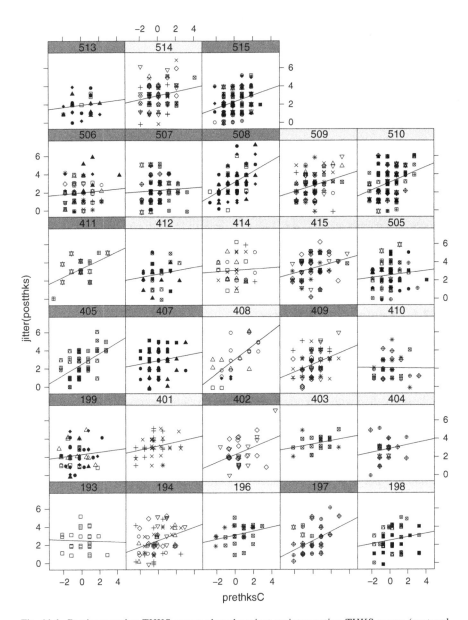

Fig. 11.1 Postintervention THKS scores plotted against preintervention THKS scores (centered by school averages). Each panel represents data from one school. Least square regression lines are plotted for each school. Different plotting symbols represent individual students nested within classes. The schools plotted in *light grey* strips were randomized to the school-based intervention, while schools in *dark grey* strips were not

```
+   {
+   panel.superpose(x, y, ...)
+   panel.lmline(x, y, ...)
+   },
+   strip = function(..., which.panel, bg)
+   {
+   strip.default(..., which.panel = which.panel,
+   bg=rep(bg.col, length = which.panel)[which.panel])
+   }        )
```

The strip = function(...) controls the appearance of the strip for each
school. By looking at the plot, there appears to be no visible difference between
schools that were randomized to the school-based intervention condition (with light
grey strips) and schools that were not (with dark grey strips). The color of each strip
is indexed by which.panel.

The individual panel.lmline(x, y, ...) plots the linear relationships
between pre- and post-THKS scores in each school. The association is strong in
some schools (e.g., school ids 405, 408, and 510) but less so in other schools (e.g.,
193, 410, and 505). Later in this chapter we will model one unique slope between
the pre- and post-THKS scores in each school.

The tapply() commands below calculate the average postintervention
changes in THKS scores. The "Neither" group (the tv.n and sr.n combination)
had an average change of 0.21. School-based intervention alone showed a 0.92
change. TV-alone showed a 0.45 change. The combined school and TV-based
intervention produced a 0.88 change. School-based intervention alone yielded the
greatest change of nearly one point in the THKS score.

```
> attach(tvsfp.df)
> tapply(postthks - prethks, list(schtx, tvtx), mean)
          tv.n      tv.y
sr.n 0.2090261 0.4519231
sr.y 0.9184211 0.8433420'
> tapply(postthks - prethks, schtx, mean)
     sr.n      sr.y
0.3297491 0.8807339
> tapply(postthks - prethks, tvtx, mean)
     tv.n      tv.y
0.5455680 0.6395494
```

Next we examine the group differences quantitatively, taking into consideration
the intraclass correlations among members of the same class and members of the
same school.

11.3 Testing Intervention Efficacy with Linear Mixed-Effects Models

The first model to try is guided by Fig. 11.1. It contains the fixed treatment effects schtx*tvtx and the random slopes and intercepts between pre- and post-THKS scores for each school. Also because the classes are nested within schools, we try a random slope per class in (1 + prethksC | school/class). But we see a problem right away. The Random effects: portion of the output shows a correlation of 1.0 between the random slopes and intercepts. A correlation of 1.0 implies complete overlap between the estimates of the slopes and intercepts, a sign of model overparameterization (Baayen et al. 2008). The problem remains after the clustering by class is simplified to (1 + prethksC | school). Thus, the random slopes model hinted by Fig. 11.1 is not feasible.[1]

```
> library(lme4)
> tv.lmer1 <- lmer(postthks ~ prethksC + schtx*tvtx +
+                   (1 + prethksC | school/class),
+                   data = tvsfp.df)
>
> summary(tv.lmer1, corr=F)
Linear mixed model fit by REML
Formula: postthks ~ prethksC + schtx * tvtx +
    (1 + prethksC | school/class)
   Data: tvsfp.df
  AIC  BIC logLik deviance REMLdev
 5394 5459  -2685     5355    5370
Random effects:
 Groups       Name        Variance Std.Dev. Corr
 class:school (Intercept) 0.06853  0.2618
              prethksC    0.00143  0.0379   1.000
 school       (Intercept) 0.07951  0.2820
              prethksC    0.01244  0.1115   1.000
 Residual                 1.58148  1.2576
Number of obs: 1600, groups: class:school, 135;
    school, 28

Fixed effects:
                Estimate Std. Error t value
(Intercept)       2.2899     0.1201   19.07
prethksC          0.2888     0.0341    8.47
schtxsr.y         0.5841     0.1633    3.58
```

---

[1] The same model, if instead fitted by lme() in the nlme package, causes a convergence error because of model overparameterization.

```
tvtxtv.y               0.2438      0.1584     1.54
schtxsr.y:tvtxtv.y    -0.1771      0.2267    -0.78

Correlation of Fixed Effects:
            (Intr) prthkC schtx. tvtxt.
prethksC     0.315
schtxsr.y   -0.664 -0.006
tvtxtv.y    -0.680  0.010  0.502
schtxsr.y:.  0.478  0.003 -0.721 -0.699
```

To simplify `tv.lmer1`, we drop the random slopes.

```
> tv.lmer2 <- lmer(postthks ~ prethksC + schtx*tvtx +
+                  (1 | school/class), data = tvsfp.df)
```

Next, we fit a third model `tv.lmer3` which has no random `class` effects.
A model comparison shows that dropping the `class` clustering would produce
considerable difference in the likelihood ratio statistic, a rationale to keep the
`class` effect.

```
> tv.lmer3 <- lmer(postthks ~ prethksC + schtx*tvtx +
+                  (1 | school), data = tvsfp.df)
> anova(tv.lmer2, tv.lmer3)
Data: tvsfp.df
Models:
tv.lmer3: postthks ~ prethksC + schtx * tvtx +
          (1 | school)
tv.lmer2: postthks ~ prethksC + schtx * tvtx +
          (1 | school/class)
          Df  AIC  BIC logLik Chisq Chi Df Pr(>Chisq)
tv.lmer3  7 5392 5430  -2689
tv.lmer2  8 5385 5428  -2684  9.55      1      0.002
```

The `tv.lmer2` model is preferred over `tv.lmer3` because it has a smaller AIC
and BIC statistic (Pinheiro and Bates 2000, Sect. 2.4.1). The `Chisq` statistic
for the likelihood ratio test also shows a significant difference between the two
models. Generally, model comparisons based on the REML likelihood statistic
and the likelihood ratio test by `anova(tv.lmer2, tv.lmer3)` only makes
sense between models with the same fixed-effects structure and the same contrast
coding for factors within the fixed-effects structure (Pinheiro and Bates 2000,
Sects. 1.2.1, 5.4).

Model assumptions should be checked before we settled with `tv.lmer2`. The
main assumption is that the residuals are normally distributed, which can be checked
with `qqnorm(resid(tv.lmer2))`.

The `qqnorm.lme()` function in the `nlme` package provides convenient
features. To demonstrate how to use some of these features, the same model is fitted
with `lme()`.

Fig. 11.2 Normal plot of residuals for the `tv.lmer2` model

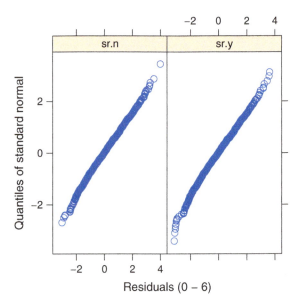

```
> detach(package:lme4) # avoid conflicts
> library(nlme)
> tv.lme <- lme(postthks ~ prethksC + schtx*tvtx,
+               random = ~ 1 | school/class,
+               data = tvsfp.df)
> qqnorm(tv.lme, ~ resid(.) | schtx)
```

The residuals in Fig. 11.2 seem to follow a normal distribution. No visible differences between students who had and had not received the school-based treatment.

The effects in the `tv.lmer2` model can be tested by the `HPDinterval()` function. There is a statistically significant `schtx` treatment effect but no `tvtx` treatment effect.

```
> set.seed(13)
> samp1 <- mcmcsamp(tv.lmer2, n=1000)
> HPDinterval(samp1)
$fixef
                        lower  upper
(Intercept)             2.082  2.612
prethksC                0.242  0.343
schtxsr.y               0.230  0.983
tvtxtv.y               -0.125  0.571
schtxsr.y:tvtxtv.y     -0.887  0.115
attr(,"Probability")
[1] 0.95
```

```
$ST
        lower upper
[1,]  0.0545 0.270
[2,]  0.1283 0.322
attr(,"Probability")
[1]  0.95

$sigma
        lower upper
[1,]    1.22   1.32
attr(,"Probability")
[1]  0.95
```

The Wald F test and *p*-values for the fixed effects can be obtained from the nlme package (*p*-values not available from the lme4 package). The conclusions are comparable to those drawn from the HPDinterval() simulations above.

```
> anova(tv.lme)
              numDF denDF F-value p-value
(Intercept)       1  1464 1517.47  <.0001
prethksC          1  1464  127.53  <.0001
schtx             1    24    9.56  0.0050
tvtx              1    24    0.06  0.8123
schtx:tvtx        1    24    1.79  0.1941
```

11.4 Model Equation

Let Y_{ijk} denote the postintervention THKS score of the ith student nested within the jth classroom within the kth school. The final tv.lmer2 model follows this symbolic form:

$$Y_{ijk} = \beta_0 + \beta_1 \text{PreTHKSC} + \beta_2 \text{CC} + \beta_3 \text{TV}$$
$$+ \beta_4 \text{CC} \times \text{TV} + b_k + b_{jk} + \epsilon_{ijk},$$
$$b_k \sim N(0, \sigma_2^2); \quad b_{jk} \sim N(0, \sigma_3^2); \quad \epsilon_{ijk} \sim N(0, \sigma_1^2). \tag{11.1}$$

Each student's postintervention THKS score is a function of the following:

- β_0: an intercept representing the estimated postthks score for a student in the "Neither" group and whose prethks score is at his or her school's average.
- β_1: the estimated postthks score for a student who scored at baseline 1 point higher than the school average.

- β_2: estimated postthks score difference between the "school" and "no school" conditions (effect of school-based social resistance curriculum).
- β_3: estimated postthks effect due to TV, and
- β_4: effect of delivering school-based curriculum by TV versus not by TV.

So far the model formula is straightforward and should be familiar to someone who has taken a course on multiple regression. These are the fixed effects – specific contrasts between the treatment conditions of a 2x2 factorial design.

There are three additional terms in the model, b_k, b_{jk}, and ϵ_{ijk}. The b_k coefficient can be thought of as fitting individual postthks intercepts for each of the kth school, in a way similar to the intercepts of the individual regression lines in Fig. 11.1. The notation $b_k \sim N(0, \sigma_2^2)$ means that b_k is assumed to follow a normal distribution with a mean of zero and a variance of σ_2^2. In other words, we do not try to solve for the individual intercepts, which would take up many degrees of freedom. Rather, we assume that the b_k parameters are a *random* sample of population parameters which belong to a normal distribution with mean zero and variance σ_2^2. We only need to spend one degree of freedom on finding an estimate for σ_2^2.

Similarly, the variance associated with the clusters of classes, b_{jk}, are assumed to follow a normal distribution with a mean of zero and a variance of σ_3^2. The residual error $\epsilon_{ijk} \sim N(0, \sigma_1^2)$ has a mean of zero and a variance of σ_1^2. We are interested in the variance components associated with the classes and schools.

```
> summary(tv.lmer2)
Linear mixed model fit by REML
Formula: postthks ~ prethksC + schtx * tvtx +
    (1 | school/class)
  Data: tvsfp.df
  AIC   BIC  logLik deviance REMLdev
 5399  5442  -2691     5369    5383
Random effects:
 Groups        Name         Variance Std.Dev.
 class:school  (Intercept)  0.0692   0.263
 school        (Intercept)  0.0779   0.279
 Residual                   1.6008   1.265
Number of obs: 1600, groups: class:school, 135;
                                    school, 28


Fixed effects:
                    Estimate Std. Error t value
(Intercept)            2.346      0.137   17.08
prethksC               0.293      0.026   11.27
schtxsr.y              0.610      0.196    3.12
tvtxtv.y               0.213      0.192    1.11
schtxsr.y:tvtxtv.y    -0.365      0.274   -1.34
```

```
Correlation of Fixed Effects:
            (Intr) prthkC schtx. tvtxt.
prethksC    -0.007
schtxsr.y   -0.702 -0.005
tvtxtv.y    -0.715  0.015  0.502
schtxsr.y:.  0.502  0.002 -0.716 -0.702
```

The random effects (1 | school/class) are unpacked behind the scene into ~ 1|school for b_k and ~ 1|class %in% school for b_{jk}.

The estimated postthks score is 2.35 (β_0) for a child who is in the reference condition (no TV, no social resistance curriculum) and whose pre-THKS scores are at the school average. For each unit increase in the baseline prethks score from the school average, the postthks scores are estimated to increase by $\beta_1 = 0.29$. Intervention delivered along with a social resistance curriculum is expected to boost postthks scores by $\beta_2 = 0.61$ (in comparison with no social resistence curriculum). Intervention delivered by television is expected to boost postthks scores by $\beta_3 = 0.21$ (in comparison with no television). Television-delivered social resistance curriculum shows a slightly lower score of $\beta_4 = -0.37$ than curriculum not delivered by TV. The t-statistics indicate that the social resistance curriculum but not the TV-delivered intervention show a statistically significant effect.

The "Random effects" section of the output shows that $\sigma_2 = 0.279$, $\sigma_3 = 0.263$, and $\sigma_1 = 1.265$.

There are 27 degrees of freedom for the 28 schools, 24 of them are for the schtx treatment effect. That is because one degree of freedom each is used for σ_1^2, σ_2^2, and σ_3^2. By contrast, 1464 degrees of freedom are associated with the prethksC scores from the students. The point of checking the degrees of freedom is to show that, in a group-randomized trial, the statistics for the intervention effects is associated with the number of randomized groups.

Controlling for the preintervention THKS scores, school-based intervention is associated with a significantly higher postintervention THKS scores.

11.5   Multiple-Level Model Equations

Equation (11.1) can also be represented in a multiple-level model by Bryk and Raudenbush (2002). We begin by modeling each student's post-THKS score as a function of a classroom mean, baseline THKS score, and a random error.

Level 1 Model (individual student i):

$$Y_{ijk} = \alpha_{0jk} + \alpha_1 \text{PreTHKSC}_{ijk} + \epsilon_{ijk}, \tag{11.2}$$

where α_{0jk} is the mean postintervention THKS scores of classroom j in school k. There is only one overall slope α_1 for the baseline THKS scores.

Level 2 Model (class j): Each classroom average score α_{0jk} is further modeled in the second-level model as a function of a school mean plus random variability for classes:

$$\alpha_{0jk} = \beta_{00k} + r_{0jk}, \tag{11.3}$$

where β_{00k} is the average postintervention THKS scores in school k.

Level 3 Model (school k): The school means β_{00k} are modeled as a function of treatment interventions and a random error per school. The treatment effects are specified at the school level because the unit of random assignment is the school.

$$\beta_{00k} = \gamma_{000} + \gamma_{100}CC_k + \gamma_{200}TV_k + \gamma_{300}CC_k \times TV_k + u_{00k}, \tag{11.4}$$

where γ_{000} represents the grand mean, γ_{100} the school-based intervention effect, γ_{200} the TV-based intervention effect, γ_{300} the extent to which the two interventions combined produces a synergistic effect, and u_{00k} represents the random variability for schools.

Substituting the school-level (11.4) into the class-level (11.3) and then into the individual-level (11.2), we get

$$
\begin{aligned}
Y_{ijk} = \;& \gamma_{000} + \alpha_1 \mathrm{PreTHKSC}_{ijk} + \gamma_{100}CC_k + \gamma_{200}TV_k \\
& + \gamma_{300}CC_k \times TV_k + u_{00k} + r_{0jk} + \epsilon_{ijk}, \\
& u_{00k} \sim N(0,\sigma_2^2); \quad r_{0jk} \sim N(0,\sigma_3^2); \quad \epsilon_{ijk} \sim N(0,\sigma_1^2).
\end{aligned}
\tag{11.5}
$$

The combined equation (11.5) bears a close resemblance to (11.1). In fact, they are equivalent. The differences are only notational. The `lme4` and `nlme` packages can handle multiple-level modeling. Beginners may find the multilevel approach particularly useful because it helps to unpack the model into more manageable components. But the underlying model is the same.

11.6 Model Equation in Matrix Notations

We can rewrite (11.1) in matrix notation. Matrix notation is the standard in the literature (e.g., Cnaan et al. (1997); Pinheiro and Bates (2000); Diggle et al. (2002); Fitzmaurice et al. (2004b)). Laird and Ware's (1982) seminal paper on mixed models use matrix notation. It helps to have a basic appreciation of matrix notation because it is used by many tutorials and manuals of statistical computer software programs. This section covers how to convert (11.1) and its equivalent multilevel (11.5) into matrix notation. Baayen et al. (2008) also provides an exposition using example data from linguistics research. More details can be found in Pinheiro and Bates (2000).

We can condense the fixed effects, $Y_{ijk} = \beta_0 + \beta_1 \mathrm{PreTHKSC} + \beta_2 CC + \beta_3 TV + \beta_4 CC \times TV$, into $Y_{ijk} = \mathbf{X}_{ijk}\beta$, where

$$
\mathbf{X}_{ijk} =
\begin{array}{c}
i = 1 \\
i = 2 \\
\vdots \\
i = 1{,}599 \\
i = 1{,}600
\end{array}
\overset{\text{intercept}\quad \text{preTHKSC}\quad \text{CC}\quad \text{TV}\quad \text{CC}\times\text{TV}}{
\left(
\begin{array}{ccccc}
1 & 2 & 1 & 0 & 0 \\
1 & 4 & 1 & 0 & 0 \\
  & \vdots & & & \\
1 & 3 & 0 & 0 & 0 \\
1 & 3 & 0 & 0 & 0
\end{array}
\right)}
, \qquad (11.6)
$$

$$
\text{and} \quad \beta =
\begin{pmatrix}
\beta_0 \\
\beta_1 \\
\beta_2 \\
\beta_3 \\
\beta_4
\end{pmatrix}.
$$

The $\mathbf{X}_{ijk}$ matrix is the "model matrix" or "design matrix," derived from adding columns to the data matrix to accommodate the model specifications. In this case, two columns are added – a column of 1's to represent the overall intercept β_0 and a column of the CC × TV interaction to represent the schools that received both interventions. The four separate parameters β_0 to β_4 are collected in one column vector β.

To see how matrix multiplication simplifies the calculation, we begin by extracting a fraction of the model matrix in (11.6). This simple model matrix will be used to estimate the group means of the four intervention groups – neither intervention, school intervention only, TV intervention only, and both school and TV interventions combined. We begin by this simple model matrix:

$$
\mathbf{X} =
\begin{array}{c}
\text{no CC} \\
\text{yes CC}
\end{array}
\overset{\text{intercept}\quad \text{CC}}{
\left(
\begin{array}{cc}
1 & 0 \\
1 & 1
\end{array}
\right)},
\quad \text{and } \beta =
\begin{pmatrix}
\beta_0 \\
\beta_2
\end{pmatrix}
=
\begin{pmatrix}
2.3459 \\
0.6097
\end{pmatrix},
$$

where $\mathbf{X}$ consists of a column of 1's to represent β_0, the overall average of postthks scores; and a column of 0 and 1 to represent the contrast between school-based intervention (coded 1) and the reference, no school-based intervention (coded 0). Therefore, when $\mathbf{X}$ and β are multiplied together, the result is an overall average of postthks score (the column of 1 times 2.3459 which yields [2.3459, 2.3459]), plus adjustments due to the contrast (the column of [0, 1] times 0.6097, which yields [0, 0.6097]). By matrix multiplication $\mathbf{X} \cdot \beta$ equals:

$$
\begin{bmatrix} 1 & 0 \\ 1 & 1 \end{bmatrix}
\begin{bmatrix} 2.3459 \\ 0.6097 \end{bmatrix}
=
\begin{bmatrix} 1 \cdot 2.3459 + 0 \cdot 0.6097 \\ 1 \cdot 2.3459 + 1 \cdot 0.6097 \end{bmatrix}
=
\begin{bmatrix} 2.3459 \\ 2.9556 \end{bmatrix}.
$$

The matrix multiplication can be done in the following R command.

```
matrix(c(1, 1, 0, 1), ncol = 2) %*%
    matrix(c(2.3459068, 0.6097407), ncol = 1)
          [,1]
[1,] 2.345907
[2,] 2.955647
```

The result of this multiplication, [2.3459, 2.9556], represents the model's best estimates of group means given that there is no TV intervention. Additional adjustment will have to be made to account for the TV-intervention contrast, which is explained next.

From the output of summary(tvlme1) we know that the TV-intervention contrast is 0.2130955. Thus, we adjust the no-TV group means [2.3459, 2.9556], by the same amount of 0.2131 to get [2.5590, 3.1687]. Also, the CC:TV interaction entails a contrast of −0.3654. We add this adjustment to the mean of the group with both school and TV interventions to get $3.1687 - 0.3654 = 2.8033$. Thus, the model's estimates of the four group means are

$$
\begin{array}{c}
 & \begin{array}{cc} \text{no TV} & \text{yes TV} \end{array} \\
\begin{array}{c} \text{no CC} \\ \text{yes CC} \end{array} & \left(\begin{array}{cc} 2.35 & 2.56 \\ 2.96 & 2.80 \end{array} \right).
\end{array}
$$

The estimates are close to the observed group means below.

```
tapply(tvsfp.df$postthks,
    list(tvsfp.df$schtx, tvsfp.df$tvtx), mean)
          tv.n       tv.y
sr.n 2.361045 2.538462
sr.y 2.968421 2.822454
```

Our matrix calculations do not produce an exact fit, in part because we have not taken into consideration the prethksC covariate and the b_k and b_{jk} random effects. But this is just a simple illustrative example to show how (11.1) can be streamlined, and to set things up for a general formulation of a mixed-effects model as described originally in Laird and Ware (1982).

Equation (11.7) below adds two random effects and their model design matrices. The two random effects are $\mathbf{Z}_{ik} \, \mathbf{b}_k$ for the school clusters and $\mathbf{Z}_{ijk} \, \mathbf{b}_{jk}$ for the class clusters, respectively. The $\mathbf{Z}_{ik}$ model matrix fits one constant per school and the $\mathbf{Z}_{ijk}$ model matrix fits one constant per class.

$$\mathbf{Y}_{ijk} = \mathbf{X}_i\,\beta + \mathbf{Z}_{ik}\,\mathbf{b}_k + \mathbf{Z}_{ijk}\,\mathbf{b}_{jk} + \epsilon_{ijk}, \tag{11.7}$$

$$b_k \sim \mathcal{N}(\mathbf{0}, \sigma_2^2), \quad b_{jk} \sim \mathcal{N}(\mathbf{0}, \sigma_3^2), \quad \epsilon_{ijk} \sim \mathcal{N}(\mathbf{0}, \sigma_e^2 \mathbf{I}).$$

$$\mathbf{Y}_i = \begin{bmatrix} 3 \\ 4 \\ 3 \\ \vdots \\ 3 \\ 3 \end{bmatrix}, \mathbf{X}_i = \begin{bmatrix} 1\ 2\ 1\ 0\ 0 \\ 1\ 4\ 1\ 0\ 0 \\ 1\ 4\ 1\ 0\ 0 \\ \vdots \\ 1\ 3\ 0\ 0\ 0 \\ 1\ 3\ 0\ 0\ 0 \end{bmatrix}, \mathbf{Z}_{ik} = \begin{matrix} \text{Sch01} \\ \text{Sch02} \\ \text{Sch03} \\ \\ \text{Sch27} \\ \text{Sch28} \end{matrix}\begin{bmatrix} 1 \\ 1 \\ 1 \\ \vdots \\ 1 \\ 1 \end{bmatrix}, \text{and } \mathbf{Z}_{ijk} = \begin{matrix} \text{Sch01.cls01} \\ \text{Sch01.cls02} \\ \text{Sch01.cls03} \\ \\ \text{Sch28.cls05} \\ \text{Sch28.cls06} \end{matrix}\begin{bmatrix} 1 \\ 1 \\ 1 \\ \vdots \\ 1 \\ 1 \end{bmatrix}.$$

The school matrix $\mathbf{Z}_{ik}$ and the class matrix $\mathbf{Z}_{ijk}$ can be combined into one single matrix $\mathbf{Z}$. Likewise, the school and class random effects b_k and b_{jk} can be combined into a single vector b. The result is a general mixed-model equation:

$$\mathbf{Y} = \mathbf{X}\beta + \mathbf{Z}b + \epsilon. \tag{11.8}$$

$$b_k \sim \mathcal{N}(\mathbf{0}, \sigma_2^2), \quad b_{jk} \sim \mathcal{N}(\mathbf{0}, \sigma_3^2), \quad \epsilon_{ijk} \sim \mathcal{N}(\mathbf{0}, \sigma_e^2 \mathbf{I}).$$

Statistical computer packages on linear mixed-effects models support this general equation. In R, the lme() function uses the fixed parameter to represent $\mathbf{X}, \beta$, and the random parameter to represent $\mathbf{Z}, b$. Similar syntax rules apply in SAS and SPSS. Although in this particular example two separate RANDOM statements are needed in SAS and SPSS to account for the class clusters and the school clusters, respectively. For example, the SAS code for the same lme() analysis can be found on Donald Hedeker's website at http://tigger.uic.edu/~hedeker/tvsfpmix.sas.txt (last accessed June, 2011).

In R, the school and class random effects b_k and b_{jk} can be printed. They represent the estimated adjustments to postthks scores for each school and class.

```
ranef(tvlme1)
Level: school
      (Intercept)
193   0.05632247
194   0.10514216
196   0.06918219
[... skipped ...]
514   0.09993460
515  -0.06579224

Level: class %in% school
                (Intercept)
193/193101   0.0500300619
194/194101  -0.0595581908
```

```
194/194102   0.0044636599
[... skipped ...]
515/515112   0.0927875423
515/515113  -0.2986458234
```

11.7 Intraclass Correlation Coefficients

The Intraclass Correlation Coefficients (ICCs) can be calculated for both the class clusters and for school clusters, using the formula in Smeeth and Ng (2002):

$$\hat{\rho} = \frac{\mathrm{MS}_b - \mathrm{MS}_w}{\mathrm{MS}_b + (m-1)\,\mathrm{MS}_w}, \tag{11.9}$$

where m is the average cluster size (e.g., average number of students nested within a class). MS_b and MS_w are the between- and within-cluster mean squares, respectively, obtained from the output of a one-way ANOVA table. For example, for school clusters, we do `aov(postthks ~ school, data = tvsfp.df)`. The Sum of Squares for `school` divided by its degrees of freedom is the MS_b, the mean square error attributable to different schools. The Sum of Squares for the `Residuals`, divided by its degrees of freedom, is MS_w. Because the clusters varied in size, an average cluster size m_0 is estimated:

$$m_0 = \frac{1}{k-1}\left(n - \sum_{i=1}^{k} m_i^2/n\right),$$

where k is the number of clusters and m_i is the size of each of the k clusters.

The R code below shows how to calculate the ICCs associated with schools and classes, respectively. Note that these are the ICCs without adjustments of covariates such as the treatment assignments and preintervention THKS scores. Considerations of covariates are likely to affect the variance components associated with school and class clusters and thus the ICCs. In the next section we will explain how to calculate ICCs from the output of mixed models.

```
# Estimated ICC of students nested within schools
> aov(postthks ~ school, data = tvsfp.df)
Call:
   aov(formula = postthks ~ school, data = tvsfp.df)

Terms:
                    school Residuals
Sum of Squares    248.6751 2809.3993
Deg. of Freedom         27      1572
```

```
Residual standard error: 1.336843
Estimated effects may be unbalanced
> MSb <- 248.6751 / 27
> MSw <- 2809.3993 / 1572
> k <- tapply(tvsfp.df$postthks,
+         list(tvsfp.df$school), length)
> m0 <- (1 / (length(k) - 1)) *
+       (1600 - sum(k^2) / 1600)
> (MSb - MSw) / (MSb + (m0 - 1) * MSw)
[1] 0.06842898
> # Estimated ICC of students nested within classes
> aov(postthks ~ class, data = tvsfp.df)
Call:
   aov(formula = postthks ~ class, data = tvsfp.df)

Terms:
                   class Residuals
Sum of Squares   549.5563 2508.5180
Deg. of Freedom       134      1465

Residual standard error: 1.308548
Estimated effects may be unbalanced
> MSb <- 549.5563 / 134
> MSw <- 2508.5180 / 1465
> k <- tapply(tvsfp.df$postthks,
+         list(tvsfp.df$class), length)
> m0 <- (1 / (length(k) - 1)) *
+       (1600 - sum(k^2) / 1600)
> (MSb - MSw) / (MSb + (m0 - 1) * MSw)
[1] 0.1054988
```

As expected, the 0.11 ICC for classes is slightly greater than the 0.07 ICC for schools. Smeeth and Ng (2002) discuss the pros and cons in making a statistical test of two ICCs (p. 413). Equation (11.9) is similar to the "Case 2" equation in Shrout and Fleiss (1979, p.423).

11.8   ICCs from a Mixed-Effects Model

ICCs can also be calculated by lme() or lmer(). The ICC for schools is the between-school variance, σ_2^2, divided by the total variance (sum of σ_1^2, σ_2^2, and σ_3^2). The ICC for classes uses the same denominator. The numerator is the sum of two variances, the between-class variance and between-school variance. We calculate the $\sigma_1^2, \sigma_2^2, \sigma_3^2$ variance components without adjusting for treatment and baseline THKS scores:

```
> tvlme0 <- lme(postthks ~ 1,
+              random = ~ 1 | school/class,
+              data = tvsfp.df)
> summary(tvlme0)
Linear mixed-effects model fit by REML
 Data: tvsfp.df
       AIC        BIC      logLik
  5513.224  5534.733  -2752.612

Random effects:
 Formula: ~1 | school
         (Intercept)
StdDev:   0.3414634

 Formula: ~1 | class %in% school
         (Intercept) Residual
StdDev:   0.2915119 1.312856

[... Fixed effects skipped... ]

Number of Groups:
              school class %in% school
                  28              135
> 0.341^2 / (0.341^2 + 1.313^2) # school ICC
[1] 0.06318761
> (0.341^2+0.292^2)/(0.341^2+0.292^2+1.313^2) # class
[1] 0.1046708
```

The ICCs are:

$$\text{ICC}_{i|k} = \frac{\sigma_2^2}{\sigma_1^2 + \sigma_2^2 + \sigma_3^2} = \frac{.341^2}{1.313^2 + .341^2 + .292^2} = 0.063$$

$$\text{ICC}_{i|jk} = \frac{\sigma_2^2 + \sigma_3^2}{\sigma_1^2 + \sigma_2^2 + \sigma_3^2} = \frac{.341^2 + .292^2}{1.313^2 + .341^2 + .292^2} = 0.105$$

To interpret, the ICC for school clusters is the percentage of the total variance accounted for by the school clusters. The ICC for class clusters is percentage of the total variance accounted for by the classes nested within schools.

ICCs are often reduced if covariates are entered into the mixed-effects models. We will leave it as an exercise for the reader to show that the ICCs are smaller when baseline THKS scores are included:

```
lmer(postthks ~ prethksC + (1 | school/class),
     data = tvsfp.df)
```

If covariates are available and are likely to reduce the ICC, they may boost the statistical power of a hypothesis test involving a fixed effect. This feature is available in the `power.grouped()` function in the `grouped` package by Dimitris Rizopoulos and Spyridoula Tsonaka.

11.9   Statistical Power Considerations for a Group-Randomized Design

Donner and Klar (1996) provides a formula to estimate the statistical power of a group-randomized study with two parallel intervention arms. The R function can be found in Sect. 7.7 on page 135. Here we briefly repeat how to use it. The function needs the standardized difference between the two treatments (effect size), the number of groups per treatment condition, the estimated ICC among members of the same group, and the number of individual members per group. In their Table 1, they found a 72% statistical power for a study with 6 groups in each of the two intervention conditions, an ICC of 0.005, and 100 individual participants per group, if the estimated effect size is 0.20. A call to `dk.pow(d=0.20, m=6, rho=0.005, n=100)` yields an estimated statistical power of 0.72.

11.9.1   Calculate Statistical Power by Simulation

Estimating statistical power by simulation is useful when the assumptions in the power formulae are untenable. Let us begin with a hypothetical example. Suppose we want to estimate the statistical power in training health care providers in detecting depression among patients diagnosed with cancer. Because of practical considerations we will be able to offer training to 40 health care providers. For each trainee, we will be able to recruit four patients, two before and two after the trainee has completed the depression training class. Patients of the health care provider trainees will fill out a questionnaire assessing depression symptoms before they see the provider. We will only recruit patients who score above a cutoff and thus are candidates for referral to a psychiatrist or a clinical psychologist. The trainee will not be told the score. The primary outcomes are whether or not a patient receives a referral from the provider, and whether or not the patient actually sees a psychiatrist/psychologist within a specific time. It is anticipated that, before the training, 30% of possibly depressed patients receive a referral. After the training, 50% of patients receive a referral. We assume a Pearson correlation of 0.45 among the four patients nested within the same health care provider.

We need the `bindata` package to generate correlated multivariate binary random variables. Then we use `lmer()` to test the training effect on the probability

of a referral. The simulated test is repeated 1,000 times. Statistical power is the
percentage of finding a significant training effect.

```
require(bindata)
require(lme4)
pre   <- 0.30    # pre depression detection training
post  <- 0.50    # post training
corr  <- 0.45    # Pearson correlation coefficient
nsim  <- 1000    # number of simulations
ndoc  <- 40      # number of health care providers
npatn <- 4       # number of patients per provider
sig   <- 0.05    # two-sided, Type-I error rate
vmat  <- matrix(c(1, corr, corr, corr,
                  corr, 1, corr, corr,
                  corr, corr, 1, corr,
                  corr, corr, corr, 1), nrow=npatn)
docs  <- rep(paste("doc", 1:ndoc, sep=""), each=npatn)
# 1 = post-training
ptrain <- rep(rep(c(0, 1), each = 2), ndoc)

set.seed(733)
quiet <- TRUE
power <- rep(NA, nsim)
for (i in 1:nsim) {
   if (!quiet) cat(i, " ")
   y <- rmvbin(nnur, margprob=c(pre, pre, post, post),
         sigma = vmat)
   datc <- data.frame(y=as.vector(t(y)),ptrain,docs)
   lmeR <- lmer(y ~ ptrain + (1 | docs),
                  data = datc, family = binomial)
   sink("tmp", append=FALSE)
   show(lmeR)  # print results into file tmp
   sink()
   lmerOut <- readChar("tmp", 20000)
   p.str <- strsplit(lmerOut, "\n")[[1]][14]
   p.str <- strsplit(p.str, split="[[:space:]]+")[[1]]
   pval <- as.numeric(p.str[length(p.str)])
   if (is.na(pval))
     { cat("\nNA found in pval:", p.str, "\n")}
   power[i] <- pval <= sig
}
print(sum(power, na.rm = TRUE)/nsim)
[1] 0.868
```

The estimated statistical power is 87%. In the simulation, we need to sink() the
output to an external file tmp, then we need to read it back in and find the *p*-value

using `strsplit()`. This step is needed because `lmer` does not return a list object (as of version 0.999375-39, dated 2011-03-07). Thus, we cannot use the method of extracting the *p*-value in Horton et al. (2004).

Exercises

11.1. Changes in ICC when a covariate is added.
Run the model below and get the between-class variance, the between-school variance, and the residual variance. This mixed model differs from the one in Sect. 11.8 because it includes a covariate `prethksC`.

```
lmer(postthks ~ prethksC + (1 | school/class),
    data = tvsfp.df)
```

(a) What is the ICC for school clusters?
(b) Compare your results with `tvlme0` in Sect. 11.8. Does the incorporation of the covariate `prethksC` increase or decrease the estimated ICC for school clusters?
(c) What is the ICC for class clusters nested within schools?
(d) Does the `prethksC` covariate increase or decrease the ICC for class clusters?
(e) Does the inclusion of the `prethksC` covariate change the ICC for classes more or the ICC for schools more? Or about the same?

11.2. The ICC is comparable to the Pearson correlation coefficient.
Run the following code to generate a simulated dataset of 1,000 couple dyads. Suppose the `y` variable represents the score of a relationship satisfaction assessment. The two columns of the simulated data, `m[, 1]` and `m[, 2]`, represent the relationship satisfaction scores of the first and second person in the couple dyads, respectively. For example, person 1 in the first couple dyad has a score of −0.556 and person 2 has a score of 0.285. Person 1 in the second couple has a score of 0.056 and person 2 has a score of 0.366, and so on. The `mvrnorm()` function purposefully sets both variables to follow a standard normal distribution with a covariance of 0.30. The Pearson correlation between the two standard normal variables is thus 0.30, as can be checked in the output of `cor(m)`. In this exercise, we use the simulated data to illustrate that the ICC calculated from a linear mixed-effects model is also 0.30, comparable to the Pearson correlation coefficient. We set `options(digits = 9)` to print out many decimal points in the variance estimates.

```
> library(MASS)        # mvrnorm() below
> options(digits=9)
> set.seed(11)
> S <- matrix(c(1,.30,.30,1), ncol = 2)
> m <- mvrnorm(n = 1000, mu = c(0,0), Sigma = S,
          empirical = T)
```

```
> round(m[1:7, ], 3)
         [,1]    [,2]
[1,] -0.556   0.285
[2,]  0.056   0.366
[3,] -1.475   0.142
[4,] -1.413 -0.684
[5,]  1.236   0.871
[6,] -0.983 -0.583
[7,]  1.456   1.611
> cor(m)
       [,1] [,2]
[1,]   1.0  0.3
[2,]   0.3  1.0
```

(a) Fit a linear mixed-effects model with a couples random effect. Write down the model equation for the R code below.

```
> t.df <- data.frame(subj=paste("s",1:2000,sep=""),
+              y = as.vector(m),
+              couple=rep(paste("c",1:1000,sep=""),2))
> library(lme4)
> lmer.t1 <- lmer(y ~ 1 + (1 | couple), data=t.df)
```

(b) Calculate the ICC for couples.
(c) Is the ICC 0.30, the same as the Pearson correlation coefficient?
(d) Fit the same model using the lme() function in package nlme.
(e) Find the numerator and denominator for the ICC for couples in the output. Are the numerator and denominator the same as in lmer.t1?
(f) Calculate the ICC. Is it also 0.30?
(g) Change the covariance matrix in the simulated data so that the covariance between the two columns is 0.65. Verify that the ICC calculated from a revised lmer() model is also 0.65.

11.3. Simulate statistical power in training health care providers in depression screening.
In Sect. 11.9.1 we run a simulation to estimate the statistical power of a study to help health care providers recognize signs of depression. We assume a Pearson correlation coefficient of 0.45 among patients seeing the same health care provider.

(a) What is the estimated statistical power if the correlation is higher, at 0.60? All other things being equal, does a higher correlation make the statistical power go higher, lower, or about the same?
(b) If the higher correlation decreases statistical power, then we need more data to compensate for the loss in power. Would it help to increase the number of health care providers to 45 (keeping the same the four patients per provider)?

(c) If we cannot increase the number of health care providers in the study, then would it help to increase the number of patients per health care provider from the original 4 to 8?

(d) Which helps more, increasing the number of health care provider to 45 or increasing the number of patients to 8?

11.4. Statistical power estimation by formula and by simulation.

The simulation code in Sect. 11.9.1 can be modified to estimate the statistical power for a cluster-randomized study. We can then compare the estimated power figures by simulation and by formula (Donner and Klar 2000). The rmvnorm() function in the mvtnorm package may be used to generate simulated multivariate normal data.

(a) Make the necessary modifications to the code to simulate a cluster-randomized study with an estimated effect size of 0.20, six groups in each of the two intervention conditions, an ICC of 0.005, and 100 individual participants per group. Set the statistical power for a two-sided Type-I error rate of 0.01.

(b) Using the dk.pow() function above, calculate the statistical power at a two-sided Type-I error rate of 0.01.

(c) What is the estimated statistical power by simulation? Does it agree with the statistical power calculated from the formula?

Appendix A
Data Management with a Database

This appendix contains the source code for creating the database in Fig. 2.1 on page 34. Here we use an open source database software program called PostgreSQL (http://www.postgresql.org/). The source code should also work with other open source database software programs (e.g., MySQL) and proprietary database software programs (e.g., ACCESS and SQL server by Microsoft).

A.1   Create Database and Database Tables

The first step is to create a database. This can be done by clicking "New" on a database software program with a graphical user interface. From that new database you can add database tables. New database tables can be added by point and click, or by syntax:

```
CREATE TABLE subjchar (
        id    char(4) NOT NULL PRIMARY KEY,
        sex   char(1) NOT NULL,
        edu   integer,
        race char(1)   );
CREATE TABLE baseassess (
        id    char(4) NOT NULL,
        bsi   integer,
        bdi   integer,
        bdate   date   );
CREATE TABLE ema (
        id      char(4) NOT NULL,
        tstamp  timestamp DEFAULT current_timestamp,
        smoke   integer CONSTRAINT con1
                CHECK ( smoke >= 0 AND smoke <= 1) );
```

These three statements are written in the Structured Query Language (SQL), the standard language for relational databases. These commands should work across most software programs. Note that the variable `smoke` in the last table `ema` has a debug feature. The value of `smoke` must be an integer of either 0 or 1. Any other value would produce an error during data entry.

Creating a new database is slightly more complicated in postgreSQL. You first create a new user and assign the new user a database management role. This is important for security. Users with different roles are allowed to do different things. The role of "superuser" is typically reserved for the system administrator only. For those who like a graphical user interface, there is a database management tool called pgAdmin for PostgreSQL. Free tutorials of pgAdmin can be found online (http://www.pgadmin.org/).

A.2   Enter Data

The following SQL script inserts the data into the tables. A script is probably the most transparent way to share data. In most cases, it works seamlessly across different database programs on different hardware platforms. Usually, we use a graphical tool like pgAdmin to enter data. When we need to share data, we use pg_dump to dump the data into a script. The script is also useful for data backup.

```
INSERT INTO subjchar VALUES ('s001', 'F', 3, 'W');
INSERT INTO subjchar VALUES ('s002', 'F', 2, 'A');
INSERT INTO subjchar VALUES ('s003', 'M', 1, 'W');
INSERT INTO subjchar VALUES ('s004', 'M', 4, 'B');
INSERT INTO subjchar VALUES ('s005', 'F', 2, 'B');

INSERT INTO baseassess VALUES ('s001', 10, 13,
    '2009-06-28');
INSERT INTO baseassess VALUES ('s002', 12, 15,
    '2009-06-17');
INSERT INTO baseassess VALUES ('s003', 12, 10,
    '2009-07-09');
INSERT INTO baseassess VALUES ('s004', 14, 16,
    '2009-07-12');
INSERT INTO baseassess VALUES ('s005', 11, 10,
    '2009-07-12');

INSERT INTO ema VALUES ('s001',
    '2009-06-29 09:20:25', 1);
INSERT INTO ema VALUES ('s001',
    '2009-06-29 09:35:35', 1);
```

```
INSERT INTO ema VALUES ('s001',
    '2009-06-29 09:50:35', 0);
INSERT INTO ema VALUES ('s001',
    '2009-06-29 10:15:05', 1);
INSERT INTO ema VALUES ('s001',
    '2009-06-29 10:35:55', 1);
INSERT INTO ema VALUES ('s002',
    '2009-06-19 07:35:35', 1);
INSERT INTO ema VALUES ('s002',
    '2009-06-19 08:05:15', 1);
INSERT INTO ema VALUES ('s002',
    '2009-06-19 08:35:35', 0);
INSERT INTO ema VALUES ('s002',
    '2009-06-19 09:05:55', 0);
INSERT INTO ema VALUES ('s002',
    '2009-06-19 09:42:32', 0);
INSERT INTO ema VALUES ('s003',
    '2009-07-10 11:42:30', 0);
INSERT INTO ema VALUES ('s003',
    '2009-07-10 12:02:30', 1);
INSERT INTO ema VALUES ('s003',
    '2009-07-10 12:25:17', 0);
INSERT INTO ema VALUES ('s003',
    '2009-07-10 13:02:19', 0);
INSERT INTO ema VALUES ('s003',
    '2009-07-10 13:34:49', 1);
INSERT INTO ema VALUES ('s004',
    '2009-07-13 06:34:30', 1);
INSERT INTO ema VALUES ('s004',
    '2009-07-13 07:11:33', 1);
INSERT INTO ema VALUES ('s004',
    '2009-07-13 07:43:27', 1);
INSERT INTO ema VALUES ('s004',
    '2009-07-13 08:11:46', 1);
INSERT INTO ema VALUES ('s004',
    '2009-07-13 08:47:03', 1);
INSERT INTO ema VALUES ('s005',
    '2009-07-14 11:07:03', 1);
INSERT INTO ema VALUES ('s005',
    '2009-07-14 11:32:23', 1);
INSERT INTO ema VALUES ('s005',
    '2009-07-14 12:02:33', 0);

INSERT INTO ema VALUES ('s005',
    '2009-07-14 12:42:19', 0);
```

```
INSERT INTO ema VALUES ('s005',
    '2009-07-14 13:29:07', 1);
INSERT INTO ema (id, tstamp) VALUES ('s005',
    '2009-07-14 14:03:54');
```

In the last data entry, the variable smoke is missing. Missing values are stored internally as NULL. NULL values are automatically converted by R into NA. Some data analysts use different values to capture types of missing data (e.g., −99 for survey nonresponse, and −66 for refusal). Sometimes, a blank entry is used to represent missing data, causing the software program to convert a numeric variable into a character string. These steps should be avoided because they are typically counterproductive.

The SQL query below retrieves all EMA assessments of smoking and matches them to each subject's characteristics and baseline assessments.

```
SELECT subjchar.id, sex, edu, race, bsi, bdi, tstamp,
            smoke FROM subjchar, baseassess, ema
    WHERE subjchar.id = baseassess.id
      AND subjchar.id = ema.id
    ORDER BY subjchar.id, tstamp;
```

Below is the output of the SELECT statement. It is in long format. There is no need to run merge().

```
  id  | sex | edu | race | bsi | bdi |      tstamp         | smoke
------+-----+-----+------+-----+-----+---------------------+-------
 s001 | F   |  3  | W    | 10  | 13  | 2009-06-29 09:20:25 |   1
 s001 | F   |  3  | W    | 10  | 13  | 2009-06-29 09:35:35 |   1
 s001 | F   |  3  | W    | 10  | 13  | 2009-06-29 09:50:35 |   0
 s001 | F   |  3  | W    | 10  | 13  | 2009-06-29 10:15:05 |   1
 s001 | F   |  3  | W    | 10  | 13  | 2009-06-29 10:35:55 |   1
 s002 | F   |  2  | A    | 12  | 15  | 2009-06-19 07:35:35 |   1
...
 s005 | F   |  2  | B    | 11  | 10  | 2009-07-14 12:42:19 |   0
 s005 | F   |  2  | B    | 11  | 10  | 2009-07-14 13:29:07 |   1
 s005 | F   |  2  | B    | 11  | 10  | 2009-07-14 14:03:54 |
```

A.3   Using RODBC to Import Data from an ACCESS Database

R can use library(RODBC) to import data tables from a Microsoft ACCESS file, or from any other ODBC-compliant database management systems. This section covers how to do it on a standalone PC running Windows XP. We assume that you have already created a database using ACCESS. It is saved in the file systbl.mdb.

The process involves three steps. The first step is to give the ACCESS file a Data Sources definition.

A.3.1 Step 1: Adding an ODBC Data Source Name

The first step is to create an "ODBC Data Source Name" (DSN) using the Control Panel of the Windows XP machine. Go to Start → Control Panel → Administrative Tools. Under Administrative Tools (see a screenshot below), you double click the "Data Sources (ODBC)" icon to set up a new "ODBC data source name."

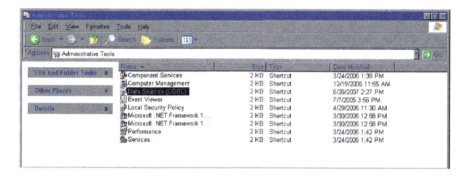

A.3.2 Step 2: ODBC Data Source Name Points to the ACCESS File

Clicking on the "Data Sources (ODBC)" icon opens the "ODBC Data Source Administrator" window. In the example below the system already has a couple of DSNs, including one for dBASE files, one for Excel files, and one for generic MS

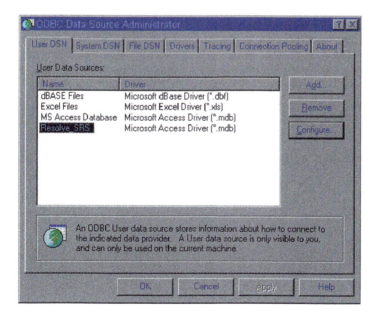

Access Databases. We need to create a new DSN that points to where the ACCESS file is saved on the hard drive. This is done by clicking the "User DSN" tab and then "Add."

In the "Data Source Name" field, a name can be given to the new data source. Here we call it "Resolve_SRS." Next you need to specify where the DSN points to by clicking "Create." A simple file browser pops up (not shown here). You use the file browser to locate where the ACCESS file is saved, in this example it is H:\Resolve Database\SystemTbl\systbl.mdb. The "H:" drive is a shared hard drive. Close the file browser. The "Database" box should show an abbreviated path that points to where the .mdb file is. The "Description" field can be left blank, or filled in with a short description of the DSN. Here for simplicity we enter the directory path to the ACCESS database file.

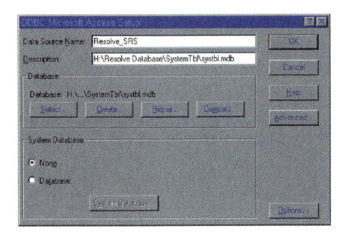

The "Resolve_SRS" data source name (and the systbl.mdb file it points to) is now available to RODBC. RODBC can connect to "Resolve_SRS," which points to where the systbl.mdb file is saved. It helps to think of "Resolve_SRS" as a translator. Any computer program that understands ODBC and the SQL language can connect to it.

A.3.3   Step 3: Run RODBC to Import Data

Finally, you load RODBC (line 1), make a connection to "Resolve_SRS" (line 2), display simple information about the connection (line 3), and fetch a database table called tblSRS_Data (line 4).

```
library(RODBC)
ch <- odbcConnect("Resolve_SRS")
odbcGetInfo(ch)
```

```
         DBMS_Name                DBMS_Ver   Driver_ODBC_Ver
          "ACCESS"            "04.00.0000"           "03.51"
  Data_Source_Name             Driver_Name        Driver_Ver
      "Resolve_SRS"          "odbcjt32.dll"    "04.00.6304"
          ODBC_Ver             Server_Name
      "03.52.0000"                "ACCESS"
df1 <- sqlFetch(ch, "tblSRS_Data")
odbcClose(ch)    # close connection
save(df1, file = "C:/data/SRS.RData")
```

The sqlFetch() function fetches the whole table. A standard SQL query can be
used, like df1 <- sqlQuery(ch, "select * from tblSRS_Data")
or   df1 <-sqlQuery(ch, "select * from tblSRS_Data limit
10"). (if you only want the first ten entries). Other more sophisticated SQL
queries can be used, such as selecting several variables from one table and merge
them with other variables from another table, matched by id numbers. The save()
command saves df1 into an external R data file. Later this file can be restored by
load().

References

Agresti, A. (2002). *Categorical data analysis*. Hoboken, NJ: Wiley.

Akaike, H. (1974). A new look at the statistical model identification. *IEEE Transactions on Automatic Control*, *19*(6), 716–723.

Albert, J. H. (1992). Bayesian estimation of normal ogive item response curves using gibbs sampling. *Journal of Educational Statistics*, *17*, 251–269.

Allison, P. D. (2002). *Missing data*. Thousand Oaks, CA: Sage Publications, Inc.

Atkins, D. C. (2005). Using multilevel models to analyze couple and family treatment data: Basic and advanced issues. *Journal of Family Psychology*, *19*, 98–110.

Atkins, D. C., & Gallop, R. J. (2007). Rethinking how family researchers model infrequent outcomes: A tutorial on count regression and zero-inflated models. *Journal of Family Psychology*, *21*(4), 726–735.

Baayen, R., Davidson, D., & Bates, D. (2008). Mixed-effects modeling with crossed random effects for subjects and items. *Journal of Memory and Language, special issue on Emerging Data Analysis Techniques*, *59*, 390–412.

Baker, F. B., & Kim, S.-H. (2004). *Item response theory: Parameter estimation techniques*. New York: Marcel Dekker, Inc.

Baldwin, P., Bernstein, J., & Wainer, H. (2009). Hip psychometrics. *Statistics in Medicine*, *28*, 2277–2292.

Baron, J. (2010). Looking at individual subjects in research on judgment and decision making (or anything). *Acta Psychologica Sinica*, *42*(1), 88–98. Available from http://journal.psych.ac.cn/xuebao/qikan/epaper/zhaiyao.asp?bsid=3056, last accessed April, 2011.

Baron, R. M., & Kenny, D. A. (1986). The moderator-mediator variable distinction in social psychological research: Conceptual, strategic, and statistical considerations. *Journal of Personality and Social Psychology*, *51*, 1173–1182.

Bock, R., & Lieberman, M. (1970). Fitting a response model for n dichotomously scored items. *Psychometrika*, *35*, 179–197.

Bock, R. D., & Aitkin, M. (1981). Margnal maximum likelihood estimation of item parameters: Application of an em algorithm. *Psychometrika*, *46*(4), 443–459.

Bond, T. G., & Fox, C. M. (2001). *Applying the rasch model: Fundamental measurement in the human sciences*. Mahwah, NJ: Lawrence Erlbaum Associates.

Breiman, L. (1992). The little bootstrap and other methods for dimensionality selection in regression: X-fixed prediction error. *Journal of the American Statistical Association*, *87*, 738–754.

Bryk, A. S., & Raudenbush, S. W. (2002). *Hierarchical linear models* (2 ed., Vol. 1). Newbury Park, CA: Sage Publications, Inc.

Chambers, J. M., & Hastie, T. J. (1993). *Statistical models in s*. New York: Chapman & Hall.

Y. Li and J. Baron, *Behavioral Research Data Analysis with R*, Use R,
DOI 10.1007/978-1-4614-1238-0, © Springer Science+Business Media, LLC 2012

Chu, S. (2001). *Pricing the C's of diamond stones* (Vol. 9) (No. 2). http://www.amstat. org/publications/jse/v9n2/datasets.chu.html; last assessed: January, 2011.

Clark, H. H. (1973). The language-as-fixed-effect fallacy: A critique of language statistics in psychological research. *J. of Verbal Learning and Verbal Behavior*, *12*, 335–359.

Cnaan, A., Laird, N. M., & Slasor, P. (1997). Using the general linear mixed model to analyze unbalanced repeated measures and longitudinal data. *Statistics in Medicine*, *16*, 2349–2380.

Cumming, G. (2006). *How the noncentral* t *distribution got its hump.* http://www.stat.auckland. ac.nz/ iase/publications/17/C106.pdf, last accessed April, 2011.

Curtis, S. M. (2010). Bugs code for item response theory. *Journal of Statistical Software*, *36*, 1–34.

Dalgaard, P. (2007, October). New functions for multivariate analysis. *R News*, *7*(2), 2–7.

de Ayala, R. J. (2009). *The theory and practice of item response theory.* New York, NY: The Guilford Press.

Diggle, P., Heagerty, P., Liang, K. Y., & Zeger, S. L. (2002). *Analysis of longitudinal data.* Oxford, Great Britain: Oxford University Press.

Donner, A., & Klar, N. (1996). Statistical considerations in the design and analysis of community intervention trials. *J Clin Epidemiol*, *49*(4), 435–9.

Donner, A., & Klar, N. (2000). *Design and analysis of cluster randomization trials in health research.* London: Arnold.

Embretson, S. E., & Reise, S. P. (2000). *Item response theory for psychologists.* Mahwah, NJ: LEA.

Faul, F., Erdfelder, E., Lang, A.-G., & Buchner, A. (2007). G*power 3: A flexible statistical power analysis program for the social, behavioral, and biomedical sciences. *Behavioral Research Methods*, *39*, 175–191.

Fitzmaurice, G. M., Laird, N. M., & Ware, J. H. (2004a). *Applied longitudinal analysis.* Hoboken, NJ: John Wiley & Sons.

Fitzmaurice, G. M., Laird, N. M., & Ware, J. H. (2004b). *Applied longitudinal analysis.* Hoboken, NJ: John Wiley & Sons.

Flay, B. R., Miller, T. Q., Hedeker, D., Siddiqui, O., Britton, C. F., Brannon, B. R., et al. (1995). The television, school, and family smoking prevention and cessation project. viii. student outcomes and mediating variables. *Prev Med*, *24*(1), 29–40.

Fox, J. (2002). *An R and S-Plus companion to applied regression.* Thousand Oaks, CA, USA: Sage Publications. Available from http://socserv.socsci.mcmaster.ca/jfox/ Books/Companion/index.html (ISBN 0-761-92279-2)

Fox, J.-P. (2010). *Bayesian item response modeling: Theory and applications.* New York: Springer.

Gelman, A., & Hill, J. (2007). *Data analysis using regression and multilevel/hierarchical models.* New York: Cambridge University Press.

Gelman, A., & Rubin, D. B. (1992). Inferene from iterative simulation using multiple sequences. *Statistical Science*, *7*(4), 457–511.

Graham, J. W. (2009). Missing data analysis: making it work in the real world. *Annual Review of Psychology*, *60*, 549–76.

Graham, J. W., Hofer, S., Donaldson, S., MacKinnon, D., & Schafer, J. (1997). Analysis with missing data in prevention research. In K. Bryant, M. Windle, & S. West (Eds.), *The science of prevention: methodological advances from alcohol and substance abuse research* (p. pp. 325–366). Washington, D.C.: American Psychological Association.

Hardin, J. M., Anderson, B. S., Woodby, L. L., Crawford, M. A., & Russell, T. V. (2008). Using an empirical binomial hierarchical bayesian model as an alternative to analyzing data from multisite studies. *Eval Rev*, *32*(2), 143–56.

Harrell, J., F. E. (2001a). *Regression modeling strategies: with applications to linear models, logistic regression, and survival analysis.* New York: Springer-Verlag.

Harrell, J., F. E. (2001b). *Regression modeling strategies: with applications to linear models, logistic regression, and survival analysis.* New York: Springer-Verlag.

Hays, W. L. (1988). *Statistics* (4th ed. ed.). New York: Holt, Rinehart and Winston.

Hedeker, D., & Gibbons, R. D. (1997). Application of random-effects pattern-mixture models for missing data in longitudinal studies. *Psychological Methods*, *2*, 64–78.

Hoaglin, D. C., Mosteller, F., & Tukey, J. W. (1991). *Fundamentals of exploratory analysis of variance*. New York: John Wiley & Sons.

Hoenig, J. M., & Heisey, D. M. (2001). The abuse of power: The pervasive fallacy of power calculations for data analysis. *The American Statistician*, *55*, 19–24.

Honaker, J., & King, G. (2010). What to do about missing valu3s in time series cross-section data. *American Journal of Political Science*, *54*(2), 561–581.

Horton, J., N, Brown, E. R., & Quian, L. (2004). Use of r as a toolbox for mathematical statistics exploration. *The American Statistician*, *58*, 343–357.

Horton, N. J., & Kleinman, K. P. (2007). Much ado about nothing: A comparison of missing data methods and software to fit incomplete data regression models. *Am Stat*, *61*(1), 79–90.

Horton, N. J., & Lipsitz, S. R. (2001). Multiple imputation in practice: comparison of software packages for regression models with missing variables. *The American Statistician*, *55*(3), 244–254.

Jackman, S. (2009). *Bayesian analysis for the social sciences*. Chichester, United Kingdom: John Wiley & Sons, Ltd.

Janega, J. B., Murray, D. M., Varnell, S. P., Blitstein, J. L., Birnbaum, A. S., & Lytle, L. A. (2004). Assessing intervention effects in a school-based nutrition intervention trial: which analytic model is most powerful? *Health Educ Behav*, *31*(6), 756–74.

Karabatsos, G. (2003). Comparing the aberrant response detection performance of thirty-six person fit statistics. *Applied Measurement in Education*, *16*(4), 277–298.

King, G., Honaker, J., Joseph, A., & Scheve, K. (2001). Analyzing incomplete political science data: An alternative algorithm for multiple imputation. *American Political Science Review*, *95*(1), 49–69.

Kraemer, H. C., Mintz, J., Noda, A., Tinklenberg, J., & Yesavage, J. A. (2006). Caution regarding the use of pilot studies to guide power calculations for study proposals. *Arch Gen Psychiatry*, *63*, 484–489.

Laird, N. M., & Ware, J. H. (1982). Random effects models for longitudinal data. *Biometrics*, *38*, 963–974.

Lazzeroni, L. G., Schenker, N., & Taylor, J. M. G. (1990). Robustness of multiple-imputation techniques to model misspecification. *American Statistical Association Proceedings of the Survey Research Methods Section*, 260–265.

Levin, J. R., & Serlin, R. C. (2000). Changing students' perspectives of mcnemar's test of change. *Journal of Statistics Education*, *8*(2). (http://www.amstat.org/publications/jse/secure/v8n2/levin.cfm)

Li, Y. (2006). Using the open-source statistical language r to analyze the dichotomous rasch model. *Behavioral Research Methods*, *38*, 532–541.

Little, R. (1993). Pattern-mixture models for multivariate incomplete data process,. *Biometrics*, *44*, 175–188.

Little, R. J. A. (1988). Missing-data adjustment in large surveys. *Journal of Business & Economic Statistics*, *6*, 287–301.

Little, R. J. A., & Rubin, D. B. (2002). *Statistical analysis with missing data* (2 ed.). New York: John Wiley & Sons, Inc.

Lord, F. M. (1980). *Application of item response theory to practical testing problems*. Hillsdale, NJ: Erlbaum.

Lunn, D. J., Thomas, A., Best, N., & Spiegelhalter, D. (2000). Winbugs – a bayesian modelling framework: concepts, structure, and extensibility. *Statistics and Computing*, *10*, 325–337.

MacKinnon, D. P., Lockwood, C. M., Hoffman, J. M., West, S. G., & Sheets, V. (2002). A comparison of methods to test mediation and other intervening variable effects. *Psychol Methods*, *7*(1), 83–104.

Masters, G. N. (1982). A Rasch model for partial credit scoring. *Psychometrika*, *47*(2), 149–174.

Masters, G. N., & Wright, B. D. (1996). The partial credit model. In W. Linden (Ed.), (pp. 101–121). New York: Springer-Verlag.

Maxwell, S., & Delaney, H. (1990). *Designing experiments and analyzing data*. Belmont, CA: Wadsworth Inc.

Mittal, Y. (1991). Homogeneity of subpopulations and simpson's paradox. *Journal of the American Statistical Association, 86*, 167–172.

Moore, D., & McCabe, G. P. (1993). *Introduction to the practice of statistics*. New York, NY: W. H. Freeman and Co.

Muraki, E. (1992). A generalized partial credit model: Application of an em algorithm. *Applied Psychological Measurement, 16*, 159–176.

Murray, D. M. (1998a). *Design and analysis of group-randomized trials*. New York: Oxford University Press.

Murray, D. M. (1998b). *Group-randomized trials*. New York: Oxford University Press.

Murray, D. M., Varnell, S. P., & Blitstein, J. L. (2004). Design and analysis of group-randomized trials: a review of recent methodological developments. *Am J Public Health, 94*(3), 423–32.

Ntzoufras, I. (2009). *Bayesian modeling using winbugs*. Hoboken, NJ: John Wiley & Sons, Inc.

Patz, R. J., & Junker, B. W. (1999). Applications and extensions of mcmc in irt: Multiple item types, missing data, and rated responses. *Journal of Educational and Behavioral Statistics, 24*(4), 342–366.

Peduzzi, P., Concato, J., Kemper, E., TR, T. H., & Feinstein, A. (1996). A simulation study of the number of events per variable in logistic regression analysis. *Journal of Clinical Epidemiology, 49*(12), 1373–9.

Pinheiro, J. C., & Bates, D. M. (2000). *Mixed-effects models in S and S-Plus*. New York, NY: Springer. (ISBN 0-387-98957-0)

Pinheiro, J. C., & Bates, D. M. (2004). *Mixed-effects models in s and S-Plus*. New York: Springer-Verlag.

CRAN. (2011). *Cran task view on psychometric models and methods*. `http://cran.r-project.org/web/views/Psychometrics.html`. last accessed: January, 2011.

Quintana, S. M., & Maxwell, S. E. (1994). A Monte Carlo comparison of seven ϵ-adjustment procedures in repeated-measures designs with small sample sizes. *Journal of Educational Statistics, 19*(1), 57–71.

Raaijmakers, J. G. W., Schrijnemakers, J. M. C., & Gremmen, F. (1999). How to deal with "the language-as-fixed-effect" fallacy: common misconceptions and alternative solutions. *Journal of Memory and Language, 41*, 416–426.

Raftery, A., & Lewis, S. (1992). How many iterations in the gibbs sampler? In J. Bernardo, J. Berger, A. Dawid, & A. Smith (Eds.), *Bayesian statistics* (Vol. 4, pp. 763–774). Oxford, UK: Claredon Press.

Rasch, G. (1980). *Probabilistic models for some intelligency and attainment tests*. Chicago: The University of Chicago Press.

Revelle, W. (2010). psych: Procedures for psychological, psychometric, and personality research [Manuel de logiciel]. Evanston, Illinois. Available from `http://personality-project.org/r/psych.manual.pdf` (R package version 1.0-90)

Rubin, D. (1987). *Multiple imputation for nonresponse in surveys*. Hoboken, NJ: John Wiley & Sons.

Rubin, D. (1996). Multiple imputation after 18+ years. *Journal of the American Statistical Association, 91*, 473–489.

Schafer, J. L. (1997). *Analysis of incomplete multivariate data*. New York: Chapman & Hall.

Schafer, J. L., & Graham, J. W. (2002). Missing data: our view of the state of the art. *Psychological Methods, 7*, 147–177.

Schafer, J. L., & Olsen, M. K. (1998). Multiple imputation for multivariate missing-data problems: a data analyst's perspective. *Multivariate Behavioral Research, 33*, 545–571.

Scheipl, F. (2010). *Exact (restricted) likelihood ratio tests for mixed and additive models*. `http://cran.r-project.org/web/packages/RLRsim/index.html`, last accessed June, 2010.

Searle, S., Casella, G., & McCulloch, C. E. (1992). *Variance components*. New York: John Wiley & Sons.

Shoukri, M. M., & Pause, C. A. (1999). *Statistical methods for health sciences* (2nd ed.). Boca Raton, FL: CRC Press LLC.

Shrout, P. E., & Fleiss, J. L. (1979). Intraclass correlations: uses in assessing rater reliability. *Psychological Bulletin, 86*(2), 420–428.

Smeeth, L., & Ng, E. S.-W. (2002). Intraclass correlation coefficients for cluster randomized trials in primary care: data from the mrc trial of the assessment and management of older people in the community. *Controllled Clinical Trials, 23*, 409–421.

Stevens, J. (1992). *Applied multivariate statistics for the social sciences.* Hillsdale, NJ: Lawrence Erlbaum Associates, Inc.

Student. (1908). The probable error of a mean. *Biometrika, 6,* 1–25.

Su, Y.-S., Gelman, A., Hill, J., & Yajima, M. (in press). Multiple imputation with diagnostics (mi) in R: Opening windows into the black box. *Journal of Statistical Software.* Retrieved Sept. 30, 2011, from `http://www.stat.columbia.edu/~gelman/research/published/mipaper.rev04.pdf`.

Thissen, D., & Steinberg, L. (1986). A taxonomy of item response models. *Psychometrika, 51*(4), 567–577.

Torre, J. de la, Stark, S., & Chernyshenko, O. S. (2006). Markov chain monte carlo estimation of item parameters for the generalized graded unfolding model. *Applied Psychological Measurement, 30*(3), 216–232.

Venables, W. N., & Ripley, B. D. (2002). *Modern applied statistics with s* (4th ed.). New York: Springer.

Vittinghoff, E., & McCulloch, C. E. (2007). Relaxing the rule of ten events per variable in logistic and cox regression. *American Journal of Epidemiology, 165*(6), 710–718.

Wickens, T. D. (1989). Multiway contingency tables analysis for the social sciences. In (p. 78). Hillsdale, NJ: Lawrence Erlbaum Associates.

Wonnacott, T. H., & Wonnacott, R. J. (1987). *Regression, a second course in statistics.* Malabar, FL: R.E. Krieger Pub. Co.

Wright, B. D., & Stone, M. H. (1979). *Best test design.* Chicago: MESA Press.

Zigmond, A. S., & Snaith, R. P. (1983). The hospital anxiety and depression scale. *Acta Psychiatrica Scandinavica, 67*, 361–370.

Index

A
AIC, 118, 186, 211
Akaike information criterion, *see* AIC
Amelia package, 171
AmeliaView(), *see also* Amelia package,
    171
aov(), 81
apply(), 14, 15, 21
aregImpute(), *see also* Hmisc package,
    163
augPred, 189

B
barplot(), 55
Bayesian Information Criterion, *see* BIC
BIC, 186, 211
binom.test(), 43
bioconductor package, *see* Packages
by function, 21

C
casewise deletion, 162
character strings, 10
    search and replace, 11
cluster randomized trials, 205
coda.samples(), 156
comparePred, 190
conditional independence in contingency
    tables, 46
contrasts, 27
coplot(), 56, 113
corSymm, 192

D
data layout
    long format, 19, 21, 31
    wide format, 19, 21, 31, 37
data.frame(), 2, 22
datasets
    bfi dataset, 147
    sleep dataset, 1
    tvsfp dataset, 206
date data type, *see* POSIX date
density, 39
dev.copy2eps(), 56
dev.off(), 59
dev2bitmap(), 56
difftime(), 11

E
Error(), 24, 81, 83
eval(), 12
event per variable (EPV), 123
exactRLRT, 200
example(), 6

F
Fisher information, 144
Fisher's exact test, 47
fisher.test(), 47
fixed effects
    degrees of freedom, 215
    highest posterior density intervals, 202, *see*
        also HPDinterval(), 212
    Wald test, 213
floating point arithmetic, 3, 7

Lightning Source UK Ltd.
Milton Keynes UK
UKOW06f1802220914

238977UK00002B/5/P